Mt. Fuji From Our Window

Mt. Fuji
From Our
Window

*A Forty-Year Adventure
at the International Christian University*

Benjamin Duke

iUniverse, Inc.
New York   Bloomington

Mt. Fuji From Our Window
A Forty-Year Adventure at the International Christian University

iUniverse books may be ordered through booksellers or by contacting:

iUniverse
1663 Liberty Drive
Bloomington, IN 47403
www.iuniverse.com
1-800-Authors (1-800-288-4677)

Because of the dynamic nature of the Internet, any Web addresses or links contained in this book may have changed since publication and may no longer be valid. The views expressed in this work are solely those of the author and do not necessarily reflect the views of the publisher, and the publisher hereby disclaims any responsibility for them.

ISBN: 978-1-4502-4784-9 (sc)
ISBN: 978-1-4502-4785-6 (hc)
ISBN: 978-1-4502-4786-3 (ebk)

Library of Congress Control Number: 2010911831

Printed in the United States of America

iUniverse rev. date: 08/10/2010

Table of Contents

INTRODUCTION
MT. FUJI FROM OUR WINDOW
- THE TROYER HOUSE -

I magine a 28-foot long living room with large sliding windows running from wall to wall. Picture a near-perfect volcanic cone rising over 12000 ft. through the magnificent Japan Alps appearing precisely in the middle of the windows. Envision the sky turning brilliant red as the sun sets behind the snow-covered mountain sixty miles away on a late afternoon from October to March. That was the view of Mt. Fuji we enjoyed for over thirty years from our home on the campus of the International Christian University in Tokyo.

When Mike Wallace visited our home in the 1980s for an interview for the most popular CBS program Sixty Minutes on my book, The Japanese School, he experienced that magnificent scene. As if prearranged, the sun was setting behind Mt. Fuji with the sky turning red over the long mountain range when he entered the living room through the sliding shoji door. His reaction when viewing Mt. Fuji through our window was typical of first-time visitors. "Awesome." It provoked a sense of quietness and meditation among not a few visitors to our home who had the good fortune to be there at the right moment.

We moved to that home in 1966 when the first Vice President for Academic Affairs at ICU, Dr. Maurice Troyer, retired and returned to America with his wife Billie. When we moved in, the house was affectionately known on campus as the 'Troyer house,' and for good reason. Maurice and Billie Troyer, an extraordinarily gracious couple, set a standard of hospitality for students and faculty that few others equaled.

The Troyer House had become a symbol of the goals and aspirations of ICU as a bilingual liberal arts 'university of tomorrow' founded on Christianity and democracy. There was a steady stream of ICU students and faculty from throughout the world who visited the Troyer House to consider matters of great concern to a unique institution struggling for its very existence in a nation recovering from wartime devastation. Maurice, of humble American background, was among the ICU founders who could articulate the vision of the institution most appealingly. He was, in fact, the primary figure who designed the original academic program. An impressive number of us who visited the Troyers at home were drawn into their vision of the 'ICU Family,' determined to commit ourselves to its fulfillment, as were the indefatigable Maurice and the vivacious Billie.

The atmosphere within the Troyer House went well beyond academic interests. Their home became a social center of the university as well. Students were invited to dine with the Troyers not only to enjoy their kindness and open hospitality but to experience western customs of dining. To not a few students from rural Japan skilled in the use of ohashi (chopsticks), manipulating a knife and fork in the 1950s was a unique experience. The Troyers in their homespun manner were seeking to prepare students for an international career beginning with the basics.

When we arrived on campus in the late 1950s to join the ICU faculty, the Troyer House soon became a delightful venue to enjoy an evening of relaxation in a comfortable setting beyond the spectacular site of Mt. Fuji at dusk. Billie and Maurice Troyer were thoroughly enjoyable to be around. They loved to laugh and loved to make other people laugh. And that's what the Dukes did when we visited the Troyer House. We enjoyed many an evening of humor and gaiety that remain vividly in our memories to this day. Our relationship with the Troyers, and the many academic and social events that we participated in at the Troyer House, was one of the decisive factors in our decision to commit to a lifetime career at ICU.

Billie and Maurice Troyer at home

When Maurice retired in 1966, the Vice President for Financial Affairs, Hallam Shorrock, American missionary recently from the World Council of Churches who was responsible for assigning ICU houses to faculty members, called us. He informed us that we had been chosen to move from the old apartment house on campus, East Grove where we had lived for six years, to the Troyer House if we so desired. We were taken by surprise. As the youngest foreign faculty member at ICU, and an assistant professor, it seemed incredulous that we would be considered to live in the revered Troyer House. As it turned out, all of the other foreign faculty members with families had already been assigned to a campus house and were pleased with their accommodations.

When Hal notified us about the housing assignment, he revealed that one of the factors in the selection process was the expectation that the Dukes would carry on the tradition of the Troyer House that Maurice and Billie had nurtured so carefully. Regardless of our deep concern about living up to the standards the Troyers set during their fifteen years in the Troyer House, we accepted Hal's generous offer. Even with great trepidation, we could not pass up the opportunity to move into the Troyer House with our daughter Noriko Susan.

For over thirty years we enjoyed the Troyer House immensely. We brought up our three children virtually from birth in that glorious home in the woods within the great metropolis of Tokyo. It was an ideal environment for our kids to roam through the paths and lanes that laced the campus. We entertained countless numbers of students from throughout the world for 'open house,' for dinners, for Halloween parties, for tutorials, for advisee barbecues, etc. And we entertained faculty for parties, dinners, backyard barbecues, home piano concerts, etc. Gradually the Troyer House became the Duke House.

During those thirty years in that home we also had the wonderful experience of viewing Mt. Fuji from our window thousands of times. How grateful we remain to this day to Maurice and Billie Troyer who chose the site of their home in 1953. They loved to tell the story of walking along the bluff of the 360 acre wooded site of the new university selecting the site where the view of Mt. Fuji was most impressive. Who could have imagined that in 1959, when a letter reached us at Penn State University from Vice President Maurice Troyer inviting me to join the faculty of ICU, that so many adventures would transpire while living in a home chosen for its exquisite view of Mt. Fuji? The following thirty-five memoirs have been chosen from among them.

The Troyer – Duke House

MEMOIR 1

THE CALL TO ADVENTURE

JOINING THE ICU FACULTY IN 1959

- THE HARVARD OF JAPAN -

ICU campus shortly before our arrival

On December 8th, 1959, we arrived at the Tokyo International Airport to begin a three-year contractual appointment on the faculty of the International Christian University. At ages twenty-eight, June and I were eager to begin a new adventure in a strange land we knew little about, and at a university we had never heard of until six months previously. Who could have foreseen on that fateful day in 1959 that we would remain at ICU for the rest of the 20th century, and experience a life of adventure unimaginable when we left our small hometown of Berwick, Pennsylvania for Tokyo, Japan?

In retrospect, our working-class family background and small-town upbringing may have been a critical factor underlying our long and enjoyable life in Japan. We arrived in Japan having never met a Japanese, and with no preconceptions of the Japanese with whom we would spend decades as our neighbors, colleagues and students. Moreover we did not think of the Japanese in terms of World War II since the war had little direct influence on our hometown during childhood. In addition, we had no desire to impose strongly held religious beliefs or opinions on the Japanese. In a word, we were a young inexperienced small town American couple.

Originating from families with fathers and mothers who had completed schooling after the eighth grade, we were brought up by caring hard-working parents who struggled valiantly to keep our families in tact during the Great Depression. Our fathers lost their jobs in the local factory for long periods of time. Nevertheless we were reared with the simple virtues of honesty, trustworthiness, diligence, respect for others, and a strong dose of plain common sense. As it turned out, many of the Japanese, and non-Japanese as well, that we encountered at ICU cherished those same virtues. The so-called 'ICU family,' often used to characterize relations between faculty and students at that time, unexpectedly turned out to be a perfect fit for us from the first day at ICU.

Academically, however, there was some apprehension that I was ill prepared to join the faculty of the International Christian University in 1959 from several aspects. First of all I had no teaching experience at the university level. By the age of 28, I had spent two mandatory years in the United States Army during the Korean War era after graduation from college. I then spent two years as a teacher in the public schools of the small community of Hershey, Pennsylvania, the famous chocolate town. From there I entered the graduate school at Penn State for the Ph.D. and directly from there joined the faculty of ICU.

Unexpectedly, rather than being inappropriate for university teaching, my only classroom teaching experience at a public school in Hershey proved an invaluable asset as a professor in the Division of Education. Not a few of our divisional students earned the certificate required to teach in Japanese public schools. Much to my surprise I was the only faculty member in our division who had teaching experience at the pre-university level.

When I observed and evaluated ICU seniors during their mandatory student teaching classes in public schools of Tokyo over the decades, I responded from personal classroom experience which the students greatly appreciated. Later, as Chairman of the ICU Graduate School Division of Education, experience as a public school teacher served me well in focusing our Japanese scholars on the practical as well as the theoretical foundations of education.

On the other hand, I was inadequately prepared to teach at a private liberal arts university. As the son of a factory worker I attended a nearby Pennsylvania state college that prepared teachers for the public schools. In contrast to a liberal arts curriculum at ICU, my undergraduate education was highly specialized in teacher preparation. General education as the foundation of a liberal arts education was something I had never experienced when I was assigned to teach a general education course on education, Social Science 3, during my first year at ICU, which I taught until retirement.

As I soon learned, ICU faculty meetings and retreats were often devoted to the topic of the role of general education in a liberal arts university. I found myself learning and appreciating the meaning of those grand concepts from senior Japanese and American scholars who had different interpretations of them. I had little appreciation of them at the beginning. I developed it after we arrived at the Tokyo International Airport on December 8, 1959.

On that memorable December day, our adventure at ICU began when no one was at the airport from the university to meet us. A telephone call to ICU produced a long delay. Finally the reply: "What are you doing here?" "We came to join the faculty. We sent you a letter last month." Silence. Finally a reply: "I found your name. We were not expecting you. Please wait two hours for a car from ICU." Our first reaction was instinctive. We may have made a huge mistake in signing a multi-year contract to teach at an institution in Japan that did not have the courtesy to meet us upon our arrival.

As we later learned, ICU was not at fault for the arrival confusion. Three weeks earlier we airmailed a letter with precise arrival information to the vice president's office. Two weeks after we arrived in Japan, the letter was delivered to the university rerouted from the Philippines where it had been mistakenly sent. It was symbolic of the state of international mail to Asia in the late 1950s.

A brief review of the process for employment that had been initiated in June, 1959, amidst the completion of the requirements for the doctorate at the Pennsylvania State University, is relevant. We first learned of the name International Christian University from a curious letter from the Vice President of the International Christian University in Tokyo offering a position on the faculty. The institution was described as a new adventure in liberal arts education at a young university only six years old launched by a coalition of Christians from Japan and North America. It was characterized as an experiment in Christian higher education in postwar Japan.

Looking toward the future, the recruitment of 'promising young academics' with the Ph.D. from throughout the world to balance senior scholars already on the faculty was underway. The straightforward terms: a three-year contract at the annual equivalent in yen of $4,800 with travel expenses provided both ways, and a sabbatical leave after three years with tenure if invited back. Curiously, our salary would be paid by the Japan International Christian University Foundation, an institution we had never heard of, and located in, of all places, New York City. Who would have imagined that over fifty years later I would currently serve as a member on the Board of Trustees of that foundation?

At that time we had no interest in Japan. The only Japanese word we knew was sayonara. In the frenetic moments of fulfilling the doctoral requirements for the 1959 June graduation from Penn State, particularly the stressful final defense of the Ph.D. thesis, our first response to the letter from ICU was negative. The idea of moving to Japan to teach at an unknown institution for three years seemed absurd. Although in a short accompanying flyer it was noted that some observers referred to ICU as the 'Harvard of Japan,' we brushed that aside as preposterous.

The American Vice President for Academic Affairs at ICU, Dr. Maurice Troyer, noted in his recruitment letter that academic experience was not a significant factor since the goal of recruiting young academics precluded experience as a qualification. Indeed my experience by the age of 28, academic or otherwise, was unimpressive. As the first and only one in my family to attend college, I graduated from an inexpensive nearby state school financing my full tuition with tips as a desk clerk at a Pocono Mountain resort hotel during the summers. Upon graduation I was immediately drafted into the United States Army for two years stationed mostly in Texas as the Korean War came to a close. During that stint I married my high school sweetheart, June Smith, who joined me in a small apartment off base in Texarkana, Texas.

Upon discharge from the Army in 1955 we moved to Hershey, Pennsylvania, where I began a teaching career in the public school system at a salary of $3300. After receiving the first paycheck which we assumed covered two weeks, on learning that it was our monthly salary, the decision was made early on that public school teaching would not be my life's work. Graduate degrees were essential for a professional career.

I immediately enrolled in graduate courses offered by Penn State University in nearby Harrisburg. In 1957, upon resigning from the teaching position in Hershey, we moved to State College to complete the doctorate in two years financed by the G.I. Bill as a veteran of the United States Army. June worked as a receptionist at a local doctor's office to make ends meet. It was at the end of the two-year course of study when the unsolicited recruitment letter from ICU arrived. On second thought we rashly, and naively, reasoned why not go to Japan. After all it was a 25% increase in salary as a public school teacher in Hershey when I resigned two years previously.

The decision made at Penn State in 1959 to accept the offer to join the ICU faculty in Japan for a three-year period was not only an act of faith, it was a risky gamble on the part of ICU. Incredibly no one representing ICU interviewed us. At the same time it was equally risky on our part to accept the offer without any interest in Japan or knowledge about ICU. Moreover we had no access to anyone who could tell us what to expect as a young faculty member and wife at a new university located in far-off Mitaka, Tokyo, Japan. In hindsight, we attribute the fateful decision to go to Japan in 1959 as the call of adventure.

We followed directions outlined in a letter from the university in applying for passports and a visa for the September semester, 1959. The process took longer than anticipated and so informed the university that a delay in our arrival was inevitable. When the documents finally arrived we immediately made travel reservations and notified the university by letter that we were to arrive at Tokyo International Airport on December 8, 1959.

Unaware that our letter had been misdirected to the Philippines, the critical decision made at Penn State six months previously seemed all the more questionable while we patiently waited for a car from ICU to pick us up at the Tokyo International Airport. There were no other foreigners in the waiting room when an assistant and driver from ICU quickly located us. Since neither could speak English, we drove to the campus virtually in silence.

As we rode through the countryside for nearly two hours from Haneda Airport to ICU near dusk, we were shocked at the economic conditions of Japan. The Japanese people were dressed very poorly. The houses we passed were nearly all one-story tiny dark brown wooden buildings. Nearly all of the tiny stores on the street corners were open to the cold winter weather with goods chosen off the shelves from the street or from the rare sidewalk. There were many three-wheeled cars and trucks on the roads, something we had never seen before. There were still former soldiers from World War II standing on the corners dressed in white, often with a limb missing, begging for food and money. As we drove to ICU we asked ourselves what are we doing here.

We were particularly fascinated with the farmland covered with rice paddies that extended right up to the ICU campus, another sight we had never seen before. We also became aware of strange odors in varying degrees. We later learned that most Japanese farmers at that time applied human waste to their fields as fertilizer stored in open vats near the fields. Flush toilets had reached few areas beyond central Tokyo such as, fortunately, ICU, indicative of the economic development of Japan in 1959. Trucks with long suction hoses cruised the suburbs collecting their goods from private houses to sell to the farmers.

It was dark when we arrived on campus in front of our assigned apartment in East Grove. We soon learned that it was an old warehouse converted into six apartments mostly for foreign faculty. This would be our home for the first six years at ICU.

East Grove shortly before we arrived

Much to our surprise a rather large blonde middle-aged women came to the door of apartment number three and introduced herself with an engaging smile as Sunshine Henna from Norway. She was the head of the welcoming committee for new foreign faculty having only learned two hours previously that we had arrived in Japan. She had come to make our beds and take us to her home on campus for a mutton dinner, Norwegian style, our first meal in Japan. And that was the unexpected beginning of what turned out to be an unlikely forty-year adventure at the International Christian University.

We walked across the ICU campus to the Henna home through the woods in the darkness of our first evening in Japan. Our Norwegian host chatted all the way with a charm that immediately endeared her to us. We then met her husband, Henry Henna, a distinguished scholar in linguistics from Bergen, Norway, who spoke five languages with an ability to be very amusing in English. I was deeply impressed, especially when I compared it to my academic background and experience. Who would have thought that several years later we would visit the Hennes at their Norwegian home in Bergen during a sabbatical leave?

After dinner the Hennas guided us back to our apartment in the dark pushing their bicycles all the way. We quickly found that bicycles were indispensable on the 360 acre ICU campus. We rode them nearly every day from then on for forty years. About fifty meters from our apartment the first ICU library building was under construction funded mostly by a gift of a quarter of a million dollars from the Rockefeller family. Little did we know that Jay Rockefeller had just completed three years of Japanese language study at ICU. Who would have thought at that moment that we would meet him twenty years later as United States Senator Jay Rockefeller on a nostalgic visit to ICU with his wife?

Bright lights were glowing at the construction site as the workers, including elderly women during this era of economic depression, labored throughout the night in order to meet the deadline by the opening of the next academic year in April. Who could have imagined that first evening on campus that fifteen years later I would be appointed Interim

Director of the new ICU Library for two years when the professional head librarian, the venerable Tane Takahashi, suddenly resigned? That was an adventure in itself for one who had no background in library science?

With the cost of fuel double that of America, and ICU in deep financial difficulties from the very beginning, the central heating from an old coal furnace was turned off in our apartment house at 10 o'clock each evening. With ill-fitting windows that let in the cold as well as the dust and dirt from the nearby construction site, we spent our first night at ICU huddled under the covers. It was frontier living at best. For the second time that day we seriously considered whether we had made a terrible mistake in joining the ICU faculty.

In front of our East Grove Apartment

The next morning we were pleasantly surprised to find two bottles of milk on our front door step. An original herd of Jersey cows with one bull, a gift from America that arrived on a ship in 1952, produced enough milk to supply the local community as well as campus residents and students with fresh milk. Nearly fifty acres of the campus were devoted to farming. ICU hired several local farmers to take care of the cows, the chickens and pigpens as well as the rice paddies.

During that first morning on campus we met our neighbors from the adjoining apartment, Roy and Dorothy Morrell from England who were in their late fifties. They brought us tea and sweets for breakfast. Roy, a graduate of Cambridge University, was one of the world's leading scholars on the great British writer Thomas Hardy, with a home in Dorset where the Hardy novels were written. He had taught in several countries in Africa and in Singapore for the British Council before joining the ICU faculty.

I was deeply impressed with the first British scholar I ever met. Roy would shortly introduce us to the world of Thomas Hardy beginning with his great novel Tess. Who would have thought that several years later, after their retirement, the Morrells would meet our ship, the SS United States sailing from New York, at Southampton during our summer vacation and take us to their charming cottage in Dorset? Meeting my first ICU colleagues, Henry Henne from Norway and Roy Morrel from England, was exhilarating as well as somewhat intimidating.

We then met our neighbors in the apartment on the other side, a Japanese several years older than we were named Carl (Yasuo) Furuya with an American wife Sachi of Japanese ancestry. We were deeply impressed since Carl had just earned a Ph.D. at a premier American institution, Princeton Theological Seminary, in a foreign language of course. Carl had arrived two weeks earlier to serve as the ICU church pastor. Who would have thought that four years later Carl would baptize our first daughter, Noriko Susan, in the ICU Church? Moreover who could have imagined that that baby girl would in fact be a Japanese child we had adopted three weeks after her birth, a rare occurrence in the early 1960s?

I must digress briefly to note that not long afterwards, a young promising Japanese scholar by the name of Owada Yasuyuki, wise beyond his years, moved in next door with his American wife Judy when the Furuyas moved to the newly completed pastor's house. Yasuyuki, first year graduate from ICU, returned to campus as assistant to the president with a new doctorate from America. We were impressed.

Judy Owada turned out to be the perfect friend for June since it was the first opportunity for her to have an American friend near her age living nearby. These two young American women living in Japan far from home hit it off perfectly. They were both unassuming and quietly adventurous wives who made the important decisions in both families. Who would have thought that some years later Judy would give birth to a baby girl and name her June Owada, or that Yasuyuki and I would become members of the Japan International Christian University Foundation Board of Trustees in New York, he the President of the Board no less?

On our first morning in Japan another neighbor in the same old apartment building came to meet us. Dr. Bill Newell, a native of New Zealand with wife Pauline from Britain, had come to ICU from the faculty of Manchester University, England. He had carried out extensive onsite research on Chinese and Malay societies. I was deeply impressed. Who would have thought that years later Bill, as a Visiting Professor at Oxford University from ICU, would invite me while on leave to complete a Ph.D. at London University, to have dinner with the faculty and students at Churchill College, Oxford University?

We were then greeted by a tiny frail dark-skinned soft-spoken woman from India, Miss Akhtar Qamber, in her beautiful sari. She had come to ICU from Isabella Thoburn College in India, in the field of literature. She turned out to be an absolute delight with a great sense of humor. Who would have thought that during our first summer at ICU when we were having a badminton tournament behind our apartment, she would come dressed in jeans and beat the daylights out of everyone? In fact she was quietly aggressive and shockingly athletic. She endeared herself to all of her colleagues.

At eleven o'clock the first Japanese faculty member to meet us, my department head, Nishimoto Mitoji, arrived to introduce himself and show me to my office, only about 150 meters away. Professor Nishimoto, in his mid-60s, was a curious Japanese in many ways. First of all he had a deep booming voice coming out of a small body. But his prewar background proved fascinating. In 1924, with limited English skills, he daringly set sail for America to study under the great American educator, John Dewey, then on the faculty of the University of Chicago.

The young Nishimoto promptly fell under the spell of the leading progressive educator in the world. When Dewey moved to Teachers College in New York City, Nishimoto transferred his student status to continue his studies under the great educational philosopher in New York where he earned the master's degree from Teachers College, Columbia University, in 1926. In the process Nishimoto became one of the foremost Japanese pioneers in the field of progressive education long before World War II when modern theories of education were not well received in his home country. He also became well known as the Japanese translator of the educational classics that formed the progressive education movement, particularly those of William Kilpatrick, Dewey's primary collaborator, who later visited Japan with Nishimoto as his guide and translator.

Professor Nishimoto in class

As one who had taken a course at Penn State on Dewey's controversial educational theories, and had read one of Kilpatrick's books on progressive education which Nishimoto had translated into Japanese, I was deeply impressed. When I signed a contract to join the faculty of ICU in 1959, I did not expect to have a personal disciple of John Dewey and William Kilpatrick as the chairman of my department. By this time during my first morning on the faculty, I began to marvel at what kind of an institution ICU was.

Professor Nishimoto showed me to my office located, of all places, in the hastily refurbished former laboratory of the Nakajima Aircraft Company, later to become the Fuji Heavy Industries, that built fighter planes for World War II. I must confess that I did not appreciate at that moment the fact that turning a laboratory for designing military aircraft during wartime into the Honkan, the Main Building, of a Christian university in postwar Japan exemplified the adage of turning swords into plowshares. I had unknowingly become part of an historical moment when I joined the ICU faculty.

My office was located on the third floor of the Honkan which gave me my first view of Mt. Fuji rising majestically in the distance above the trees that covered the campus. It was an awesome site. Who could have imagined on that first morning in Japan in 1959, looking out from my shabby office at Mt. Fuji from a former wartime military laboratory, that I would write these memoirs in the 21st century entitled Mt. Fuji From Our Window?

Next to my office separated only by a temporary partition was the office of Hidaka Daishiro, Dean of the Graduate School of Education. Professor Nishimoto introduced him as the former Vice Minister of Education. He explained that in the structure of the Japanese government the Minister of Education was a politician from the ruling party who was frequently replaced when the Prime Minister shuffled his cabinet for political purposes. The Vice Minister of Education, however, was a long-term professional appointment held by the senior official from within the Ministry. The Vice Minister administered the Ministry of Education and its policies and thereby held enormous power and influence in determining educational policy for the country.

My immediate response to the first meeting with Dean Hidaka was, in retrospect, natural. I thought of the contrast between my educational experience as a public school teacher in Hershey, Pennsylvania, for two years and that of Dean Hidaka's as the senior government official responsible for a nation's school system. It was a humbling as well as an intimidating thought to say the least. Who could have imagined on that day that Dean Hidaka would be instrumental in my decision nearly a decade later to earn the second Ph.D., this time at the University of London, the topic of a later memoir? We will learn more about Dean Hidaka in that memoir.

Professor Nishimoto introduced me to my other office neighbor, Mrs. Cho Kiyoko Takeda, the first Japanese female professor I ever met who was destined to serve as President of the World Council of Churches years later. During that first short meeting I was impressed with her English that grew out of her student days in America before World War II. I was also somewhat intimidated by Mrs. Cho who, although friendly toward me, exuded the aura of a decisive figure.

As a colleague in her division I soon learned that Mrs. Cho, a leading authority on the history of Japanese thought, was not only a distinguished scholar in the field, she was a powerful figure in divisional matters held in great esteem by her Japanese colleagues. During the countless divisional and departmental meetings I attended over the years with Mrs. Cho, I was often impressed when the senior Japanese male professors deferred to her, as I did. Without doubt she was and is one of the most concise and thoughtful Japanese scholars with whom I would have the privilege of serving at ICU. Who would have thought that when I met her long after retirement, when she was writing a perceptive history of ICU in the late 1990s, she recalled vividly our first meeting in 1959?

Professor Cho

We then ran into one of the Japanese faculty members in my department who fit into the same category as I did, young scholars with academic potential. Tsuru Haruo, who preferred to be called Harry by non-Japanese, had just returned from Teachers College, Columbia University, with a doctorate in psychology majoring in the new field of counseling. He was on the ICU faculty prior to his American graduate education and had been sent to Teachers College in New York in order to introduce the field of counseling in Japan. For a young man a few years older than I, his assignment to launch a new academic discipline in his country struck me as particularly challenging.

Harry's wife, Nobuko, trained as a nurse, was the founder of the ICU Clinic before the couple went to America. Who could have imagined on our first day at ICU in 1959 that Nobuko and Harry would become our dearest Japanese friends? But of enormous significance, Nobuko, with Harry's support, would play the pivotal role in the beginning of our family just four years later in the adoption of Japanese baby girls, the topic of another memoir. Harry and Nobuko fittingly became the god-parents of our first daughter.

Professor Nishimoto then ushered me around for brief introductions beginning with the President and on to the chairmen of the four divisions. My first meeting with President Yuasa Hachiro was unforgettable from several aspects. First of all he was a tiny frail-looking man with a commanding voice. Secondly his English was impeccable from his years in America from age 18 working on a farm for several years to earning the Ph.D. in entomology from the University of Illinois in 1920, and well beyond.

President Yuasa Hachiro

Professor Nishimoto briefly outlined Dr. Yuasa's background before we entered his office. After returning to Japan before World War II, Dr. Yuasa was appointed Professor of Agricultural Science at Kyoto

University and then President of the leading Christian university in the land, Doshisha. He had become well known in Japan before the war when he was forced to resign the presidency of Doshisha University under intense political pressure by an increasingly militaristic government. On a peace mission to the United States when World War II broke out, he remained in America returning to Japan shortly after the war ended to be reelected to the presidency of Doshisha. He resigned that post to assume the Presidency of ICU at its inauguration in 1953.

It was the manner in which Dr. Yuasa used the Japanese and English languages in personal meetings and in formal situations such as faculty meetings or graduation speeches that was so impressive. What I also found intriguing was his extemporaneous comments before a mixed Japanese-non-Japanese audience. He would begin his remarks in splendid English in his usual style in which the intonations went from the low to the high and to the low in a musical-type sequence. However in the middle of the English sentence he would insert the Japanese version with its conclusion, and then end with the conclusion in English. It was mesmerizing to hear whether you were Japanese- or English-speaking, or both.

Dr. Yuasa could effortlessly speak to Japanese and non-Japanese with powerful and often inspirational ideas in sharing his vision of ICU as a 'university of tomorrow' using Japanese and English in every sentence which was understood in both languages. It was an uncanny use of language that, in part, made him so effective as president of a new and unique institution founded on bilingualism. He was warm and very friendly in personal meetings with a disarming sense of humor, and yet profound and most thought-provoking in formal situations.

For the first time in my life, I was aware that I was before a natural born leader in the presence of Dr. Yuasa who exemplified Christian living. I never imagined that my initial encounter with someone who combined those unique qualities would be a Japanese. Dr. Yuasa and his endearing wife treated June and me as members of their family that began with dinner at their home the following evening.

Professor Nishimoto then took me on a tour of divisional offices beginning with Social Science in which my Department of Education was located. Dr. Ayusawa Iwao, Chairman, who spoke flawless English from his years of study in America, had served as Japan's representative to the International Labor Office in Switzerland. He was a most pleasant soft-spoken man who had distinguished himself as an effective negotiator in labor relations. He was well known abroad. One instantly liked Dr. Ayusawa, who had been greatly influenced by the Quaker faith, as a kind and thoughtful individual. His distinguished career in international circles made him that much more deserving of respect, which this young American recognized at the first meeting.

The meeting with the second Chairman, Dr. Kanda Tateo of the Humanities Division, was memorable. Dr. Kanda spoke impeccable British English from his Oxford days. His manner was also impeccably aristocratic in the finest sense. Even the manner in which he rode his bicycle on campus, that is, as he quietly rode by it appeared as if he wasn't pedaling so straight was his body, seemed somehow aristocratic. As one of Japan's leading scholars in classics from a most distinguished family of scholars from the Meiji period, his father a graduate of Amherst College and an outstanding Christian scholar in English before the War, Dr. Kanda was in a class by himself.

Having resigned from his senior position in literature at Tokyo University to join ICU from its beginning in the early 1950s, Dr. Kanda with his charming wife from a leading Japanese family were the personal links between ICU and the Imperial Family. Through a long-standing relationship between the Kanda family and the Imperial Household, the Kandas had developed a close relationship with the Emperor's brother, Prince Chichibu and his wife Princess Chichibu who survived her husband.

In an act of kindness the following week, Dr. Kanda brought a bag of apples to our door explaining that, "They're ordinary apples, but they came from Princess Chichibu." The implication was that they were royal apples. As I would soon learn Princess Chichibu had taken a deep interest in ICU attending major events such as graduation ceremonies where we had the opportunity to meet her. Dr. Kanda was the epitome of a Japanese scholar with deep roots in the Greek and British world of classical thought.

The next Japanese scholar to meet was the Chairman of the Natural Science Division, Dr. Sinoto Yoshito. He was the first Japanese on the faculty I met with limited ability in English. Nevertheless his self-effacing manner, always with a smile, masked his scholastic ranking. He, a devout Christian, was the leading geneticist at Tokyo University who resigned his prestigious position to join the faculty of the International Christian University. I would have the privilege of serving with him as he later became President of ICU during its darkest days of student turmoil, the topic of a later memoir.

Finally I met Dr. Robert Gerhard, an American, who chaired the Language Division. A former missionary born in Japan who had taught at a Christian college, Tohoku Gakuin, in northern Japan before and after the war, his knowledge of the Japanese language and the Japanese people was unequalled among the non-Japanese faculty. During our first summer in Japan, 1960, he would help us get settled in a cottage at Takayama near Sendai where we enjoyed a vacation at the Japanese shore on the Pacific Ocean next to his lovely summer cottage.

At the end of the short tour of chairman's offices on December 9, 1959, I realized that each undergraduate division at ICU was headed by a senior scholar who ranked among the leading figures in their respective fields. Beyond their academic distinction, they treated this young American who had attained little academic distinction and had insignificant educational experience with kindness and respect that I could not have imagined when I signed the contract to join the faculty of a university that I had never heard of six months previously.

That evening several American faculty couples, who had just learned that the Dukes from Pennsylvania had unexpectedly arrived on campus, paid us a visit each bearing gifts of food aware that we had no opportunity to get to a store of which there were few in the neighborhood. They were:

Dr. Donald Worth, Professor of Physics, Ph.D., Yale University, and wife Ardyce

Dr. J. Edward Kidder, Professor of Oriental Art and Archeology, Ph.D., Washington University, and wife Cordelia

Dr. Alan Gleason, Professor of Economics, Ph.D., University of Rochester, and wife Emily

Dr. Roger Geeslin, Professor of Mathematics, Ph.D., Yale University, and wife Lois

Dr. Richard Linde, Director of the ICU Freshman English Program, and wife Janet

ICU Friends

What a joy it was to meet these American couples, all except the Geeslins older than we were, who virtually engulfed us into the ICU family from that evening onward. They would become our dearest friends as well as colleagues. They immediately set up a schedule of dinners at their homes during our initial adjustment period when obtaining food we were accustomed to was a challenge. For example there were no nearby meat shops. A boy came to our door twice a week to take meat orders to be delivered the next day. Only after seeing the meat upon delivery did you know what you were getting.

It was such a comfort to have these American friends on campus who so generously assisted us in adjusting to a foreign country we knew virtually nothing about in December, 1959. It should be noted here that several months later Dr. Maurice Troyer, with his magnetic personality as Vice President, and gracious wife Billy returned from leave in America. They took us into their family from the moment we met them.

Who could have imagined on December 9, 1959, that in the next century in the year 2003 in retirement, we would hold an 'ICU mini-reunion' at our summer home in the beautiful Endless Mountains of Pennsylvania on Lake Mokoma? The Kidders drove up from North Carolina, the Worths flew in from California, and the Gleasons drove down from Rochester, New York, for several memorable days reminiscing about our early days together at ICU.

When we finally retired in the evening of my first full day on the faculty of ICU we were exhausted and yet exhilarated. It had been a long but memorable day in which I met over two dozen colleagues, adjusting to many styles of accented English. They included, among others, British, New Zealand, Indian, Norwegian, and Japanese. The day had also been filled with fascinating moments as I learned about the incredible diversity of the ICU faculty. Not only did my non-Japanese colleagues originate from countries as diverse as India and Norway, that is, from Asia to Europe including a significant contingent from the United States, the Japanese faculty had diverse experiences abroad before and after World War II that were profoundly impressive.

Further, the standard of English fluency among the Japanese faculty defied expectations. The vast majority could be categorized as fluent in English. My Japanese colleagues proved particularly fascinating not only because of their diverse backgrounds and facility in English, both unexpected, but their sense of humor took us by complete surprise. I simply did not expect to have senior Japanese scholars who enjoyed a good laugh, and could provoke a smile in others, as colleagues. Not only were my new Japanese colleagues very serious about, and dedicated to, the goals and purposes of their new institution, they were warm, friendly, and oftentimes disarmingly humorous in Japanese and English.

By the end of the day I realized that we were already being drawn into the 'ICU family.' We read about the concept of the ICU family in one of the brochures but could not imagine what it meant. However, after meeting two dozen of my colleagues on that cold December day in 1959, we had the exhilarating as well as comforting feeling of being part of a family of dedicated scholars and their wives who had committed themselves to an ideal of Christian higher education that I had never envisioned before.

I also realized at the end of my first day at ICU that the characterization of ICU as the 'Harvard of Japan,' which we dismissed as hyperbole in one of the early pamphlets, had a remarkable degree of validity. There was an international academic elite on the faculty of ICU made up of outstanding scholars from around the world. There was also a Japanese academic elite on the ICU faculty made up of outstanding bilingual Japanese scholars, many of whom had broad experiences overseas. Harvard University would have been proud to have them on its faculty. Who would have thought during our first full day in Japan in December, 1959, that we would remain at the International Christian University for the rest of the 20th Century?

MEMOIR 2

MY FIRST CLASS IN THE HONKAN
- A ONE-BUILDING UNIVERSITY ON
A VAST TOKYO CAMPUS -

Several days after I joined the faculty of the International Christian University in early December, 1959, classes convened for the third semester of a tri-semester system. Since our arrival was unexpected, no courses had been assigned for me to teach with the beginning of the December term. It was impossible to schedule an undergraduate course three days before term. Therefore a course listed in the graduate school catalog for visiting scholars entitled Seminar in Education I was hastily chosen for me to teach as I saw fit. I had not expected that my first course at ICU would be at the graduate level. Who would have thought that I would eventually serve as Chairman of the Graduate Division of Education for many years?

The course was scheduled for Monday evenings, 6 to 9 o'clock. The timing was arranged so that it would not interfere with the regularly scheduled classes thereby making it possible for graduate students to register for it at the last minute. An announcement was placed in all graduate student mailboxes. Surprisingly five students, about average for graduate seminar courses, signed up for my first course assigned to a small seminar room on the 4th Floor of the Honkan, the Main Building. Little could I have imagined that I would teach nearly all of my courses for the next forty years in the Honkan.

As I learned early on, the name of the Honkan, the Main Building, was not only apt, it was misleading. The Honkan was, in reality, the only academic building on campus. It not only included all of the classrooms, the Honkan also housed the library, the science labs, the administrative offices, and the faculty offices, including mine on the third floor. The faculty offices were located in refurbished rooms from the old aircraft laboratory designed for regular classroom use. Those assigned as offices were simply divided into three with movable partitions providing little privacy. In effect, ICU, the Harvard of Japan, was a one-building university.

The Honkan

To continue with the unusual situation I found myself in joining the ICU faculty in 1959, the Main Building where my office and classroom were located was a huge imposing four-story structure 375 feet long by 100 feet wide with over one hundred rooms. Noted above, it had been originally built as a research laboratory for an airplane company during

World War II which became the Fuji Heavy Industry Corporation. In
1949, during the postwar economic depression, a unique combination of
Japanese Christians and non-Christians was able to collect under great
odds enough money to purchase the estate of the Fuji Corporation where
the military laboratory was located. The Main Building symbolized the
very founding purpose of ICU in the proverbial turning swords into
plowshares. I did not fully appreciate that symbolism when I entered my
seminar room in the Honkan for the first time during a cold December
evening in 1959.

The physical setting of ICU was a contrast unimaginable. The
Main Building was located on a 360 acre wooded site within the city
limits of Tokyo, already one of the most heavily populated cities in the
world. The property would eventually become unbelievably valuable
as real estate prices increased many times during our years on campus.
However at the time of our arrival in 1959, the country had not yet
recovered from the devastation of World War II. The so-called Japanese
economic miracle had not yet taken off. Consequently ICU was a
very poor university economically although physically situated on an
enormous metropolitan campus. Academically, however, it was a first-
rate institution with one of the finest faculties on a standard with
leading foreign universities in Europe and North America including,
arguably, Harvard.

When I entered the small classroom on the 4th Floor of the
Honkan for my first class at ICU, not only did I not know what to
expect from my students, I had received no advice or instructions
what to teach, how to teach, how to evaluate the students, or what
to require of them to complete the course. I was on my own, which
was particularly challenging since I had never taught a course at the
university level, let alone a graduate course, and to Japanese graduate
students no less. My only teaching experience by 1959 was, as noted
previously, a two-year term as a public school teacher in Hershey,
Pennsylvania.

My first class.

I did receive one bit of advice from a young Japanese colleague who had graduated from ICU and knew of the physical conditions of the 4th Floor of the Honkan in the evening during the winter. It would be cold. His advice: "Be sure to take your top coat. You may even want to wear long underwear." I took the later warning as a feeble attempt at humor. It turned out to be otherwise.

To heat the four-story Main Building that extended over a hundred yards long required an enormous amount of fuel. ICU simply did not have the budget to accomplish this adequately in a land where fuel routinely costs twice or more as that in the United States. Consequently the classrooms were barely heated during the daytime. The heat was then further turned down each afternoon at 5 o'clock. By 6:30 or so, when few classes were scheduled, there was little difference between the temperature outside the building with that in the classrooms. An overcoat was essential. In fact I wore long underwear from the second class onward.

The small classroom contained a large round table for a seminar atmosphere. The five students, three males and two females, were already seated around the table when I arrived, with one exception. One of the Japanese female students, about my age, sat three feet back from the round table which caught my eye. I also noticed that she had an unusual western dress that resembled a Japanese kimono. As I walked by her chair I happened to notice a cord running from the bottom of her long dress back toward the wall plugged into the electrical outlet. I realized that she had a heating pad wrapped around her frail body. Since the electrical cord could not quite reach the round table, she sat a few feet away from the other students so the cord could reach the wall outlet.

From the moment I began my first lecture as a faculty member at ICU I had to adjust to the traditional atmosphere of the Japanese classroom. I was sensitive about the lack of response of my graduate students during class. I lectured. They listened. When I posed a question or asked if anyone had a question, there was little or no response. I became concerned that my students were not able to follow my English. I began to slow the pace of my presentations and to speak clearly and distinctly in order for them to have the best opportunity to follow the English lectures. I covered the black board with supplementary material hoping that the written English would aid the students who had, I assumed, problems with verbal English.

Although I did not appreciate it, I accepted the reality that Japanese students are reluctant to participate in class by asking questions or responding to questions posed to them. This attitude is even more difficult to alter when the class is taught in a foreign language. Since ICU was established as a bilingual institution, the use of English in the classroom by all non-Japanese faculty set the university apart from all the others in Japan.

However, it also rendered it more difficult to conduct discussions or stimulate responses in English with Japanese students who had come through high schools engrossed in university entrance examination preparation where little time is available for discussions. In that kind of an atmosphere teachers do not encourage questions. I learned from my Japanese colleagues that they also found their Japanese students reluctant to ask questions during class in Japanese. Nearly a decade later I introduced the tutorial system used at Cambridge and Oxford in an attempt to overcome lack of student participation that I encountered from my first class onward, considered in a later memoir.

When I reminisce about my first class at ICU over fifty years ago, I cannot recall the content or precisely how I handled that initial experience as a university teacher. Nevertheless I like to think of the quality of my first students according to their accomplishments. From this aspect I take considerable pride in being a part of their advanced education. One of the male students became a professor at Japan's leading national institution, Tokyo University. Another male student became a professor at Chiba University, a major prefectural institution. The third became a faculty member of a Canadian university from where he retired after a long and distinguished career.

One of the two female students married a Christian minister who served at the ICU Church. She became, in effect, the wife of our pastor. The couple then moved to South East Asia where they devoted many years in the mission field with a Christian organization headquartered in Singapore. They remain our dear friends to this day. And finally, the other female student in the class was the wife of an American professor at ICU. She taught Japanese at the American School in Japan. She was the student with the heating pad wrapped around her body to keep warm during the cold winter of 1959 in the Main, and only, Building during my first class at ICU.

MEMOIR 3

THE FIRST EDUCATION DIVISION RETREAT

- A MISADVENTURE WITH THE OFURO (BATH) AT A JAPANESE RYOKAN -

Two weeks after my arrival in Japan in early December, 1959, to join the faculty of ICU, our Division of Education held the annual Christmas Retreat at a Japanese Inn at the hot spring resort of Atami. Fifteen members boarded a mini bus for the two hour drive south from Tokyo arriving before dinner on a Saturday evening. It was my first opportunity to join my colleagues for a divisional retreat in what I expected to be a non-academic atmosphere to celebrate the joy of Christmas. This was also my first opportunity to experience the customs of the famed ryokan, the Japanese Inn, in this case one related to a consortium of private universities frequented by ICU groups.

Upon arrival it was announced that the ofuro was available to those who wished to bathe before dinner. Most of the faculty put on a hakata or ryokan robe for the bath. I donned mine but decided to take my bath before retiring for the evening, my usual routine. The dinner was a bit painful since it was my first experience eating on a tatami (straw mat) floor. I simply could not comfortably bend my legs under my body as the Japanese faculty did. I had to stretch them out under the low table.

Even that was awkward but I managed to eat a great deal of the many dishes except raw fish. That would take a period of time to get used to, although I grew to love it.

That evening we all met in a large room with tatami straw mats on the floor, that is, without chairs. Again sitting on the floor, we launched into the evening session discussing the future of the 'C' in the International Christian University. The discussion was completely in Japanese. Since I was the only non-Japanese faculty in the Department, a young Japanese instructor sat next to me quietly providing a simple translation.

The seriousness of the meeting to celebrate Christmas took me by surprise. I would eventually become accustomed to these seemingly endless intense faculty discussions designed in part to form a close relationship among us. However it had already become a tradition at ICU retreats to devote session after session on the topic of the I, or the C, or the U in ICU. As a relatively new institution in Japan founded on the concept of integrating Christianity and internationalism within a university context, few faculty members had a clear understanding what that entailed.

During the prolonged discussions at the Christmas retreat, each member was expected to participate in a discussion to clarify the meaning of Christianity in a university context. As I learned later there was a certain ambivalence in discussing the so-called C-Code, the requirement that all ICU faculty be baptized Christians. In a few instances it was rumored that baptism took place to fulfill the requirement for employment. The C-Code remained a topic of controversy throughout my tenure at ICU.

By midnight I was virtually in a daze as the discussion continued. My translator and fellow instructor could see that I was dozing off. He mercifully suggested that I go down and take my bath since everyone else had already done so. I thought that was a good idea. As inconspicuously as possible I crawled across the tatami to the door and left the meeting, picked up a towel and wash cloth from my room, and headed for the ofuro, my first experience with the famed Japanese bath.

Upon entering the ofuro area I was impressed by the size of the bath itself, obviously designed to accommodate families or small groups. It measured about six feet wide and eight feet long already filled with water up to one's shoulders when sitting on the bottom. It was beautifully designed and edged with stone masonry. My first thought was that this is truly a hot spring resort since the water was steaming hot straight from the ground.

Along one side of the bath itself was an area about four by eight feet long with faucets protruding from the wall. Several tiny wooden stools were stacked against the wall. I had no idea what the area was used for. I surmised that it was a place for women to wash their hair. I ignored it.

I then disrobed placing my yukata in a basket and stuck my foot into the bath. It was far too hot, scalding hot, in fact, for me to get in. I turned on the cold water faucet and let it run and run. Finally when the water temperature was reduced so that I could stand it, I slowly entered an ofuro for the first time in my life. What a glorious feeling it was when I finally submerged myself up to my neck.

I instinctively began to soap up and then rinse off by submerging my body into the bath over and over again. At last I could understand why the Japanese and many foreigners enjoyed the Japanese ofuro. This was a Japanese custom to love. Finally my body started to turn a bit red. I was also becoming drowsy from the hot water. I stood up, pulled the plug, and stepped out to towel off.

As I left the ofuro I took one last glance at the bath and thought what a wonderful custom it was, but what a waste of water. The bath was still more than half full by the time I had dried off. There was much water to run out. I figured it would take at least fifteen more minutes for all that water to run down the drain. I left with a wonderful feeling of relaxation and headed for my first night in Japan sleeping on a tatami floor. I concluded that the Japanese ryokan was truly a wonderful institution, but what a waste of water in the ofuro.

The next morning appointed members conducted a Christian service with a sermon followed by a continuation of the serious discussion on the C in ICU, all in Japanese of course. Most of my Japanese colleagues had already taken a morning bath. Unaccustomed to morning baths or showers I decided against it. However after an hour of discussion in Japanese, I decided once again to enjoy the wonderful ofuro by myself. I quietly crawled across the tatami and left the meeting headed for the ofuro.

I naturally followed the same wonderful routine of the night before by cooling down the temperature of the steaming bath with cold water, soaping up and rinsing off in the ofuro, and finally pulling the plug completing the second exhilarating experience of the Japanese bath. Upon departing the ofuro I again thought how wasteful of water it is as the gallons gurgled slowly down the drain. But I then thought that since it naturally flowed up from the underground hot spring, it was free. From that aspect it made sense. I returned to ICU from my first experience at a Japanese ryokan (inn) with a profound admiration for the Japanese custom of bathing in the ofuro.

And now the rest of the story . . .

Three months later June and I were preparing to leave Tokyo on a two-week site-seeing trip to the northern island of Hokkaido during our first spring break at the end of the Japanese academic year. We had engaged one of our graduate students to accompany us as guide and interpreter. While waiting in the train to depart from Tokyo Station a young faculty member from our Division suddenly appeared on the platform knocking excitedly on our compartment window. In the early 1960s long-distance trains in Japan were propelled by steam with the old-style windows that opened upwards from the inside. Our student-guide immediately pushed the window up to talk to my colleague who was by now out of breath from running to catch us before departure.

After a short rather animated discussion between the two in Japanese, the whistle blew for our departure and the train slowly moved forward as the steam engine huffed and puffed. My colleague ran along the platform keeping up with us while continuing the animated conversation with our student-guide. When he got to the end of the platform we were moving at a good pace. We all called out goodbye and the graduate student pulled the window down.

With a look of astonishment he turned and posed a question that baffled me. After I got out of the ofuro at the Atami ryokan during the Division Christmas retreat, "Did you pull the plug?" I replied that of course I did since I was finished taking a bath. Again in disbelief he asked, "Did you pull the plug twice?" With the same sense of conviction, and by now growing a bit irritated with such a line of questioning, I replied that of course I did when I took a bath again the next morning. "What else do you do when you finish bathing?" I asked our baffled young friend.

He then explained that the divisional colleague had come all the way to the station to catch us before we left on a two-week trip, when we would be staying at Japanese ryokans throughout, with an urgent message. It seems that his wife, an ICU secretary, had just returned from a spring retreat of secretaries held at the same ICU-affiliated ryokan as our Education Division had for the Christmas retreat. One of the ryokan staff mentioned to her that several months ago they were dismayed when a strange foreigner who stayed at the ryokan shortly before Christmas with a group from ICU left the water out of the ofuro after bathing, not once but twice.

On the way home she told the other secretaries about the ofuro story which provoked much consternation as well as laughter among them. By that time she recalled that I had been at Atami with her husband for the divisional Christmas retreat. She realized that the strange foreigner was surely her husband's American colleague. When she arrived home rather late from the trip on a Sunday evening, she immediately informed him about the unbelievable use of the Japanese ofuro by his foreign colleague.

Since her husband had arranged for our graduate student to accompany us on our two-week trip departing early the following morning with reservations at various ryokan, he realized that he must catch us at the train station before we departed. He had to notify our guide so he could explain to us how to properly use the Japanese ofuro. Otherwise he assumed that we would surely pull the plug in the ofuro at every ryokan where we were planning to stay.

As we picked up steam heading north from the station after our guide verified that it was indeed I who pulled the plug not once but twice at Atami, he quietly but with the most serious look on his face began his explanation with a simple statement of fact. "You do not pull the plug in the ofuro." And then he described the proper procedure in using the bath at a ryokan.

In taking a bath at a Japanese inn, one first soaps up outside the ofuro itself using the water from the faucets coming out of the wall beside the ofuro. To do so you sit on one of those tiny wooden stools that I had noticed stacked up against the wall by the ofuro at the Atami inn. After rinsing off the soap completely again with water from the faucets, one then enters the ofuro not for actual washing purposes, which is by that stage completed, but purely for relaxation. When one is totally relaxed you step out of the ofuro which remains full, and devoid of soap suds, for the next guest who will relax in the same water. You do not pull the plug.

Our graduate student, wise beyond his years who later became the principal of the elite Peer's Elementary School (Gakushuin), then concluded his lesson on Japanese customs for his foreign professor and wife with this profound statement. The procedure for using the Japanese ofuro handed down over the centuries works well when all bathers know and follow it. It fails when it is not. For the next forty years we appreciated the ofuro as one of the great customs of the Japanese by carefully following the proper procedure. We never pulled the plug.

MEMOIR 4

OUR FIRST CHRISTMAS – NEW YEARS AT ICU

- AN INTRODUCTION TO JAPANESE HOLIDAY CUSTOMS -

Two weeks after we arrived in Japan in 1959, we celebrated our first Christmas–New Years holiday at ICU. It began precisely at 8 o'clock, Christmas morning, when two workmen unexpectedly showed up at our doorstep each holding a can of paint and a paint brush. Obviously they had come to paint our apartment. Since Christmas fell on a weekday, and it's not an official holiday in Japan with schools, factories, and offices open as usual, the painters contracted from outside ICU had showed up for work unaware that it was Christmas Day. Christmas was obviously not part of the Japanese tradition. As we learned, New Years was the major holiday of the year when the country shuts down for family get-togethers.

We hastily arranged the bedroom for painting so we could prepare breakfast in the kitchen and have our Christmas breakfast in our dining room-living room area. We then settled down for a Christmas morning engulfed with the strong odor of fresh paint. It was not how we had hoped to begin our first Christmas in Japan.

Fortunately we had been invited for lunch and dinner at the homes of two American faculty members. We looked forward to that in part because we had no Christmas decorations. It was the first time in our lives that we did not have a Christmas tree in our house. In addition we had yet to become accustomed to using the old kerosene stove in our apartment for cooking and baking. Several times while trying to light the stove, a plume of smoke erupted from the strange device. It was clearly a fire hazard that intimidated us. And finally we were relieved to get out of the apartment for much of our first Christmas day in Japan to escape the smell of paint.

Our American hosts, Roger (Yale, mathematics) and Lois Geeslin for our first Christmas lunch, and the elderly Vice President for Finance Glen Brunner and wife for dinner, were most gracious. We had a wonderful time with both couples. We also experienced the ICU tradition of student caroling at Christmas time. Students, many of whom are not Christians, join in the traditional Christmas caroling on campus. Each holding a lighted candle they wind their way through the woods in long lines on the narrow lanes from one faculty home to the next. Stopping in front of each one they sing two or three carols before moving quietly on to the next. It remains one of the most endearing memories of our many years at ICU.

We did not look forward to returning to our apartment after dinner on our first Christmas Day at ICU not only because of the strong smell of paint. The noise from the construction of the new library underway less than fifty meters from our bedroom windows, as well as the lack of heat after 10 o'clock in our apartment building converted from a warehouse, was not something to look forward to.

The following day we received an invitation to a traditional Japanese New Year dinner at the campus home of Professor and Mrs. Nishimoto. A Japanese couple on campus also invited us to join them for a visit to the local temple on New Years eve. These were two opportunities to learn about Japanese customs about which we knew so little. We eagerly accepted both invitations as we approached our first major holiday in Japan.

On New Years eve, 1959, we hopped on our bicycles at 11:15 headed for Jindaiji, the major Buddhist temple in our area located about two miles from the ICU campus. Riding through the back streets of Osawa, the community surrounding ICU, we were struck by the silence. This was not a night of revelry as in the west. This was a night of quiet enjoyment with families.

As we approached Jindaiji, we ran into heavy traffic barely moving on the major road leading to it. By the time we rode past the cars to park our bikes near the temple, we had become engulfed in a river of Japanese quietly walking toward the entrance of the temple grounds. From that moment onward, we became part of an amorphous mass moving slowly toward the majestic temple. We had to stay with the flow.

Several thousand people that evening were all headed for the front of the temple where there was a special wooden container running across the steps leading to the temple entrance. We were advised to bring coins to throw into the box. As we slowly worked our way to the front, we got out our coins and threw them in the box, then veered off to the left and back out of the compound. The Japanese, as they approached the front not only threw their coins into the box, they paused, bowed, clapped their hands three times, and then veered off to the right or left to exit the compound. It took over twenty minutes to reach the front of the temple, one slow step at a time. The act of reverence was over in twenty seconds. Who would have thought that evening in 1959 that decades later, we would perform the same ritual, bicycles and all, during our last New Years at ICU in the 1990s?

The next day we had our second experience with Japanese customs at New Years. All non-Japanese on the ICU faculty were invited to experience food customarily associated with New Years in Japan at Professor Nishimoto's home on campus. That meant that it was served cold. As we were told, in agrarian Japan when relatives traveled long distances to return home for New Years, the demands on the hostess on New Years day were so great that she had little time to prepare a cooked meal for the guests. Hence the tradition of cold food for New Years prepared days ahead became a popular custom.

Professor Nishimoto, elderly chairman of my department, was a unique Japanese figure in many ways. As described previously, he had gone to America as a young man in the 1920s to study the most progressive theories of education in the west under the great John Dewey, first at the University of Chicago and then at Teachers College in New York City. He was famous as a Japanese pioneer in the new teaching methods founding the Audio-Visual Center at ICU, the first of its kind in Japan. It attracted many students especially at the graduate level. Nishimoto was a leading progressive in the field of Japanese education but deeply conservative otherwise.

Although often curt and condescending with his Japanese colleagues, Nishimoto san was generous and thoughtful of his non-Japanese colleagues. As a young American in his department, I came under the careful guidance of the chairman. He treated me, and June as well, with great consideration. For example, since there were few stores in our area when we arrived, he took us to the great Takashimaya Department store in downtown Tokyo assisting in the selection of furnishings for our apartment. He was committed to taking care of his young faculty member from America which I greatly appreciated.

In contrast, Nishimoto san's personal life style was one of tradition. In his relationship with his family, especially his wife, he followed the custom of maintaining the superiority of male over female in all matters. His wife seemed to appreciate her status and revered her husband. The three children endured it all while carving out distinguished careers for themselves. One, who became professor of Italian at Tokyo University, was also fluent in English and French. The other son became a scholar of modern education at another university in the footsteps of his father. The daughter studied in America attaining fluency in English. She came to my farewell lecture many years later presenting me with a magnificent scroll from her then-late father's collection with the comment that, "I know he would want you to have it." It hangs in our living room in America today.

That gift was indicative of Professor Nishimoto's special interest in high quality Japanese antiques such as scrolls, pottery, etc. When we first entered his campus home on New Years in 1960, we were immediately impressed with the Japanese antiques that adorned his home and of which he was very proud. Without being an authority, you knew they were of good quality, as was the scroll we received from his collection upon our departure long after his death.

Mrs. Nishimoto had obviously spent many hours preparing the traditional Japanese New Years dinner. There were a dozen splendid red and black lacquer trays of cold food artfully arranged on a table buffet-style. They included a variety of sweet red bean concoctions, fried beans and peas, a variety of tiny fish with beady eyes, vegetable dishes including lotus root and pickled turnip, dried squid rings, slices of raw fish, and rice cakes wrapped in seaweed. It was truly a site to behold.

Professor Nishimoto, dressed in traditional Japanese style in kimono or hakata, ardently wanted his non-Japanese colleagues to sample all of the traditional Japanese dishes to appreciate this great winter custom. He also had beautifully designed black ohashi (chop sticks) with which to eat the delicacies Japanese-style. His enthusiasm made it difficult not to try everything in moderation.

In one of the more embarrassing moments in our early days at ICU, while eating one of the beady-eyed fish with the delicate chop sticks which I could not yet properly use, I bit into one breaking the end off. Under the circumstances it provoked a sickening feeling. I had just damaged beyond repair a Japanese antique that my department chairman cherished. With great reluctance I sheepishly confessed my transgression which was gratuitously accepted by our hosts.

By the time we finished our first traditional New Years day Japanese dinner at ICU in the middle of the afternoon, we were beginning to feel the outcome of combining such an unusual assortment of foods with which we were unfamiliar. We excused ourselves after giving assurances that we had thoroughly enjoyed the dinner in appreciation of the hospitality of our kind Japanese hosts. By the time we returned to our cold apartment around four o'clock, we felt so badly that we took medicine for upset tummies. We went to bed early to recover from experiencing Japanese customs on our first New Years at ICU.

MEMOIR 5

PROCTORING THE GRUELING TWO-DAY ICU ENTRANCE EXAMINATION

- EXAMINATION HELL! –

In early January, 1960, one month after joining the ICU faculty, an announcement was circulated to all faculty and staff members concerning the 1960 entrance examination. Every year the exam in Japanese is administered in February to select the ICU freshman class for the Japanese school year beginning in April. All faculty members and assistants were expected to serve as proctors for the two-day examination. Specific room assignments for the proctors were listed. A bag lunch would be provided for the faculty each day. Classes were suspended during this period for three days, including one for the preparation, since every classroom was needed to accommodate over 1,800 applicants to fill the 180-student quota for Japanese. Non-Japanese applicants entered ICU in September and were handled through a documentary procedure.

I had no idea what to expect on examination day. I heard from colleagues that it was known to all Japanese as Examination Hell. I learned that a multi-billion yen industry had sprouted up around the annual university entrance examination season. Magazines with advice on taking the exams had proliferated with some specializing on specific entrance examinations such as Tokyo University with sample questions from previous year's exams.

Private preparatory schools called juku had increased sharply offering candidates a multiplicity of courses designed to sharpen the test-taking skills of eager high school students and their parents willing to pay the special fees. Most candidates devoted many an evening and weekend in prep classes no matter the sacrifice. College students earned extra income tutoring students to prepare for the exam. It had reached a fever-pitch level of competition among high school seniors and graduates. Some spent a year or two after graduation enrolled in jukus. The term Examination Hell was understood by all as an appropriate characterization of the state of affairs each February in Japan.

The final stage, the two-week period of examinations in late February, further intensified the examination frenzy. Candidates applied to take up to ten entrance examinations each with a fee of around $50 depending on the prestige of the institution. Rare was the student with sufficient confidence to apply for only one entrance examination.

Private universities profited from the annual examinations. It was reported that the prestigious private university Waseda earned enough income from the entrance examination with tens of thousands of applicants to construct a new building every year. Consequently maximum effort was made to schedule the exams to avoid conflicts with other universities at the same level of prestige. The entrance examination had become a highly competitive instrument that all universities had to devote significant time and effort to perfect.

University entrance examinations had also become a defining instrument for high schools, especially elite public and private institutions, whose popularity depended overwhelmingly on their success at placing graduates in the most famous universities. The primary PR statistic of virtually all leading high schools was the number of graduates who entered the elite national institutions, Tokyo or Kyoto University, or the private institutions, Waseda and Keio. In 1960 ICU was struggling to break into that elite category.

The key factor underlying Examination Hell in postwar Japan throughout the rest of the 20th century was curious in itself. Every Japanese high school student was well aware of the reputation that virtually all Japanese universities have, which includes ICU: It's difficult to enter the university but not difficult to graduate from it. That attitude has been one of the major motivating forces that drove the vast majority of high school applicants to devote countless hours in academic preparation for the exam, and parents to spend large sums of money to enable their sons and daughters to secure a place at as prestigious a university as possible since graduation was virtually assured.

The examination fee was not the only expense incurred by the applicant. Those registering for the ICU entrance examination who did not live in Tokyo had to find accommodations at a hotel or, if fortunate to have a relative living in Tokyo, stay with them. In addition, transportation costs plus meals for every examination added up to the basic expenses. Some students who lived outside Tokyo spent a week or ten days in the city to enable them to take several tests during that period at great expense to their families.

Each university chose a date for the examination so as to reduce the competition with other universities that would potentially attract a similar type of student. That was not an easy task since the examination period covered a fairly set time schedule when senior high schools suspended classes to enable their students to take the exams. In effect, all senior high schools and universities in Japan came to a halt during the annual entrance examination season in February each year.

On the appointed day of my first experience with the ICU entrance examination, I reported to my assigned classroom along with three other proctors at 8:40, twenty minutes before the beginning of the morning tests in the area of humanities. As I walked through the hallway of the huge Honkan or Main Building, I was struck at the quiet atmosphere in a building with nearly two thousand students in it. When I entered my assigned room it was eerily silent and tense with eighty applicants already seated in their assigned numbered seats sent out from the ICU examination office several weeks previously. Barely a word was spoken among them since they didn't know each other coming from high schools all over Japan. The majority, however, came from Tokyo high schools.

The regular proctors' duties were simple. We passed out and collected the examinations row by row in precise numbered order. We were not to talk to the students during the examination except to respond individually to a question. Otherwise we were either to sit quietly in the rear of the room with breaks of ten minutes staggered during each hour. At 8:50 two proctors walked between the rows of students with pictures taken from their application packets. The face on the numbered picture had to conform to the faces of the applicants in the assigned seat number to verify the identity of the test taker. That process was carried out quickly and in complete silence.

Meanwhile the chief proctors reported to the test headquarters to pick up the test papers, and to adjust their watches to the minute with the official clock. The chief proctor carrying the examination papers then entered our room with a brief greeting to the tense applicants, a simple statement usually about the weather, and handed the exam papers to the proctors to pass out.

At the assigned moment of 9 o'clock, the chief proctor in each room began reading the instructions as each applicant followed along on the front page of the exam, and asked for any questions with rarely a response. Outside the door sitting in the hall was an assistant who was informed at 9:05 that all was ready. If for any reason there was a problem, the assistant was to hurriedly notify the test headquarters which would turn on the loud speaking system in each room and notify all proctors to wait for further notification to begin the test. During the many exams I proctored at ICU, there was rarely a delay.

Then, while carefully checking their watches, at a precise moment all proctors as if in unison instructed the students to begin. As one, all 1,800 applicants lurched forward to begin two days of examinations that included humanities, social sciences, natural sciences, Japanese,

English, and an interview. With that, my first experience as a participant in Japan's notorious Examination Hell was underway at ICU.

My initial impression was one of amazement at the precision and solemnity of the procedure. This was indeed very serious business. However the precision of it all, with exact timing according to the minute to begin and end the examination, had a special purpose that I soon came to respect. It was meant to provide an equal opportunity for each applicant. No matter how rich or poor, how far away one lived, etc., every applicant who took the ICU entrance examination received precisely the same treatment. No one could use family or political influence to enter ICU. The process represented democratic education in the Japanese tradition.

I found the first morning of the exam of great interest. The shear intensity of it all fascinated me. At the end of the first exam at the same moment, the students were told to stop. They all leaned back with a sigh of relief when the ten minute bathroom break was announced. However the opportunity to actually use the facilities was limited although portable toilets had been rented. Students on the upper floors of the huge Main Building had no opportunity to run down the steps to use them. The lines, especially in front of the girl's bathroom on each floor, discouraged most female applicants from even attempting a bathroom break.

After the second exam that morning, a lunch hour was scheduled. Virtually all students brought an obento, a lunch box, to be eaten at their desks. The lines in front of the bathrooms, particularly in front of the girl's bathroom, predictably wound down through the corridors. By this time a few students seated next to each other began to converse with each other. Otherwise even during the lunch hour, solemnity prevailed.

I had by now come to feel enormous empathy with the eighty candidates in my assigned room since I had never experienced anything remotely resembling the Japanese entrance examination. I marveled at how each candidate coped with the intensity of the environment surrounding him. I wondered how many realized the odds of passing the ICU examination. In our room it averaged one from each row. When I mentioned my reaction to a Japanese colleague during the lunch break, he reminded me that many of the applicants in our room were 'veterans' of the examination hell having taken other exams already. Not a few were also going through the process for the second or third year. Even then I wondered how they adapted to the pressure.

By the end of the first day the students were exhausted. It was a grueling experience to be sure. They filed out across the campus headed for a long line of buses and taxicabs waiting to take them from the ICU campus to the Mitaka train station. Each bus was jammed to the fullest as it pulled away for the 20-minute ride. The next morning the taxis and buses filled to capacity arrived on campus between 8 and 8:30. The candidates, slightly reduced in number from the previous day with some having already given up, headed for their assigned seats for the second day of exams. We all carefully followed the same procedure as the previous day. By now there was more interaction among the candidates and with the faculty proctors. I made a habit of opening a conversation in English during the breaks with as many as I could. Most reacted with some trepidation.

There was one major exception to the routine during the second day. The afternoon was set aside for personal interviews, a distinctive feature of the ICU exam that not only set it apart from all other institutions, it was an arduous experience that those who were accepted to ICU never forget. Not a few of the Japanese students in my classes remembered that I had served as an interviewer when they took the examination.

The interviews were difficult to manage and difficult to evaluate. Three faculty met with three students seated across from each other for a 20-minute session. It was meant to provide an opportunity for each candidate to reveal his or her special qualities that would render them the best candidate to not only benefit by the unique bilingual education ICU offered, but one who could also contribute to it. To make that critical analysis among three students in twenty minutes was extremely demanding. I was given about three minutes to ask a question in English which was always, "Why do you want to come to ICU?" To most it was a challenge to their English ability.

During the several decades that I proctored the ICU entrance examinations, there was only one serious incident that, predictably, caused an uproar within ICU with later repercussions. In the midst of the test on English literature that year, the loudspeakers in every room suddenly came alive with the announcement to stop the examination immediately. By that year the number of candidates reached over four thousand, all of whom instantly put down their pencils in astonishment. We waited for twenty minutes before the second announcement was made that the literature examination would not continue. The proctors were instructed to collect the exam papers and the answer sheets. The next examination would begin on time.

This is the incredulous story behind that event that we learned about later. The American professor of English literature who annually designed the English literature examination always chose specific questions from it to be distributed the following year to those magazines that catered to students planning to take the ICU examination. The exact questions from the previous year's test were made public as an opportunity for potential candidates to become familiar with the type of questions used in the ICU exams.

During the year of the infamous incident, questions from the previous year's exam that had been made public were mysteriously included without revision in the current examination. It was suddenly brought to the attention of a proctor during the exam when a candidate reported that he had seen the same questions with the answers in a magazine. That brought the examination to an immediate halt, which was reported in many newspapers bringing what was considered by some Japanese faculty and staff as shame upon the university.

During the faculty meeting following the notorious incident, the American professor responsible for the English literature exam who had been on the ICU faculty for many years, blamed the procedural error on his assistant. He claimed that he was not shown the section to be made public from the previous year's exam. The professor did not show remorse by accepting responsibility for the negative publicity for ICU that resulted from the mix-up. It was just one incident among several others that followed which led to his termination as an ICU faculty member. Examination Hell took its toll on professors as well as students.

The final scene in the grueling ICU entrance examination took place several weeks later when the results were made public. Each student was notified that on a certain Saturday morning at 10 o'clock, the examination numbers of the successful candidates would be posted in front of the Main Building. A notice by mail would also be sent to arrive the following Monday.

I was advised by a Japanese colleague to take advantage of the opportunity to observe the scene before the Main Building on that Saturday in February, 1960. There was a large crowd of students and parents waiting anxiously for the staff to appear. A temporary billboard about five meters wide and one meter high was already attached to tall stakes set in the ground. Several staff appeared with a five meter scroll rolled up with the numbers of the successful candidates printed in large figures in numerical order.

As the staff slowly unrolled the scroll across the billboard carefully attaching it as it went along, the students and/or parents frantically searched for the magic number. Suddenly howls of joy went up as the successful candidates spotted their numbers. Many jumped for joy, hugged friends or parents, and experienced the exhilarating feeling that Examination Hell had ended for them.

At the same time when the unfolding scroll passed the vacant slots where unsuccessful candidate numbers would fall, those who failed could be identified as easily as those who passed. With their heads down they quickly walked away toward the bus either alone or with a parent, some with tears streaming down their faces. Examination Hell was not over for them.

MEMOIR 6

FULFILLING MY MILITARY OBLIGATION AS CAPTAIN ON SUMMMER DUTY WITH THE U. S. ARMY IN KOREA

- THE ICU FRIENDSHIP BRIDGE BETWEEN JAPAN AND KOREA -

In early June, 1960, immediately after the last class at ICU as my first summer vacation began, I shed the coat and tie of a university teacher for the uniform of a Captain in the United States Army Reserve. Under orders from the Army I boarded a Military Air Transport plane at Tachikawa Air Force Base in the suburbs of Tokyo. Several hours later I arrived at Kimpo Airport in Seoul to report for obligatory summer duty at the headquarters of the U.S. Eighth Army. A new and unlikely adventure as a faculty member of the International Christian University in Japan was underway in Korea. It unexpectedly evolved into a commitment to initiate the first student exchange between Japan and Korea since World War II.

Social and political unrest was widespread in both Japan and Korea in 1960. In April, Korean student organizations provoked a national uprising against the longtime dictatorial regime of Syngman Rhee that had banned non-government travel between Japan and Korea. Political unrest continued after his resignation as the government struggled to contain student militancy. University campuses were paralyzed for prolonged periods.

Amidst the government crisis in Korea, activist students at ICU encouraged by several faculty members joined in the massive street demonstrations involving over a half million participants protesting the extension of the ten-year Japan-U.S. Security Treaty (Ampo Joyaku). Tumultuous sessions took place in the Diet when it finally ratified the Treaty on May 20. The campaign against the continuation of American military bases in Japan according to the provisions of the controversial treaty culminated at the Haneda International Airport on June 10th. President Dwight Eisenhower's Press Secretary and the American Ambassador to Japan were surrounded in their car by demonstrators and forced to evacuate by helicopter. As a result President Eisenhower had to cancel his scheduled visit to Japan the following week to commemorate the signing of the treaty by Prime Minister Kishi earlier on January 19, 1960, in Washington.

When we arrived in Japan in December, 1959, six weeks before the treaty signing, the Japanese political world was already unsettled over the proposed treaty authorizing the continued presence of American military forces in Japan. At that time I knew very little about the treaty. Since I had no interest in Japan when the unexpected letter arrived at Penn State offering me a position at ICU, I was only vaguely aware of the state of relations between the two countries. As most Americans, I had assumed that all was well since the American government considered Japan a loyal ally in the defense of western-style democracy in Asia. At the same time I had only a superficial understanding of political opposition movements in South Korea, assuming all was well with the U.S. 8th Army protecting that country from aggression by communist North Korea.

It was not long after our arrival that I learned otherwise. During the Japanese demonstrations that led up to the huge 1960 May Day protest, several of our most active ICU students were arrested and jailed by the riot police. At the same time many meetings of students and faculty were held on the ICU campus. A valiant effort was made to arrive at some understanding of the proper role of ICU students in the campaign against the government under Prime Minister Kishi, often vilified as a war criminal arrested by the American Occupation authorities for war crimes and imprisoned. By 1960, as Prime Minister in favor of the treaty, he was considered by the Americans as an ally.

Even the ICU Church became involved in the growing controversy. At one congregational meeting convened after the Sunday morning service to discuss the church's position on the treaty, an American professor of political science proposed that the church send a letter of opposition to the treaty to President Eisenhower with signatures of all members who agreed with that position. We spent a long time arguing the wisdom of such action by a church body before it was voted down.

About that time a group of activist ICU students decided to show their solidarity with the students demonstrating on the streets by conducting a peaceful march from ICU to the Mitaka train station. One of them gave a short speech critical of the treaty and the Japanese government's handling of it in the Diet. The group then quietly dispersed. Never once during this entire period did we as Americans have any concern over our personal safety either on campus or on the streets of Tokyo.

In the midst of the controversy growing more militant by the day, my orders from the United States Army to report for active duty as a Reserve officer for two weeks in Korea arrived. This was not the first time that I wore the uniform of an American soldier. When I graduated from high school in 1949, relations between the United States and the communist world of the USSR and China were so tense that the military draft of 18-year-old males was in effect. However, if accepted into college, a deferment was essentially automatic until graduation. When the Korean War broke out shortly thereafter, my deferment as a college student kept me out of the army until graduation.

I knew that after college I would be drafted into the army within a short period. Immediately upon graduation in June, 1953, as an adventure before army duty, I drove to Alaska from Pennsylvania with a buddy for summer work with a construction company. The trip to Alaska was a fascinating experience itself driving through the great Yellowstone National Park followed by the unpaved 1600-mile Alcan Highway across the Canadian Rockies to Anchorage.

When the draft notice for military duty reached me in Alaska during the middle of the summer of 1953, I had the option to undergo the physical examination at an army base in Alaska or return promptly to Pennsylvania for the examination. I choose to have it done in Alaska so that I could stay as long as possible to continue receiving the high wages paid to construction workers. Moreover, since I was working on a construction site at a military base near Anchorage, I observed recruits marching into the surrounding mountains already covered by snow for basic training. I decided to return to the States for basic training.

Having passed the physical examination in Anchorage, a notification was received that I would be drafted into the United States Army in October. In September I flew from Anchorage to Seattle and hitch-hiked across America to Pennsylvania, another adventure from another era when hitch-hiking was common in the States, to prepare for induction. I also arrived home early to propose to my high school sweetheart, June Smith, who lived only two blocks from my family home in Berwick. She accepted and we planned to get married during the first furlough after basic training. I then went off to begin the mandatory two-year service as a private in the United States Army.

After six months serving at the Red River Arsenal in Texarkana, Texas, where June joined me in our first apartment located off-base, I looked into the possibility of earning a commission as a 2nd Lt. based in part on my college degree. I learned that through correspondence courses I could qualify for a commission after passing a series of examinations. I enrolled in the course and after a year of correspondence work with many examinations I was commissioned as a 2nd Lt. in the United States Army Reserve in 1954.

At that time I was given the options of holding the commission in the Reserves while remaining an enlisted man on active duty to fulfill the two-year obligatory service, or being appointed as an active duty officer for four years. Both options included a ten-year commitment in the Reserves. I decided on the former and completed the two-year period of service and was discharged in 1955 to take a teaching position in the public schools of Hershey, Pennsylvania.

I continued to hold the commission in the Army Reserves fulfilling the yearly requirements to do so, and had been promoted to the rank of captain with a commitment of ten years service, that is until 1964, when I joined the faculty of ICU in December, 1959. At that time I did not notify anyone at ICU about my status with the Reserves since it seemed irrelevant. I also had an obligation to report for summer duty at an American military base as an officer in the Reserves during the summer vacation of 1960, my first at ICU.

When I arrived on the ICU campus I soon learned for the first time about the controversial United States-Japan military pact then under consideration in the Japanese Diet that would authorize the continuation of American military bases on Japanese soil. In effect it would sanction the many bases that had been approved in the 1951 San Francisco Peace Treaty between the two countries at the end of the U.S. military occupation of Japan following World War II in 1945.

As mentioned above, opposition to the treaty by the time of our arrival in Japan was spreading especially among labor unions and student associations. Trains were often halted during half-day strikes. Schools were also closed as militant teachers joined the workers in a display of solidarity. There were frequent demonstrations on the streets of the major cities, the most prominent ones taking place in Tokyo. Our students were well aware of the role that activist students from virtually all of the major colleges and universities were beginning to play in the demonstrations. It struck a sympathetic reaction among many.

In May, 1960, along with the orders from the United States Army Reserve to report to an American base for summer duty in 1960, a list of eligible American bases in Japan as well as the 8th U.S. Army base in Seoul, South Korea, was included. Amidst the rising tide of opposition against American bases in Japan, I chose the Korean option even though I was fully aware of the recent overthrow of the Rhee government instigated by a nationwide student campaign. Shortly thereafter I received orders to report for duty at the Headquarters of the 8th Army in Korea in early June, with reservations on a Military Air Transport plane from Tachikawa Air Force Base in western Tokyo to Kimpoo Airport in Seoul.

Meanwhile, since the Japanese Diet had ratified the Treaty on May 19, President Eisenhower planned to visit Japan in mid-June as a goodwill gesture marking the reaffirmation of the strong relations between the two countries. Since I was scheduled to leave Japan for Seoul before his arrival, I was sorry that I would not be in Tokyo when the President, whom I had never seen, would arrive. As the time grew closer to his visit, opposition to the treaty by students, labor unions, and many academics grew more intense provoking police efforts to contain it on the streets.

On the day of my departure for Seoul, as the tempo of opposition in Tokyo reached a crescendo, I dressed in the uniform of a captain in the United States Army Reserve. I borrowed the old American station wagon owned by ICU along with the driver to take June and me to the Tachikawa Air Force Base to arrive several hours prior to my departure scheduled for 4 PM. The reason we left so early was to have sufficient time to shop at the PX on base. In 1960 Japan was still in an economic depression. Very few items that we considered essential as Americans were available in the few stores around ICU. For example we could not find a simple ironing board or cooking utensils that we were used to. The trip to the American base was our first chance since we arrived in Japan six months previously to stock up on the basics. We were not about to let the opportunity pass us by.

Upon entering the huge Tachikawa Air Force Base we headed straight for the bank where we changed U.S. dollars into military script upon showing my official military orders. From there we went to the PX and found it overwhelming. Not only did it resemble a big supermarket in America, the prices were so reasonable that we couldn't resist the temptation to buy as much as would fit into the station wagon. We literally bought a station wagon full of American products. I recall that when I was dropped off at the terminal, I chuckled at how full the station wagon was with the ironing board sticking out the window as June returned to campus with the driver.

Upon arrival at Kimpo Airport I reported to the Education Center of the 8th Army and was given the assignment to survey the Education Centers at five regional American bases. I was to evaluate their effectiveness in a final report to the commander of the 8th Army. Much to my astonishment I was given a map with the location of the five basses and a telephone number to call to reserve a small single engine plane to be made available to take me to and from a particular base each day to carry out the study. A car would be sent to pick me up at my officer's billets and take me to a small nearby airport to board the plane. And that is exactly what I did during duty hours for the fifteen-day period of my assignment.

During the first week in Korea, an unexpected development took place. President Eisenhower, who had planned to visit Japan commemorating the signing of the Japan-American Peace Treaty, could not land at the Tokyo International Airport because of student demonstrations. Instead he came to Korea where a welcoming parade was held for him on the streets of Seoul which I witnessed. When he passed by, as a uniformed officer of the United States Army Reserve, I saluted my Commander-in-Chief. I could not help but think of the irony of our ICU students joining in the protest to prevent the American President from visiting Japan.

During the weekends in Seoul from Friday at five o'clock, I was off duty and on my own. In 1960 Korea was not only an extremely poor country, it was also politically unstable under virtual martial law as a result of the uprising by students and workers that overthrew the government. Policemen were everywhere guarding against protest activities especially by students. The roads were crowded with horses, wagons and carts mixed with pedestrians. Cars were a luxury of the few. Although Japan was also experiencing an economic depression, conditions in Korea were decidedly worse.

It so happens that shortly before I left for Korea I met an American missionary who attended an ICU Church service one Sunday morning. He was on his way home from teaching at Yonsei University, the great Christian institution in Seoul founded by an American Missionary, Horace Underwood. Classes had been suspended due to the protests that led to the overthrow of the Rhee government.

Over lunch I asked him many questions about Yonsei since I was scheduled to fly to Seoul in about two weeks. In the short time we had together he explained a bit about the student movement against the oppressive Rhee government expressing considerable sympathy for the students. He also strongly urged me to visit the Yonsei campus while I was in Seoul giving me his name card as a reference when calling for an appointment with a descendent of the Underwood founder currently on the faculty. He wrote down the telephone number to call.

Several days after arriving in Korea I called the number, identified myself as an acquaintance of the missionary from Yonsei that I had met as a faculty member of ICU, and made an appointment for the following Saturday. I appeared in civilian clothes at the entrance to Yonsei University in a taxi a good hour and a half before the meeting to walk around the campus to get the feel of it. To do so I had to pass through a student barricade that was erected to keep the police out of the campus after the student-led coup several months previously. Under the circumstances the university was closed.

On passing through the student barricade I took the opportunity to ask several questions about their activities. Several student representatives who had a good command of English crowded around me. I showed them my meishi, the name card in Japanese and English identifying me as a faculty member at ICU in Tokyo. They immediately found me of considerable interest and eagerly responded to my questions about their movement. But they also had many questions about Japan, ICU and student life, and especially the political opposition on campus to the Japanese government and Prime Minister Kishi. The more we talked the more I displayed a genuine interest in their activities. By the time I had to end the conversation for my meeting, I had formed a positive image of the Yonsei student leaders and a nascent sympathy for their movement.

My interest in Yonsei University was further enhanced when I met the descendent of the Underwood family instrumental in founding the institution currently on the faculty. His story of the origin of the university had a certain similarity to ICU, both with significant involvement and support by American churches and missionaries. I returned to my officer's billets on the 8th Army base with a new realization that the two institutions, ICU and Yonsei, had a great deal in common and could play a role in bringing about a new relationship, a friendship bridge, between the two countries with a bitter historical past.

The following week I called my new American friend at Yonsei expressing my desire to visit the campus again during the weekend. He invited me for the church service on Sunday followed by lunch. I jumped at the opportunity to further my knowledge of Yonsei. I asked him if possible to arrange for me to meet some Christian students during my visit, which he did. I had a most enjoyable second visit to Yonsei and a particularly enjoyable meeting with five students who were capable of expressing in English their ideas and frustrations under the prevailing political and social unrest in their country.

The students also asked me a number of questions about ICU expressing a strong desire to visit our school. Their genuine interest provoked a spontaneous response from me. I asked them if they would participate in a student exchange between Yonsei and ICU if scholarships were available. They supported the idea with enthusiasm. They were also convinced that Japanese students from ICU would be welcomed on the campus of Yonsei University now that the repressive Rhee government which banned student exchanges between the two countries had been overthrown. I left Yonsei determined to make an effort to bring this about.

Returning to my status as a United States Army Reserve officer, I completed the assignment to survey the educational program of the U. S. 8th Army on time and submitted the report of my conclusions on the final day of duty. Upon arrival at the Tachikawa Air Force Base in Tokyo, June met me with the ICU station wagon. We once again visited the PX to buy additional American goods that would make our life more convenient at ICU while I was still wearing the uniform of an American soldier. I arrived home on the ICU campus satisfied with my contribution to my country, and with a new interest in Japan-Korean relationships in the postwar era, particularly the unique role ICU could play enhancing them.

And now the rest of the story . . .

When the fall term at ICU opened in September, 1960, I learned that two ICU students had attended a Christian work camp in Korea during the summer when I was there. They were the first non-official Japanese to visit Korea since the war ended in 1945. I met with them to discuss their visit and learned that they were intent on starting a student exchange between ICU and Korean universities. I gave them my strong support and encouragement based on my recent experience at Yonsei University. I assured them that Korean students, in particular from Yonsei University, would welcome the opportunity to study at ICU and that ICU students would be welcomed to study at Yonsei, reflecting the Christian commitment of both institutions.

In October we arranged a student-faculty convocation to launch a movement on the ICU campus which the students named LIKS, Let's Invite Korean Students. The two ICU students who attended the work camp in Korea, one of whom would later study at Yonsei to become professor of Korean studies at ICU, Kawashima Fujiya, along with ICU Professor Norman Sun who visited Korea in August, and I spoke in favor of the proposal.

The following day the Mainichi Daily News carried our pictures under the headline DRIVE TO INVITE ROK STUDENTS BEGUN AT ICU. I was quoted accordingly. "Dr. Duke stated that young Koreans were tremendously interested in Japan. Any understanding, and particularly trust, must come from the younger generation of both countries." That convocation did indeed spark a movement on campus to open a "friendship bridge" between Japan and Korea. The following year three students and one professor from Korea came to ICU. It marked the first exchange of students between Japan and Korea since the war.

In one of the great ironies that grew out of my military obligation in Korea, among the exchange students from Yonsei later on was a graduate student named Byung-Yul Yoon who was assigned to me as his advisor. From that moment another adventure was set in motion that eventually resulted in the inauguration of The Dr. Duke-Dr. Yoon Scholarship Fund For Korean Students at ICU, covered in another memoir.

To move ahead with the rest of the story concerning my military commitment, when my ten-year obligation to the United States Army Reserve ended in 1964 I had to make a decision. If I signed up for another period of service, it would include a promotion to the rank of major since I had become eligible for a promotion based on the Ph.D. and experience. However, if I intended to remain on the faculty of ICU for a prolonged period, which June and I decided we would since we were enjoying our life on campus immensely, it would be prudent to terminate my relations with the United Stated Army Reserve.

In addition, student unrest was reemerging on most university campuses in Japan as the American military involvement in Vietnam increased with tacit Japanese government approval. I resigned my commission before the summer vacation. With that, my summer adventures in Korea as an officer in the United States Army Reserve came to an end. Ironically they led to a commitment to, and involvement in, the improvement in Japan-Korean relations through student exchanges between ICU and Yonsei University.

MEMOIR 7

FAREWELL PARTY ON MT. FUJI

- CHAMPAGNE TOAST TO A DEPARTING COLLEAGUE AT 13,000 FT. –

W hen we arrived at ICU in December, 1959, the differences in age between me and the graduate students in my first class was not significant. One was older than I, one about the same age, and the other three were two or three years younger. When the students in the ICU Graduate Division of Education planned a farewell party for a young instructor going to America to study for the doctorate, Nakano Terumi, and his wife, they invited June and me to join the party numbering about a dozen. Since the site of the party was planned for the top of Mt. Fuji in July of 1960, the students may have concluded that I was the only graduate faculty member physically able to climb the great mountain. Most of the others in the division except Nakano san were senior Japanese scholars.

We were told about the famous adage among Japanese that one is a fool not to climb Mt. Fuji once in a lifetime, and that one is a fool to climb it more than once. Having been in Japan for eight months, this seemed an ideal opportunity to climb Mt. Fuji once. With the assurance that mountain-climbing experience was not necessary, we accepted the student invitation with some anxiety.

We joined the party very early on a typically hot Saturday in July for the bus ride from ICU to Mitaka station, the commuter train ride on the Chuo Line to Shinjuku, and the long-distance train to Hakone near the base of Mt. Fuji. Out of curiosity we asked what was in the three wooden boxes, each about two feet long and a foot deep, carried on to the train by the male students in addition to their backpacks. We were told that we would find out at the top of Mt. Fuji.

We transferred at Hakone to a bus that took us to the fifth station, about halfway up Mt. Fuji, where most climbers begin the ascent of the famous mountain on foot. The trail was already packed full of climbers. Newspaper reports the following Monday estimated that 10,000 people climbed Mt. Fuji that weekend. The crowd was so intense that when we approached the path, we had to line up in rows of fours. And that is precisely how we climbed Mt. Fuji. In a seemingly endless line of rows of four climbers each, we began a steady but moderate pace working ourselves up a meandering path that led past four more stations.

Very shortly after departing the 5th station in our assigned rows, we became aware of one of the hazards of climbing Mt. Fuji on a weekend. Although not a dangerously active volcano today, the mountainside is covered with loose stones that were spewed out of the crater during an earlier volatile era. They ranged in size from small stones to sizable ones larger than a basketball. With the path wandering back and forth up the mountain packed full of climbers in rows of four using every inch of the path, it was inevitable that from time to time climbers knocked loose a rock of considerable size that went rolling down the mountain side.

When someone became aware of a loose rock tumbling down toward those on the path directly below, which occurred every so often, they yelled "abunai" (danger) which prompted others to join the chorus of warnings. Since the climbers below were in such tight proximity as 10,000 people ascended the great mountain, there was a moment of panic as those directly in the path of the tumbling rock lurched to get out of the way. Amazingly in only one instance did we witness a climber struck by a tumbling stone requiring first aid by the staff of the national park.

As we reached the higher altitudes, our group took periodic breaks by simply getting out of line and sitting on the ground next to the path for ten or fifteen minutes. During one break we ate our lunch brought from home. With a very polite request each time, we asked to be let back in line to continue. Hour after hour we proceeded up Mt. Fuji in a once-in-a-lifetime goal to reach the top of the mountain that is visible from the windows of our home on the ICU campus.

The plan was to continue climbing until we reached the 9th and last station before the top to buy our dinner and spend the night. At four o'clock in the morning on Sunday we were to get up and go outside to hopefully watch the sun rise, guaranteed to be a most spectacular moment well worth the trip. We would then continue to the top for the farewell party and descend on the opposite side to a bus stop at the bottom. We were scheduled to be back in Tokyo late Sunday evening.

The 9th station on Mt. Fuji at dusk was something to behold. It was simply a large building with simple facilities to provide a meal, the food having been carried up on the backs of porters. It contained one huge open room accommodating several hundred hikers with reservations. After eating we were lined up in long rows and instructed to lie down on the tatami floor as tightly as possible to enable everyone to get in. The staff then distributed blankets that were placed over each row since it gets very cold near the top of 13,000 foot Mt. Fuji at night.

What an adventure sleeping on Mt. Fuji was in itself. Every hiker was totally exhausted after many hours climbing to the 9th station. Along with several hundred others, we were then jammed together on the floor pushed tightly up against our graduate students for the night on the great mountain. It was a tedious experience. Primitive toilets were lined up outside so that when one had to use the facilities, and many did before the sun came up, you crawled out of the blanket so that it didn't come off the neighbor on either side. You then wound your way through the mass of sleeping hikers to the outside toilets, stood in line, and then retrace your way back to your tiny spot to crawl under your shared blanket. By now we realized the wisdom of climbing Mt. Fuji only once in a lifetime.

By 4 in the morning, most of the climbers who stayed over at the 9th station were perched on the side of the mountain as the sun slowly peeked over the distant horizon. With only a few clouds in the sky, we experienced an unobstructed view of the sunrise from the top of Mt. Fuji which can only be described as awesome. What added to the moment was the hush that came over several hundred climbers who, as one, were so overcome by the spectacular site that they fell silent.

By five AM we were back on the trail to complete the climb to the top of Mt. Fuji within several hours. After passing through a tori constructed over the path, signifying entry to a Shinto shrine, the first impression of the crater of the huge volcano concerned the amount of litter that covers the inner area of the cone. Thousands of climbers eat lunch at the peak. Many simply throw the plastic containers on the ground. The winter winds blow them off. That was disappointing.

Our group staked out an area on the top of the cone for the farewell party. The three wooden boxes that were carried up the mountain by the male students were then opened. The contents included several bottles of champagne, wine glasses for all, and presents for my young colleague. Farewell speeches were given by several students with a response by the guest and his wife. And then a farewell toast was made as the sun rose majestically directly over Mt. Fuji, followed by picture-taking. It was all a grand affair in an unusual venue.

Farewell party on Mt. Fuji

Finally the time to pack up and start back down Mt. Fuji had arrived. It had been decided that the descent would follow a different trail located on the opposite side of the mountain from the one used by most climbers for the ascent. The reason for using the other trail for the descent was that the base of the path consisted mostly of fine ash mixed with tiny pebbles of lava from the volcano. With the soft base one could rather effortlessly make the long descent quickly picking up speed. You felt as if you were floating with longer and longer strides. It was exhilarating the faster you went. It was also a bit scary the greater the speed.

About two hours into our descent, June struck an unseen impediment in the trail that threw her into a tailspin. When she came to a stop we rushed to her side. Her ankle was swollen and in pain. The students taking turn in pairs renewed our descent by holding June up as she gingerly hopped on one leg the rest of the way down to the bus stop at the bottom of Mt. Fuji that took the hikers back to Hakone for the train back to Shinjuku in Tokyo.

As we neared the bus stop after the descent which had taken much more time than planned because of June's accident, we found the whole area covered by people waiting for the bus that obviously came infrequently. There was a small machine attached to the bus stop sign that issued numbers. Ours were 775 and 6. We realized that we had a long wait ahead of us as it began to sprinkle. We had no choice but to sit on the ground and await our turn for the twenty-five minute bus ride.

By the time we reached the Hakone train station, the last train to Tokyo was due in five minutes. That meant that all those who arrived by bus had to get on that train or be stranded in Hakone for the night. Our students were determined to get us all on board, especially with June in such pain. As the train pulled in from Tokyo for the return trip, there were few passengers on board at that time of night. Because of the intense heat of summer, most of the windows, which in those days without air conditioning could be opened from the inside, had been pushed up by the passengers upon arrival.

Our students were well aware of the situation and quickly planned accordingly. It was all done in Japanese so we were unaware of the plan as we stood among a huge crowd of hikers all determined to get aboard. Amidst the jockeying that took place, most of our students worked their way to the very edge of the platform. As soon as the train stopped, the boys hoisted several girls up through the window to one section of four seats with two passengers facing each other. They occupied the four seats before the passengers using the doors surged on board scrambling for available seats.

Meanwhile we followed my colleague and wife in the crush to get on board forcing our way through the aisle now jammed with those who had to stand, in order to get to the section occupied by our students. Once there, the four ICU girls stood and gave us their seats. Although my colleague and I insisted that only our wives take the seats, the students vigorously protested otherwise. The Dukes and the Nakanos finally sat down for the hour and a half ride back to Shinjuku where we fortunately caught the last train on the Chuo Line to Mitaka. At Mitaka we had to wait in a long line for a taxi since the buses had stopped running well over an hour before. We finally arrived at our campus home at 1:30 Monday morning ending our adventure on Mt. Fuji. We went to bed with the unstated understanding that during our lifetime, we will not climb Mt. Fuji the second time.

MEMOIR 8

MY WEEKLY KEIDANREN SEMINAR FOR SENIOR JAPANESE BUSINESSMEN

- CHAIRED BY THE MOST INFLUENTIAL MONEYMAN IN POSTWAR JAPAN – HANAMURA NIHACHIRO -

Shortly after the beginning of the September semester, 1960, following a wonderful vacation on the Pacific beaches at Takayama, the ICU president's administrative assistant called me to her office. She had just received a telephone call from the assistant to Mr. Hanamura Nihachiro, Executive Director of Keidanran, the Federation of Japanese Industries. Keidanren was planning to start a Thursday evening English conversation seminar at the Industrial Club and was looking for an American professor to conduct it. Officially it would be called the International Studies Society (Kokusai Kenshu Kyokai). Would I be interested in the offer?

Keidanren, I was told, was the most influential business organization in Japan. Mr Hanamura was well known throughout Japanese industry for collecting enormous sums of money from industrial and financial corporations to support the ruling conservative governing party, the Jiminto, that had been in power ever since the end of World War II. He was known as 'Mr. Moneyman,' recognized by many Japanese in the business world as the most influential financial figure in postwar Japan. It would be beneficial, according to the president's assistant, for ICU to establish a connection with Keidanren. Besides, the weekly fee would be attractive. Under these circumstances, I accepted the offer.

The following Thursday I took the bus and train ride from ICU to Tokyo Station for my first Keidanren seminar. About eighty yards across from Tokyo Station stood an old red brick five-story ornate building named the Industrial Club (Kogyo Club) where Keidanren offices were then located. The Industrial Club was originally designed by a famous British architect, Josiah Condor, who was brought to Japan during the Meiji era to introduce modern architecture. He redesigned that part of central Tokyo across from Tokyo Station owned by the Mitsubishi Corporation with brick buildings to reduce the fire hazard of wooden buildings then predominant in the capital city. He modeled the Industrial Club after the gentlemen's clubs of London. When I first entered the building I was impressed by, among other features, the wide central staircase with brass railings that led from one story to the next. It was decidedly different from other Japanese buildings.

I was met at the entrance of the Keidanran office by Mr. Hanamura's assistant, a young Japanese by the name of Koike who spoke flawless English. I asked him where he learned to speak English so well. His answer: "The same place where you teach. I'm a first-year graduate of ICU." That explained why Keidanren contacted ICU for an American to conduct the seminar.

Mr. Koike then took me to Mr. Hanamura's office and introduced me to 'the most influential financial leader of postwar Japan.' With a reputation like that, I did not expect him to be a quiet, somewhat shy, reserved but very friendly Japanese businessman who treated me with great kindness. For a prewar graduate of the Tokyo University Law Department, German section, class of 1931, his English ability was fairly good. He spoke in a measured thoughtful manner. I immediately felt at ease. After pleasantries, he noted that it was time to take me to the seminar room and introduce me to my students, which I had expected to consist of Keidanran staff.

Upon entering a small classroom on the fifth floor of the Industrial Club I was greeted by five senior businessmen all dressed in dark suits. Mr. Hanamura began the introduction according to their position around an oval table. "Your first student is Mr. Suzuki, Director of the Tokyo Stock Exchange." I was startled. I couldn't imagine that I would have such a 'student' in my seminar. "Your second student is Mr. Kato, retired Director of the Mitsui Bank, whose father, Kato Kanji, was Admiral of the Japanese Navy before the war. Your third student is Mr. Moroi Ken, Professor of Economics at Tokyo University who will eventually become president of the Chichibu Cement Corporation. Your next student is Mr. Kawasaki, President of the Kawasaki Denki (Electric) Company. And the last student is Mr. Midorigawa, Vice President of Yamatane Securities Company, one of the eight major securities companies." With that Mr. Hanamura took a seat at the table and, with a twinkle in his eye, announced that, "I will be the chairman of your seminar."

The Keidanren Seminar
(Hanamura san seated at head of the table)

I was, to put it mildly, astonished to be conducting a seminar of the most powerful businessmen in Japan. It was the unprecedented equivalent in America of having in one seminar the head of the New York Stock Exchange, a retired director from the Bank of America, the President of Zerox, an Economics Professor from Harvard University, the Vice President of Charles Schwab Securities Company, and the President of the National Chamber of Congress. Little could I have imagined at that moment that this would be the beginning of a relationship between a former American public school teacher and prominent Japanese business and financial figures that would continue for the next forty years. In fact, it continues to this day.

The Keidanren Seminar proved to be an advanced lesson in Japanese industry and politics for me. According to Mr. Hanamura, ever since the end of World War II the ruling conservative political party (Jiminto) depended upon corporations to provide the party with sufficient funds to finance election campaigns. Politicians were constantly seeking financial contributions from corporations. At the national level many politicians requested funds from the same corporation depending upon the size of the company. It was an inefficient system that led to excesses and, not infrequently, abuses and, at its worst, scandals.

As head of Keidanren, Mr. Hanamura decided in the late 1950s to streamline the system in order to eliminate the persistent political pressure on corporate officers. It would hopefully eliminate most of the evil influences that plagued relationships between the political and financial world. Accordingly Hanamura san personally designed an organization with the strange title of Kokumin Kyokai, or the Peoples' Association. In reality it was an internal Keidanren organ in which the ruling Jiminto Party centralized all budgetary requests into one amount each year, or at a general election time. That figure would then be negotiated in discussions between the Prime Minister and Mr. Hanamura. The final amount represented the sum of money to be collected from the industrial and financial world by the Kokumin Kyokai for the ruling conservative party. The process came to be known among financial circles as the 'Hanamura machine.'

During our weekly two-hour Keidanren seminar, each member was asked to tell the class about some interesting event of the week. Oftentimes when it was Mr. Hanamura's turn he would quietly close the door to the hallway, a signal that he was about to reveal a confidential matter of great interest not only to me but to his fellow students who were keen on learning about Hanamura's activities. They were often shrouded in mystery.

For example, at one seminar he explained that at ten o'clock that morning he met privately with then-Prime Minister Ohira, his close friend. The Prime Minister reported to Mr. Hanamura that the Jiminto, the ruling party, needed ten billion yen to conduct the forthcoming election for the Parliament. Mr. Hanamura noted that politicians always ask for more than they need. After some discussion, he promised the Prime Minister eight billion yen which was agreed upon. None of this, he noted, was made public to the press that day.

Mr. Hanamura then revealed how he collected the eight billion yen for the next election. His Kokumin Kyokai staff ranked all of the industrial sectors of Japanese industry within Keidanren according to their profitability during the past year. Based on the ranking each industry was assigned an appropriate percentage of the eight billion yen. The next step was turned over to each industrial association, for example, the automobile industry or the iron and steel industry, which then assessed an appropriate percentage for each company within that sector according to profitability. The total amount of eight billion yen was then collected by the Kokumin Kyokai under Hanamura's office at Keidanren which turned it over to the ruling party.

One of the most interesting revelations to the members of our seminar occurred when Mr. Hanamura reported that during the most recent general election, he discretely diverted some of the political funds he had collected from industry to finance certain politicians from the Socialist as well as the Communist Party. He reasoned that it was essential for the Japanese financial and industrial world to support progressive politicians among the political opposition who represented the less radical wings of their parties. It turned out that several in that category were also classmates of Mr. Hanamura at Tokyo University during the early 1930s.

The procedure designed by Mr. Hanamura to finance the conservative political party produced truly remarkable results. The Jiminto had ruled Japan ever since World War II through the 20th century except for a short interval of Socialist Party rule. Even during that interlude, Hanamura provided funds from the Kokumin Kyokai to the more conservative members of the ruling Socialist Party (Shakaito). Nevertheless, one of the major factors in Japan's economic miracle during the postwar period when I held my weekly Keidanren seminar was the political stability within a democratic system, including a vital political opposition, brought about by the virtual uninterrupted political supremacy of the Jiminto. Keidanren under Mr. Hanamura played a key role in that accomplishment.

When I once asked how Keidanren specifically used its well-known influence on Japanese politics, Mr. Hanamura smiled and quietly said that that was a myth. Then, after closing the door, which always provoked a hush response among the others in the seminar no matter their exalted positions, he reported on his private meeting with Prime Minister Nakasone that very morning. During the inevitable discussion on fund raising for the ruling party, he reminded the Prime Minister that the Japanese corporate tax of 50% was among the highest in the world. He made it known that Keidanren's goal was 48%. About six months later the national newspapers carried the report that the Diet had approved a regulation reducing corporate tax rates from 50% to 48%. Mr. Hanamura's name was not mentioned in the article. I knew he was deeply involved in the reduction.

One evening during the seminar, Mr. Hanamura displayed the first blueprints for the new headquarters of Keidanren heretofore located within the Industrial Club where we held our weekly seminar. He had been planning on a modern headquarters for several years and had virtually single-handedly raised a large amount of money from industry to build a Keidanren Kaikan (Keidanren Building). He felt a new facility was urgently needed during the economic miracle underway, and to accommodate the rapidly expanding functions of the organization as new industries such as electronics and computers (Sony, Sharp, etc.) joined Keidanren, originally founded by basic industries such as iron and steel.

During one seminar Mr. Hanamura asked me my opinion of the building as presented in sketch form. I have no recollection of why I responded as I did. However I simply noted that it's too bad the windows didn't have a distinct look about them. Two weeks later he brought a revised set of plans with the same size building but with uniquely designed windows on both the front facing the street and the rear facing a major highway that sweeps through downtown Tokyo. Every time I pass the Keidanren Kaikan on the way to and from Narita Airport to ICU, I reminisce about the unusual but attractive windows that render the slender building distinct. It is truly a magnificent structure of 14 floors located a short distance from the Industrial Club.

With the construction of the new Keidanren headquarters underway, Mr. Hanamura decided that he should have a new English title on his business cards (meishi) which he handed out to the many visitors to his office from all over the world. Up to that time he was listed as Executive Director. He could not be called the Chairman since that title was assigned to one of the twelve company presidents who served essentially as a Board of Trustees while holding down their corporate positions as well.

Mr. Hanamura asked me to come up with a new English title that reflected his position as the fulltime administrative head of Keidanren, which I knew was the most powerful business organization in Japan. After giving it much thought I brought to the seminar a new title. When I presented it I explained that it was held by only one world figure that I knew of, and that was the head of the United Nations. I recommended that Mr. Hanamura's title become Secretary General. He was delighted and had new name cards printed the following week. From then on he took great pride at handing out his name card to the many foreign industrial and financial leaders who visited his office in recognition of his very unique position within the Japanese industrial world. His successors have used the same title ever since.

During a mid-April seminar in 1974, Mr. Hanamura brought a copy of the April 15 edition of one of the leading business journals in Japan, the Nikkei Business. He opened it to page 118-119. Spread across the two pages was a large picture of our Keidanren seminar in session. As always, Mr. Hanamura is seated at the head of the table. The Director of the Tokyo Stock Exchange is pointing to trade figures that I had written on the blackboard with my periodic question: How long can the large imbalance of trade between Japan and America, in Japan's favor, continue? Ironically, as I write this memoir over thirty years later, it has continued in Japan's favor to this day.

When Keidanren moved its offices from the 5th floor of the Industrial Club to the Keidanren Kaikan two blocks away, our seminar moved along with it to the meeting room adjacent to Mr. Hanamura's elegant office. Both the new building and his new office were fitting for the new era in postwar Japan when the country had evolved from a desperately poor defeated nation at the end of World War II to the second most powerful economy in the world. I had a privileged seat every Thursday at Keidanren to witness a super economic power emerge from wartime devastation.

Years before Mr. Hanamura retired, the ICU Vice President for Financial Affairs unexpectedly died. Since the position was traditionally held by successful Japanese businessmen who were Christians, I hatched a plan to personally find a successor. At one of the Keidanren seminars I asked the men if any of them knew of a retired Japanese businessman who was a Christian. One of them, Mr. Kato, the banker, explained that his good friend, Mr. Kamiyama was a devout Christian who had served as a senior officer of the Yokohama Bank and was currently a part-time advisor to a major securities company. I asked Mr. Kato to invite his friend to our seminar.

Two weeks later Mr. Kamiyama joined our seminar. He turned out to be a delightful man with a quiet demeanor and a great sense of humor. He fit in perfectly. After six weeks of faithful attendance I met with the ICU President explaining the situation with my new Keidanren student and recommended that he consider Mr. Kamiyama for the post of VPFA. They had dinner together shortly thereafter. Several weeks later Mr. Kamiyama from my Keidanren seminar was appointed VPFA much to the delight of Mr. Hanamura, Mr. Kato, and me.

When Mr. Hanamura retired from his position in 1988 as Secretary General of Keidanren well into his 70s, the Asahi Evening News noted that "He had controlled the flow of money from business to the ruling Liberal Democratic Party for 46 years. The system Hanamura created was called the Hanamura Machine." Our Thursday evening seminar continued with senior Japanese businessmen and ranking Keidanren officials. That included the third Secretary General. Mr. Hanamura's immediate successor was fluent in English and felt that his presence in my English seminar would inhibit the other members who had varying levels of English competency.

The death of Mr. Hanamura in his late eighties was a major event in the Japanese financial and industrial world. The funeral ceremony was conducted in the old revered Zensoji Temple in Tokyo. It was by invitation only, that is, only the leading business and political leaders of the country attended. But it also included his American seminar teacher from ICU. I received a special invitation from Keidanran to sit among this illustrious group in a reserved seat.

When the time came following the long formal ceremony for the attendees to pay their last respect by placing a flower on the altar in front of Mr. Hanamura's picture, it was led by surviving Prime Ministers. Each one was called by name over the loud speaker. Everyone, including myself, surely wondered how many Prime Ministers were in attendance since Mr. Hanamura had dealt privately with each one of them providing the financing that enabled them to become Prime Minister. They all had an enormous 'on' or debt of gratitude to Mr. Hanamura.

"Nakasone Soori Daijin" (Prime Minister Nakasone) – a long pause as everyone watched Prime Minister Nakasone walk to the front, place a flower on the altar, and then bow deeply in respect before the huge picture of Mr. Hanamura, exactly as I remembered him during the many years of our Keidanren seminar. One by one the former Prime Ministers then paid their respect to the man who played such a critical role in their successful political careers. There were five of them consisting of all surviving Prime Ministers of Japan, an appropriate testimony to the most influential financial leader in postwar Japan, and 'chairman' of my weekly Keidanren seminar.

And the rest of the story . . .

The unique relationship between this retired American professor from ICU and senior Japanese businessmen from the Keidanren seminar remains to this very day. When I return to Japan for a visit, I always meet with my last Keidanren students over lunch at the Industrial Club. Although the atmosphere within the Industrial Club remains the same as a British gentlemen's club of a bygone era, the building is new. Several years ago the original Industrial Club dating from the Meiji era was dismantled since it could not meet modern earthquake building codes.

However, due to the demands by the membership dominated by senior influential businessmen, the original façade of red bricks designed by Josiah Condor from Britain was incorporated into the new building including the ornate figures at the top of the five-story building. It stands out prominently from the surrounding high-rise buildings across from Tokyo station, all exemplifying the latest modern architectural designs. Internally the new building also retains the broad central staircase leading from one floor to the next with the brass railings, as well as the ornate dining room and lounge with large over-stuffed chairs. And on the 5th floor a small classroom resembling our old seminar room, where Mr. Hanamura revealed so many unique features about Japanese industry, was included, much to my surprise and deep satisfaction.

Every year after my retirement from ICU, we returned to ICU for a month or more to carry out research for books on Meiji education. The surviving members of the last Keidanren seminar before my retirement always arrange several luncheons at, appropriately, the Industrial Club. At the time of this writing we are planning to return to ICU later in the year. Already former seminar students, typical of those in the seminar over the years, have planned a luncheon at the Industrial Club. They include the retired Vice President of Kirin Beer, Mr. Yamamoto Yasushi, the Chairman of the Board and former president of Lintec Corporation, Mr. Shoji Kohei, retired member of the Board of Directors of the Sumitomo Trust Bank, Mr. Yoshimura Yasao, and the current Senior Managing Director of Keidanren, Mr. Tachibana Hiroshi.

As always we will pay our respects to Secretary General Hanamura Hanichiro, still remembered affectionately among the powerful businessmen who frequent the Industrial Club as the most influential financial figure in postwar Japan. I remember him as chairman of my Keidanren Seminar and dear friend.

MEMOIR 9

A NEW DIRECTION IN MY ACADEMIC CAREER AT ICU

- OBSERVING SCHOOLS IN 20 ASIAN NATIONS FROM VIET NAM TO INDONESIA TO PAKISTAN AND BEYOND -

During the first summer at ICU in 1960 shortly after the Mt. Fuji adventure, an unexpected opportunity arose destined to change the course of my academic career. The Education Division hosted an international conference on Educational Media in Asia co-sponsored by the United States Office of Education that had been scheduled before my arrival. Among the participants was the head of the research division from the Office of Education, Dr. Walter Stone. As the only two Americans among the delegates from various Asian countries, we struck up an acquaintance at the opening ceremony.

On the final day of the three-day conference I invited Dr. Stone to our home on campus for dinner where he made an intriguing proposal. He asked me if I would be interested in conducting a survey of educational media research and experimentation in the Far East for the U.S. Office of Education. Educational media was interpreted as broadcast and closed-circuit television, radio, motion pictures, slides, filmstrips, and other projected materials.

The conditions were straightforward and challenging. During a fifteen month period from February, 1961 to June 1962, I would visit public schools in nearly every Asian country excluding communist China then virtually closed to western researchers. While in each country I would search for a local educator, preferably an official in the Ministry of Education responsible for media research, to carry out the study in that country. I would provide the researcher with funds to cover the costs.

The project would end with a conference on the ICU campus to include all the local researchers who would present a report on their individual findings. My final responsibility was to write a report on Educational Media in Asia in book form to be published by the U. S. Office Education. I was assured that sufficient funds would be available to carry out the project.

I accepted the challenge on the spot on the condition that the contract be drawn up between ICU and the U.S. Office of Education, and that I would act as Principal Investigator of the project upon the appointment from ICU. The following day Dr. Stone and I met with ICU administrators to explain the proposal for their consideration. He left for Washington that afternoon to seek approval from the U. S. Government.

June and I then left for our first summer vacation in Japan during August. We rented a cottage on the Pacific coast of northern Japan at Takayama near Sendai where foreign missionaries spend summer holidays. While there I received notice that both parties had agreed to the proposal that included ICU's agreement for me to go on a halftime schedule and salary for the 15-month duration of the project. I was instructed to draw up the details of the plan including costs.

While lying on the glorious beach at Takayama on the Pacific Ocean during late August in 1960, I wrote the proposal entitled A Survey of Educational Media Research in the Far East with a budget of $15,000. That included half of my salary at $5,000 per year for the duration of the research. It was approved by ICU and sent to Washington for final approval which arrived in mid-November with a budget of $25,000, a forty percent increase over my request.

Within the proposal was a schedule of two trips each two months long. I wrote home to our families that, "I have been poring over maps for days. My first stop is Saigon, Viet Nam, to observe how the French run a school system in their colony. From there I go next door to Cambodia stopping at the capital Phnom Penh and then Siem Reap where the great Ankor Wat temple is located, and on to Bangkok and Chiang Mai in Thailand; to Burma stopping at Rangoon and Mandalay to 'see the sun come up like thunder;' to Calcutta in India to visit Mother Teresa; to Katmandu in Nepal to see the King and enjoy the Himalayas hoping to spot Mt. Everest; then back to India stopping at New Delhi and going on down to see the great Taj Mahal; from India to Karachi, Pakistan and back to Bombay, India; from there to Colombo and Candy in Ceylon; and finally over to Singapore returning to Tokyo via Hong Kong.

After a month at ICU I will take off for the second trip of two-month duration. It starts at Manila and Baguio in the Philippines, on to Papua, New Guinea, then down to Auckland and Wellington in New Zealand, to Melbourne and Sydney, Australia, to Jakarta, Bandung and Bali in Indonesia, and finally up to Kuala Lumpur in Malaysia and back to Honk Kong and Tokyo. I must also select advisors to come to ICU for a conference at the end of the project which I must organize. This will be some experience just working with all these different nationalities.

Well, there it is. You can imagine how excited I am about this project. I never dreamed I would see any of these places. And to think I'm getting paid to do this. The only drawback is that I must take these incredible trips alone. This will be my first trip in Asia since I arrived at ICU. And keep in mind, I have no background knowledge of education in any Asian country nor the time to adequately prepare myself for the trip. It will be an adventure to be sure."

Having no means of dealing in money in the local currencies of all those countries in 1960, I decided to carry U.S. dollars in cash sufficient to pay each local representative for their expenses to carry out the research. The U.S. Office of Education had budgeted for first class plane travel. However I reserved economy seats for the whole trip to allow side trips purely for sightseeing to famous sites such as Ankor Wat in Cambodia and the Taj Mahal in India. With little foresight, I divided a total of $10,000 in $20 bills into three parts. With $2,000 stowed as secretly as possible in each of two suitcases, and another $6,000 divided between my wallet, a money belt, and my briefcase, I flew off to Saigon, Viet Nam in November, 1961, to launch the research project and to begin an Asian adventure unimaginable at the time.

It began upon my arrival in Saigon to check in at the magnificent old French-run Majestic Hotel. The bellhop upon showing me my room asked in broken English whether I wanted to buy black market money. I was surprised and instantly replied no. The idea appalled me. Little could I have imagined at that moment that I would soon be dealing with black market money in several countries once I learned that the disparity between the official rates of exchange of the American dollar and the black market rates of exchange was so absurd that I simply could not ignore it. In one country, for example, the official rate of ten rupees per dollar contrasted with well over 100 rupees per dollar on the black market. Many foreigners I met traveling in these developing nations in the early 1960s avoided the official rates of exchange if the alternate possibility was readily available, which it was in most Asian countries.

The American government was just then setting up offices in Saigon to oversee the increasing aid programs being extended to help prop up French control from the communist threat supported by Mao Tse Tung in China. I contacted that office for help in arranging school visits and for an introduction to a Vietnamese official at the Ministry of Education. At that time during French control, American influence in Viet Nam was in its infancy.

My first visits to schools in developing nations in South East Asia were eye-opening. First of all the difference between the first rate schools of Saigon where the elite Vietnamese sent their children and the rural schools outside the city were so enormous that comparisons were meaningless. They reflected two different worlds. Moreover, the use of French in the elite schools was dominant. It was used superficially or not at all in rural schools. My initial impression was that although Vietnam was a third world nation under colonial rule, its good schools sharply limited in number were first rate, but that the majority of schools catering to peasant children were vastly inferior. A large but unknown number of the poor were essentially uneducated.

In my first adventure out of Saigon into the countryside to visit a rural school, I decided to use a pedicab, basically a bicycle pulling a small cab that could seat two passengers. It was very inexpensive. The first visit to a rural school was so fascinating that I stayed well after school ended asking questions of the teachers, one of whom spoke English sufficiently to translate for the others. I was then invited to visit a Buddhist temple next door.

Upon my return to Saigon on a lonely road in the late afternoon as dusk approached, about a half dozen armed men rushed out of the woods and stopped my pedicab. For the next twenty minutes or so the pedicap driver and the armed men argued loudly, obviously about my fate. I could just catch the word American off and on. At that time I had little knowledge about the communist insurgency spreading in Viet Nam against French occupation. Naively I assumed that as an American, I was not involved in the dispute and felt fairly secure even under the situation I unexpectedly found myself. Finally the men withdrew and I continued on back to the Majestic Hotel as darkness set in.

The next morning I visited the officer at the American Embassy who assisted me in making my appointments describing the event of the previous evening. He was horrified. He told me that the communist insurgency against French control of Viet Nam was growing stronger and bolder by the day with sporadic acts of violence being carried out closer and closer to Saigon. He advised me that no western foreigner, American or otherwise, should travel alone outside the city after dark. It all came as an eye opener as I began the two-month adventure through South and South East Asia in 1961.

There were many unique experiences during the four months on the two trips through twenty Asian countries. Among the most interesting were the dozens and dozens of school visits from the best to the poorest in nearly all of the countries in the project. The more schools I visited the more fascinated I became with the problems of education in these developing countries with their diverse peoples speaking many different languages. The common experience of colonial rule by European countries over many years, with the exception of Thailand, in comparison to the Japanese and American history of independence left an indelible imprint on the schools from the use of a European language in the elite schools of some countries and in all schools in others.

A good example was the Philippines where the official language of all public schools from the fourth grade was English at that time, and remains so in the elite private schools of today, in part because of the colonial history under the United States which mandated English in the classroom. Upon independence the sensitive issue of which native language among the many should be chosen as a national language, thereby favoring a privileged group, delayed the choice of a native Filipino language for the schools. I questioned how the United States, Britain, or Japan could have reached their level of development if their schools were all taught in a foreign language like the Philippines. I realized that educating the masses in Asia outside Japan was unimaginable in 1960. Illiteracy understandably prevailed through the vast rural areas in every country.

By the time I returned to Tokyo after the second two-month trip which included New Zealand and Australia that stood out in stark contrast to the Philippines before and Indonesia after, I had already decided to develop a new course in the Division of Education entitled Education in Developing Nations. I had discovered so many similarities among the South and Southeast Asian countries that I concluded they could be grouped together for educational purposes under the heading of Developing Nations. For my Japanese students at ICU, who knew so little about that part of Asia, I could draw comparisons with Japanese education that would not only demonstrate why Japan had become an economic power, it would also reveal why the so-called developing nations remained so far behind.

In April, 1962, the project neared completion when I brought to the ICU campus as many of the local advisors as possible who had been chosen to carry out the survey in their respective countries during the past fifteen months. They had been sending me reports during the project for reference in drawing up the final report for the United States Office of Education. The week-long conference proved fascinating for everyone involved since it brought together for the first time those who worked on this project. Examples of the Asians I worked with were Dr. Ambhorn Meesook, Director, Radio-Television Department, Ministry of Education, Thailand, G. K. Athalye, Director, National Audio-Visual Institute, New Delhi, India, F. Situmordng, Director, Teaching Aids Center, Bandung, Indonesia, and Victor Jesudoss, Director, Audio-Visual Division, Ministry of Education, Malaya.

The Conference of Asian Researchers at ICU

The final report was completed by June, 1962 and sent to the United States Office of Education in Washington. It was published in 1963 as New Media for Instruction: A Survey of Educational Media Research in the Far East. I wrote Chapter One, Education in the Far East, my first writing in the area of comparative and international education indicative of the new direction my career would soon take. When reading it a half century later, I realize that in the early 1960s I foresaw the rise of Asia that we now marvel in spite of the problems of education in the mid 20th century. The following are excerpts taken from my first chapter.

Education in the Far East

Asia and Asian education are in transition. A decade and a half ago nearly every Far Eastern nation was under the rule of a foreign power. In the few short years since the end of the Pacific War, this vast area from Korea to Indonesia to Pakistan is now undergoing a unique experience – that of transforming itself from subjugation into free and independent nations.

This transitional period is evident in every phase of national life. There is a new outlook and purposefulness which is gaining momentum in the majority of Asian countries. Nowhere are the manifestations of this new hope and endeavor expressing themselves so clearly as in the schools. And in no other aspect are the enormous problems facing each Asian country so glaringly evident.

To gain an appreciation of the educational situation in Asia and thereby have a better understanding of the role of educational media, several of the problems hindering educational progress in the Far East will be considered. First of all there is the extreme poverty. If they had a sufficient financial base, Asian countries could support developed school systems. The argument is also made that Asia is poverty stricken because education is undeveloped. . . . An important factor also stems from the history of colonialism when there were two distinct systems of education in most countries, one for the colonial administers and a few select natives, while the second accommodated a small percentage of natives for elementary school.

Another formidable obstacle to educational improvement is the multiplicity of languages within national boundaries with national systems of education conducted in a foreign language. In Asia millions of students in many countries must complete their entire education, or a significant portion thereof, in a foreign language. The plethora of languages within each country can be attributed to the diversity of ethnic groups. The multiplicity of ethnic peoples has placed a severe strain on the central government to effect a body politic.

In spite of the obstacles, educational progress is being made in most countries which can be recognized by some of the emerging patterns in Asian education. One of the significant patterns has been an increase in the importance of the schools. Education has become an instrument of nationalism and a concern of the state. Compulsory education is either being initiated or extended in every country, a gradual trend toward the comprehensive school is replacing the two- or three–track system, a single national language is being promoted, the upgrading of teacher training is evident, and higher education is expanding. As one travels throughout the Orient you can feel this slumbering giant beginning to stir. One overriding conclusion can be made: the truly significant and remarkable feature concerning Asian education in the early 1960s is that it is able to progress in the face of the monumental problems being encountered.

And now the rest of the story . . .

The opportunity to visit schools throughout Asia in the early 1960s motivated me to compare educational developments I witnessed with that in Japan where I was teaching at ICU, and with America where I taught in the public schools of Hershey, Pennsylvania. As a result I began to look seriously into the field of comparative and international education then receiving increasing prominence in educational journals. I learned that there were two centers of study in this field, one at Teachers College, Columbia University in New York City under Dr. George Bereday, and the other at the University of London under Dr. Joseph Lauwerys. I considered the possibility of studying this new educational discipline at both institutions.

It so happens that a year's leave of absence from ICU, granted after the first three years of service, was due from the summer of 1962. Although I joined ICU in December, 1959, rather than September because of visa delays, it was decided that I would be eligible for leave as of June, 1962. That would enable me to pursue a full year's study in a new academic direction.

I first enrolled in the 1962 summer program at Teachers College, Columbia University, New York, registering for courses under Dr. George Bereday in comparative education, my formal introduction to the field. He was a most inspiring lecturer with a unique background as a Polish soldier during World War II. Several years later I invited him to lecture in my new course on comparative education at ICU which he enjoyed immensely.

I took the opportunity to enroll in courses at the East Asian Institute at Columbia University that included Japanese literature given by a leading scholar in the field, Donald Keene. Not only was he an exhilarating lecturer, he was witty and erudite beyond description opening up a new field of interest for me in Japanese studies. It was also my good fortune to be able to take two courses on Japanese education offered by another outstanding American scholar on Japan, Herbert Passin, who wrote the classic Society and Education in Japan. He was pleased to have as his student a faculty member of the Division of Education at a university in Japan. He was very familiar with ICU.

Finally I had the great opportunity to take the course on the History of American Education by the leading scholar in the field, Dr. Lawrence Cremins. Without doubt his lectures based on his classic, The Transformation of the School, Progressivism in American Education 1876-1957, were the most stimulating I have ever experienced. He was a master at teaching. Based on his lectures I designed a new course for the Education Division at ICU entitled The Foundations of American Education which I taught for thirty years and which my students greatly appreciated.

Following an exhilarating summer at Teachers College in New York in 1962 while June stayed with her parents in our hometown of

Berwick, Pennsylvania, we took the SS United States ship to England in September. We were met at the port of Southampton by our ICU colleague and neighbor Professor Roy Morrell on leave, a leading authority on Thomas Hardy. They took us to their home in Dorset, the center of Hardy novels, for a short stay visiting sites related to his books that Roy introduced in his English literature courses at ICU.

From there we moved to a flat in north London upon enrolling in the doctoral course at the University of London Institute for Education in comparative and international education under Dr. Joseph Lauwreys, originally from Belgium, and his two assistants Dr. Brian Holmes and Dr. Edmund King. They both had already published books widely used in the field. The three of them constituted the leading team of specialists in comparative education in the world. For the next year I enrolled in courses under all three with educational field trips throughout Britain and to virtually every country in Europe. It was the beginning of my study of British and European education in contrast to the past two years devoted to the study of education in Asia.

It was also part of a transition in my teaching at ICU from educational methodology to comparative and international education. As a former teacher in American schools, to a faculty member at a university in Japan, to a Principal Investigator of Asian schools, to a doctoral student in London studying British and European education, I considered myself academically qualified to undertake the transition. Few others in the field had such a broad background. But more would follow as I engaged in research on communist education with field studies in China and the Soviet Union and made return trips to many Asian countries to follow the progress of education that I predicted in my report to the United States Office of Education in 1962.

By September 1963 I was prepared to make a new academic contribution to ICU by introducing comparative and international studies in the Education Division. From then on both my writings and teachings concentrated on this area of education.

MEMOIR 10

DETAINED FOR QUESTIONING

- AT THE AKIHABARA POLICE STATION -

I n the spring of 1966 I experienced the rather embarrassing episode
of being taken into custody by two Tokyo female police officers.
They drove me to the Akihabara police station in their tiny police car
assigned to lady policemen who carefully measure the distance from the
curb to cars suspected of parking beyond the legal limit. I was being
detained not on a parking violation since we owned no car. Rather, I
was taken in for questioning as a suspected illegal foreigner in Japan.

Akihabara is the glittering electronic mega-center of Tokyo where
you can buy the latest electronic gadgetry at wholesale prices or better,
depending on one's ability to bargain. Currently the primary products sold
at the many stores in the area are computer-related or assorted ingenious
hand-held devices. In the 1960's, when Japan was slowly recovering from
the postwar economic depression, basic household items such as TV sets,
telephones, and refrigerators were the primary attractions. When we
needed a new refrigerator in 1966, it was natural to head for Akihabara
in search of the latest model available in Japan at the best price.

In the 1960s the Akihabara commercial district was essentially
divided into two types of stores. The major outlets of electronic chain

stores were located on the main street with a wide selection of products on display. On the narrow streets behind the big stores was a maze of tiny shops each concentrating only on one or two products. These simple shops characteristically had few items on display with most of their products in boxes ready for delivery. The shop owners depended on volume in order to cut prices significantly, avoiding high rental rates and stocking large numbers of products for display. I was searching for a shop in the latter category.

I began my shopping expedition from the Akihabara train station by walking down the main street looking for big stores selling western-style side-by-side freezer-refrigerators to get an idea of the current price range. As I walked along the street an elderly Japanese man was passing out flyers for a shop on one of the side streets. I spotted a picture of a refrigerator on the advertisement and asked the man where the shop was located. He directed me to the second block ahead where I should turn left and take the second small street left for about fifty meters. The shop, he assured me, was on the left.

After checking prices and models in two of the big stores, I followed his directions to the second small street where I encountered a long row of tiny shops indistinguishable one from the other. I searched but could not find the name of the shop on the handout. Since I had passed a small koban (local police box) at the corner of the main street, I decided to ask the officer on duty for directions. One of the primary functions of the many small kobans throughout Tokyo is to give directions to the public. I showed the officer on duty the flyer and asked for directions to the shop. He checked his map on the wall and motioned that it was indeed down the adjacent street. He would show me the way.

At that moment he unexpectedly, and very politely, asked me to show him my Alien Registration card. In those days every foreigner who was not in Japan on a tourist visa was required to register at the local city hall where they took fingerprints and a picture and issued an Alien Registration card. It was to be carried at all times in lieu of the passport. Having lived in Japan for six years during which I was never asked to show my Alien Registration card, I had become accustomed to not carrying it even though I knew better.

When I couldn't produce my card giving as a flimsy excuse that I left it at home, the police officer called the Akihabara Police Headquarters asking what he should do in my case. When he hung up, again in polite language, he said that a police car would come to take me to the headquarters for questioning. About ten minutes later a tiny police car with two young female officers arrived to escort me to the headquarters.

Arriving at the station I was escorted by another police officer to the fifth floor where a sergeant questioned me about my status in Japan in a very stern demeanor. By this time I was becoming somewhat agitated since I had my weekly Keidanren seminar of businessmen two hours later at the Industrial Club across from Tokyo Station, two stops from Akihabara. After being questioned for about twenty minutes, the sergeant then called the number I gave him of the secretary of my division at ICU to confirm that I was indeed a university professor at a university in Tokyo, as I had identified myself.

When the officer returned upon verifying my status, he was now extremely polite calling me Duke Sensei, or Professor Duke, the honorific form of the language. With some embarrassment he nevertheless handed me a form in English addressed to the Ministry of Justice. It was essentially an apology for breaking Japanese laws in cases like mine. I was politely asked to sign it.

Upon reading it I realized that it was obviously written by a Japanese with limited English facility. It was sprinkled with laughable phraseology and incorrect grammar, misspellings, etc. Suddenly I saw the humor of it all and informed the sergeant that the English was so bad it could be an embarrassment for the station to use it. This was obviously quite a revelation to him.

I then asked to meet the chief of the Akihabara police headquarters about the letter. When he came, he bowed deeply calling me sensei (professor). I inquired about who had written the form letter of apology to the Ministry of Justice in English. He had no idea. It was already in use with foreigners when he became chief the previous year. When I informed him that the English was so bad it could be a great embarrassment to the precinct, he was deeply concerned. He was also grateful for my revelation.

At that moment I played my ace card. I asked the chief if he would like me to rewrite the letter using proper English. That altered the setting even further. From a foreign suspect who had broken Japanese law I was now a respected guest, a professor from a well-known university who could make a contribution to the Akihabara Police Station and its chief. He bowed in respect of his detainee and politely asked me to rewrite the letter.

I purposely took about fifteen minutes to write a formal letter of apology. I could have done it in five. When I handed the new version to the sergeant, he took it to the chief's office. In a few minutes the chief came with letter in hand to thank me profusely for the revision. I asked him whether I should sign it as the first foreigner to do so. With a smile on his face he said that wouldn't be necessary.

The chief then escorted me down to the front door of the station where the police car that brought me there was waiting to take me back to the koban from where I started. I shall never forget that scene. The chief came out to the car and bowed with a thank you as the car pulled away. Any passerby who witnessed that scene must have thought that I was a high-ranking government official from the West paying a courtesy call on the Akihabara Police Chief. They could never have imagined that I had been detained for questioning an hour earlier.

When we arrived back at the koban, the officer who sent me off to the headquarters was waiting, obviously aware of what had taken place. He bowed and thanked me for my help with his chief. Then he remembered that I had not yet found the appliance shop I was looking for. He asked to see the flyer again to confirm the address. He offered to personally take me to the shop.

Five minutes later the police officer and I entered the shop selling refrigerators that I had tried to find. When the owner saw the policeman and a foreigner come through the door, he was startled. He jumped up and bowed to the head of the local police box. In a very serious tone of voice the policeman told the shop owner that I was his friend, which impressed the owner. As he turned to leave, the officer instructed the shop owner to "Give him a good price!"

He did indeed. I had hoped for a twenty percent discount from the large store prices. The shop owner, however, gave me a discount of 40 percent on a refrigerator that we used until retirement. As it turned out, being detained at the Akihabara police station for questioning proved to be a profitable, as well as a humorous, experience during our years in Japan at ICU.

MEMOIR 11

THE AMERICAN SCHOOL IN JAPAN
MOVES TO THE ICU CAMPUS

- MY CASUAL REMARK REPOSITIONS THE SITE –

O ne afternoon in early 1964 I had a meeting with the Vice President for Finance, Miss Caroline Peckham, about an issue long forgotten. Miss Peckham was an elderly missionary from America who previously was president of a girl's Christian college in Nagasaki. Her appointment as VPAA continued the tradition of an American missionary serving in that position due to the heavy involvement of American church denominations in financing ICU in the early years of its existence.

As I was about to leave her office she inquired whether I had heard that the American School in Japan (ASIJ) had recently made a request to ICU to buy thirty acres of unused land on the campus to move from the downtown Meguro campus to build a new school. Among the foreign community in Japan, ASIJ was well known for its curriculum designed on the American pattern and offered in English by mostly American teachers. It was originally founded for children of American missionaries, diplomats and businessmen working in Japan, as well as non-Americans who wanted their children to receive an education in English. Over the years it had developed into a first-rate school from kindergarten through high school with high academic standards and many opportunities for extracurricular activities in sports, music, drama, etc.

ICU from its beginning had developed a close relationship with ASIJ. Virtually all of the non-Japanese on the faculty including those from countries other than America such as the Norwegian and British professors, sent their children to ASIJ. Early each morning during the school year, the ICU minibus driven by an ICU staff member wound through the campus picking up about a dozen foreign children for the hour and a half bus ride to the downtown Meguro campus of ASIJ. The driver remained in the area to bring the students home in the afternoon, most of whom were exhausted from the long day at school including three hours or more on the bus. Their ICU faculty parents also participated in many of the activities of the school from plays, sports events, and the ever-popular spring Broadway musicals, as well as serving on the ASIJ Board of Trustees.

By 1964, as the Japanese economic miracle began to unfold, the number of students increased as American and other western companies opened offices in Japan. The ASIJ campus in Meguro simply outgrew the facilities, many of which had become out of date. In addition the demands for a football team with an appropriate field increased the pressure for school authorities to move the campus from its crowded downtown site to the suburbs where land was so much cheaper. When the ASIJ officials became aware of the 360-acre ICU campus where only six hundred students were enrolled with literally hundreds of acres either forested or used for farming purposes, the decision to request the sale of 30 acres to ASIJ was a natural one. It would enable ASIJ to construct a modern school with sports facilities commensurate with typical high schools in America.

ICU responded positively to the request by ASIJ. Miss Peckham explained that the ICU Board of Trustees had given its approval of the land sale. The site had already been decided. At that moment in my tenure at ICU I had little interest in ASIJ since we had no children. Consequently I had no particular reaction to Miss Peckham's revelation about the plan for ASIJ to move to the campus of ICU.

As I was about to go out the door, out of curiosity I asked Miss Peckham where the site already chosen for the ASIJ campus was located within the ICU campus. She had a huge framed aerial photograph of the campus enlarged many times hanging on the wall. She pointed to an area on the upper campus close to the ICU back gate, little used at that time, as the approved site.

Without giving it any serious thought, my immediate reaction was simple. "I think it's a mistake." Miss Peckham was taken by surprise and asked why. Again with no particular emotion I simply noted that it's too close to our university facilities. ASIJ catered primarily to American teenagers. ICU catered primarily to Japanese college students. To put them so close together at our back gate is asking for trouble.

By now Miss Peckham was becoming a bit annoyed with my attitude. She then asked me where I thought the ASIJ campus should go. I looked at the map and simply pointed to the part of the campus located as far from the Main Entrance and the Honkan, the Main Building, as possible. That happened to be the southern-most section of the ICU lower campus which we used for farming purposes. In fact the very section I nonchalantly pointed to was where we had built several large pigpens. In somewhat of a huff, Miss Peckham responded with, "Well, the decision has been made." With that my meeting with the Vice President for Financial Affairs ended.

Approximately one month later I happened to meet Miss Peckham getting off at the bus stop on campus as I was about to board it for Mitaka station. She called me aside with this report. "I have just returned from a meeting of the ICU Board of Trustees. They have accepted your idea." I had no idea what she was talking about. She explained that the Trustees voted to relocate the already-approved site of the ASIJ campus near the back gate to the section of the lower campus exactly where I casually suggested. I was a bit amused with the change of plans.

And now the rest of the story . . .

It was not too long after ASIJ made the move to a splendid new campus at the far edge of the ICU campus that I began to fully realize how significant the relocation to the new site was. First of all, at that time ICU was just turning the lower campus of about 150 acres into the ICU Golf Course, minus the thirty acres for the ASIJ campus. As it turned out ASIJ was located on the opposite side of the golf course from ICU which meant that the course served as a buffer between ICU and ASIJ. Moreover since the ICU Main Entrance was located about a mile by road from the entrance to the ASIJ campus, the two institutions with different purposes and a different clientele never encountered problems that next door neighbors often incur.

In addition, within a short time after the ASIJ move, we began our family by adopting a Japanese baby girl shortly after birth, the topic of the following memoir. Within three years we adopted the second daughter and, most unexpectedly, June gave birth to a son two years after that. Although we enrolled them in the Japanese school for their basic education covered in another memoir, all three attended ASIJ for their later schooling commuting from our home on the upper campus by bicycle to the ASIJ campus at the far end of the lower campus. Their daily route took them through the great Nogawa Park that replaced the ICU Golf Course which was sold to the City of Tokyo for a public park. All three had a wonderful experience at ASIJ and we as parents enjoyed the many activities at the school located so close but yet so far from ICU.

Shortly before I retired from ICU I was asked by the ASIJ Headmaster, our dear friend Ray Downs, to speak to the ASIJ faculty at a meeting after school. I decided to tell them the story of how ASIJ was relocated at the precise location where it now stood. I began with asking how many of them knew that at the very site where we were meeting ICU kept pigs. None of them had heard the story behind the transition from pigpens to ASIJ. They found it amusing.

MEMOIR 12

WE BEGIN OUR FAMLY -
IN DOWNTOWN TOKYO

- THE ADOPTION OF NORIKO SUSAN
AND KIMIKO ANNE -

After ten years of marriage, countless tests and doctors' analyses, we accepted the inevitable. If we were going to have a child, it would have to be through adoption. But how does an American couple living in Japan in 1964 adopt a child? Our options were greatly restricted.

Pondering our predicament at great length, we came up with one potential solution however remote. We considered the possibility of adopting a Japanese baby girl. We were well aware that the adoption of a Japanese child by an American couple working for a Japanese institution in Japan was rare. But we figured that it was worth a try.

The first step was to consult with someone for advice. We turned to our close Japanese friends, the Tsurus. Harry Tsuru was a young professor in the psychology department in our Division of Education. His wife Nobuko taught nursing at the Tokyo University School of Nursing and was the founder of the ICU Clinic during the initial period of the institution. They lived in the United States for several years while Harry completed the doctoral course at Teachers College, Columbia University, in New York City.

Harry came from a well-known Christian family. Several members of his immediate family including his father held senior positions at Christian universities in pre- and postwar Japan. Nobuko also came from a distinguished family whose father served as governor of various prefectures (states) in prewar Japan. We were pleasantly surprised to learn that Nobuko's mother was an advisor to the Japanese Family Court.

Understandably our dear friends were initially startled with the idea of adoption in part because it was virtually unprecedented. But the concept of an American couple at ICU adopting a Japanese baby challenged them. Nobuko launched the search by contacting many of her former students then working as nurses in pediatric departments at hospitals all over Japan. They were asked to be on the lookout for a potential candidate baby girl, preferably one recently born, whose parents would be willing to give up the child to an unknown American couple. The search was on throughout the country for our first child.

During the fall semester of 1964 we were on leave in the United States in return for administering the summer program in Japanese studies for American teachers under a grant from the United States Office of Education. We were scheduled to return to ICU shortly after the New Year holiday. Upon our arrival in early January, 1965, we called Nobuko who was anxiously awaiting our return. One of her former students, the head nurse at the Red Cross Maternity Hospital in the downtown ward of Katsushika, Tokyo, well known as the working-class district of the city, had contacted her a week previously. She had located a 'candidate' baby girl born on December 27th. The parents had agreed to an adoption since they faced an uncertain future as the Japanese economy continued in a critical state of depression. We immediately made arrangements to visit the hospital to meet our potential daughter.

In the meantime we had asked the Tsurus to visit the natural parents of the child to explain our situation without divulging our identity, and to observe the family at home. Based on that meeting we asked that they advise us whether to proceed with the adoption process with a one-word response. Shortly thereafter Nobuko called with the answer we were hoping for. Yes. That was it. We would hopefully begin our family in downtown Tokyo.

Upon arrival at the hospital we met the head nurse who ushered us into a large room with a glass-encased nursery containing over a dozen newly-born babies in tiny cribs. They all looked the same to us. The nurse promptly entered the enclosure, picked up one baby girl and carried her to the window in front of us as we peered through the glass enclosure. Overwhelmed by the situation, we simply nodded our approval. Who could have imagined at that moment that we were looking at a future American attorney with the Commonwealth Court of Pennsylvania?

The head nurse then returned the baby to her crib. Much to our delight as well as surprise, she advised us to return to pick up the baby at our very earliest convenience since she had held the baby at the hospital specifically for our return from America. We assured her we would. Since Nobuko Tsuru, her former teacher, had introduced us to her, she accepted that without further formality. We left the hospital as if in a dream. Could it be that simple? Was this really the beginning of our family after ten years of marriage?

Since we had no time to prepare for this unexpected situation after our return from America, we went back to our campus apartment at ICU to begin preparing for the arrival of our first child. We also had to decide on a first name. June especially liked the name of Noriko, a common name in Japan, which was the name of one of her Japanese friends. With the advice from the Tsurus in choosing the appropriate Japanese characters (kanji) for Noriko, we decided to add Susan as a middle name, giving her both Japanese and American names. Our first child would be named Noriko Susan Duke.

We quickly arranged the spare room in our apartment on the ICU campus as a nursery. Since we had no baby clothes nor the necessary items for handling a baby, various friends on campus brought over hand-me-downs and we picked up a few items at a local store. Within several days we were ready for our daughter.

Nearly three weeks after the baby was born, Nobuko notified her friend at the hospital that we would come for the child two days later. Since we didn't own a car, we rented one with driver and headed for the hospital on the appointed day. We were ushered into the same room as before by the head nurse who was pleased, and surely relieved, when we showed up. She walked into the glass-enclosed nursery, picked up the baby, wrapped her for the cold January temperature, and carried her out beckoning us to follow. Our little procession then walked out the front door of the hospital to where the hired car was waiting. The nurse handed the baby to June, we got into the car, and without any further ado, we drove away with our daughter, Noriko Susan.

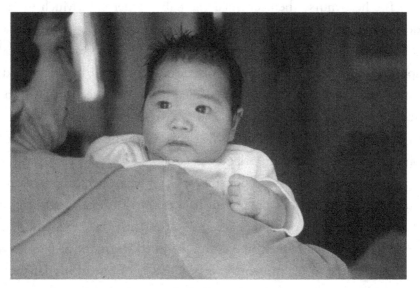

Baby Susan

Miraculously our family had been launched in the space of three weeks. In a country famous for its strict regulatory traditions, the fact that an American couple had taken custody of a Japanese baby three weeks after birth without any documentation was unbelievable. We surely set a precedent although we had the advantage of the advice of Nobuko, her mother as advisor to the Family Court, and the head nurse at the hospital.

Six months later through arrangements made by Nobuko's mother, we appeared before the Japanese Family Court judge assigned to our case. The understanding made with the biological parents was that we would not meet them nor ask for any information about their family, and they would not be given any information about our family except that we were Americans. After we attended a brief session before the judge, he gave the official approval, we signed a simple document, and the formal legalities were completed. Noriko Susan Duke legally became our daughter in the eyes of the Japanese Court. The whole process cost 100 yen, about fifty cents at that time, for the document we signed. In appreciation we made a substantial gift to the Katsushika Red Cross Maternity Hospital, never envisioning at the time that we would return three years later for our second daughter.

At this early stage in our family's development, June played the key role. I was amazed at how naturally she handled our first child. To her, Noriko Susan was not our Japanese daughter. She was our daughter. June treated her, as I did, from that moment onward as if she had given birth to the baby herself. And Noriko Susan responded as a child brought up in a family that dearly loved her.

Baptism by Rev. Furuya – with Harry and Nobuko Tsuru

During the 1965 summer vacation at ICU after Noriko Susan's birth, we decided to take her to America so her grandparents and aunts and uncles could meet our daughter. That presented the first of many procedural challenges we faced as a mixed family. Since our daughter was a Japanese citizen, she required a Japanese passport to enter the United States even though she was legally our child. We learned that in order to get a Japanese passport, proof of Japanese citizenship was necessary. That required a copy of the birth certificate and the family register (koseki) from the ward office where the individual is born. The spectacle of an American couple going through the process of securing official documents for a Japanese citizen in the Katsushika City Hall in downtown Tokyo caused much consternation among the local bureaucrats. They had never experienced such a case.

Upon receipt of the documents, all in Japanese, we learned that in fact her new name of Noriko Susan Duke was included in the family register replacing her original family name. A note was added that she was adopted into the American family of Benjamin and June Duke. Although we thought that this information was not made known to the biological parents, we learned that the family register included it since every change in the family has to be recorded by law.

With help from friends, the Japanese passport for Noriko Susan Duke was finally issued. Our family set off for America carrying two American and one Japanese passports. Even the Haneda Airport departure was confusing since Japanese citizens went through one line for processing and non-Japanese went through another, both clearly marked. When Japanese officials spotted two Americans with a baby in the line reserved for Japanese, they pointed to the next room with the English word Foreigners in large letters over the door. Upon showing them the Japanese passport for Noriko Susan, although perplexed, they allowed us to continue. Upon receiving the required exit stamp for Noriko Susan we then awkwardly went back through the line for Japanese and over to the line for foreigners to get our exit stamps.

The same problem arose when we entered the United States at the Los Angeles airport where arriving passengers were separated into an American Citizen line and a Foreigner line located in different rooms. In both instances special treatment was required to get a mixed family through the formalities of departing and entering the country. The Duke family of three came to anticipate such deviations from the normal both at home and abroad as a new adventure in our lives unfolded.

And now the rest of the story . . .

Our first year with Noriko Susan was one of great enjoyment both in Japan and in America with our relatives. Early on we began to detect signs of unusual reactions by our daughter to her surroundings. She was quick to react and long in maintaining an interest in all things in her immediate environment. The second year when we began reading to her from children's books she exhibited a keen interest. Before we realized it she was putting an A-B-C puzzle together randomly selecting a letter and placing it in the proper order.

Noriko Susan's speech patterns developed quickly. She soon began memorizing full sentences from books. We often found her on the floor by the bookcase leafing through children's books. By her third birthday she had memorized every word on the fifty-four pages of Dr. Doolittle that we read to her so often.

Learning came easily and quickly for our first daughter. To our fascination and delight, she proved not only to be extremely bright and articulate with an incredible memory, but creative and artistic. The ease with which she adapted to the Japanese elementary school becoming fluent in two languages, and the large landscape pictures she painted during her teenage years that now hang over our fireplace and in other rooms attest to that. Later she thrived on the challenges as an ICU student with a junior year at the University of Kent at Canterbury, England, where she wrote her senior thesis for graduation from ICU. It was further reinforced when she completed the law degree at an American law school honored as the best legal writer in the class. It was all the more noteworthy since her education until sixteen years old was at Japanese public schools. That led to her initial employment in the legal field as an attorney with the Pennsylvania Commonwealth Court.

Since the first several years with our first daughter proved to be so enjoyable and fascinating, we decided to search for a sister in 1968. Once again we turned to our dear friend Nobuko Tsuru who happened to be in America with her husband on leave from ICU. She contacted her old student, the head nurse at the Red Cross Maternity Hospital where Noriko Susan was born. Miraculously, the nurse notified us shortly thereafter that a child was available born as a fraternal twin of working class parents who were unprepared to bring up two more children at that time.

Following the exact procedure as before, we visited the hospital taking Noriko Susan and my ever-faithful university assistant, Tominaga Junichi, with us. We all looked through the large glass enclosure when the same head nurse picked up a tiny four-day old baby and brought her to the window. We peered down at her and shook our heads yes. Who could have imagined that we were looking at a future elementary school teacher currently teaching at a nearby public school in Mechanicsburg, Pennsylvania, who is also a Registered Nurse working at a medical clinic in Harrisburg during the summer vacations?

We were told to pick the baby up at our earliest convenience. As before, we had a Japanese friend visit the family without disclosing our identity, and to give us a 'yes or no' reaction whether she would recommend that we move forward in the adoption process. With a definite 'yes' we decided on a name and went to the Red Cross Hospital to pick up our second daughter, Kimiko Anne, then ten days old. Six months later we appeared before a Family Court judge who approved the adoption case. We now had two daughters.

Kim was an absolute delight from the moment we brought her home. With a full head of hair from birth, she was the epitome of a Japanese baby doll. Everyone wanted to hold her. And she responded happily to the attention she drew. During the first summer of her life we took her to America, on a Japanese passport of course, to meet her grandparents and uncles and aunts who all found her as adorable as we did. At that time Noriko Susan was three years old and also attracted a great deal of attention wherever she went because of her enthusiasm for life and an interest in her surroundings. We were overjoyed that our daughters turned out to be ideal children from every aspect.

To complete the rest of the family story, we spent the 1968-69 academic year at the University of London, covered in another memoir, where Noriko Susan entered a local kindergarten and Kimiko Anne stayed home with 'mummy' who was typing my doctoral thesis. After receiving the Ph.D. in the summer we spent a month high in the Alps above Lake Geneva where June had some physical discomfort which we attributed to the altitude. The most memorable moment occurred when we looked out the open window with Lake Geneva glistening under the moonlight, to gaze at the moon while listening to the voice on the radio describe the landing of the first man on its surface. That day Kim took her first steps.

On our way back to Japan for the 1969 September semester, we visited our families in Pennsylvania where June at age 38 was diagnosed as being pregnant. It came as a shock since many tests over earlier years indicated that she could not bear children, which is the reason we adopted the girls. We returned to Japan where a son was born at the Seventh Day Adventist Hospital in Tokyo in March, 1970. We named him Christopher Kenji. Who would have thought that when we saw him for the first time on that Easter weekend, we were looking at a future Japanese language teacher at the elite Columbia Grammar and Preparatory School in New York City? Chris would become the consummate outdoorsman with his fishing pole and bow and arrow at our summer home on Lake Mokoma in Pennsylvania.

The Duke family was now complete. It was also more complicated than before. With two adorable daughters of Japanese ancestry with black hair, and a blond blue-eyed son with the looks of a Gerber Baby, we attracted attention wherever we went. Our family was unique in Japan where we lived on the ICU campus from September to June each year, in America where we spent every summer with relatives on Lake Mokoma, and in all those destinations in between where we stopped on our annual trips back and forth, covered in a latter memoir.

MEMOIR 13

THE ICU STUDENT UPRISING
FOR CONTROL OF THE UNIVERSITY

- CONFINED BY OUR STUDENTS –

One morning in early March, 1967, when I arrived for my 9:30 general education class in Science Hall, I was confronted with a bizarre scene. Ten students from the ICU Hantaisha Domei, the Opposition League, had literally taken oven my classroom. They had already filled the black boards with anti-government and anti-ICU slogans and condemnations exhorting the students who had arrived early to support their movement.

I had no idea what to do. There were no instructions on how to cope with such a situation. I was on my own. I suddenly came up with what I thought was a novel idea. At 9:35, when most of my students had arrived who were as startled as I was, I walked over to the podium, unlocked the microphone from the stand with my personal key, and turned on the volume. In a firm tone of voice I announced that since this was a general education class, all opinions should be heard. I invited the student leader to take ten minutes to present his position. At the end of that period I would begin the class.

The leader was momentarily perplexed by my announcement. He then began a loud and agitated explanation of the student movement by attacking ICU's use of a new government examination for national universities called the Noken Test, essentially a Japanese version of the American SAT tests. He charged the administration with aiding and abetting monopolistic capitalism promoted by the conservative Japanese government by requiring a government examination as part of the entrance procedure, the first and only private university to do so. He raved on and on, all of which the students and I had heard over and over again during the past month.

By then, just as the student leader demanded that the faculty and administration be held accountable for condoning reactionary government policy, fifteen minutes had passed. Now the question was what should I do since I had stated clearly that a ten-minute deadline was in effect, which I had let go an extra five minutes. With considerable anxiety but with determination, I stood up and deftly grabbed the microphone from the student which took him by surprise. I announced that his time was up. My class would now begin. I invited the protesting students to take a seat and listen to my lecture as we had listened to their lecture. I paused for a moment with some apprehension wondering what they would do.

Much to my relief the student leader sat down in a front seat. His accomplices followed his lead. I began my regular class as if nothing unusual had taken place. Within five minutes they all walked quietly out the door. My ordeal was over. I found out later that the radical students had invaded about fifteen classes that morning.

My colleague, Dr. J. Edward Kidder, was determined that week to hold his archeology examination no matter the opposition. He forewarned his students that if their class was invaded by protesting students, they should follow him. When they arrived he hastily led his students across the campus to his home to avoid student disruption. The radical students surrounded his house harassing latecomers while making a great deal of noise. Nevertheless the exam was successfully administered. It marked one of the few acts of resistance to the radical student actions by individual faculty members.

Classes continued mostly in Science Hall that week since the Main Building was already occupied by protesting students. Blockades were set up in front of the main entrance by activists to stop other students from entering the building to attend class. For a week we had some difficult days as students pushed and shoved through the lines in an attempt to get to classes in the Science Hall. I well remember jostling with the activists to physically help my students break through the cordon to attend my next general education class following the unnerving episode in my classroom. By the end of the week class attendance dropped to 30%. Classes were called off.

The disruption of university operations at ICU had begun several years previously in 1965 when the first significant act of student opposition was carried out over an increase in the price of meals in the dining hall. Although short-lived with the barricades coming down after negotiations, it was an indication that more campus turmoil was forthcoming as the movement by activist students continued on campus in various forms.

It finally culminated on the morning of February 10th, 1967, when a crisis of enormous ramifications engulfed the university. A group of about sixty emboldened students protesting university policy literally invaded the Main Building. They immediately barricaded the entrances thereby prohibiting students, faculty, and administrators access to the classrooms, offices, and university documents. The dispute evolved through various stages of calmness, violence, and calmness for the next five or more years. As in previous as well as later disturbances, the issues that sparked the immediate act of protest were sometimes trivial such as a $5 rise in the entrance examination fee. Nevertheless they ultimately had the goal of shutting down the university by violent means unless student demands were met.

The demands by the radical students reached far beyond internal issues such as dining room fees or tuition increases. To the savvy student leaders at ICU, as well as those at nearly every Japanese university undergoing similar student activism, they were political. Acts of campus disruption were instruments intended to ultimately bring about the end of the governing Jiminto Conservative Party, in power since World War II.

The Jiminto was opposed for its close ties to big business led by Keidanren, and its support of American military bases in Japan fundamental to the foreign policy of the United States then involved in a military conflict in Vietnam. Campus violence was a natural evolution of the movement at ICU as our activist students became part of a national student movement being carried out on virtually every campus in Japan, some more extreme and others less than at ICU.

By the time the protesting students at ICU occupied the Main Building in February 1967, they had become effectively under the influence of the Kakumaruha, the lesser of two radical national student organizations. Spouting anti-government slogans and political theory reportedly provided by the Japan Teachers Union then under leftwing leadership, the radical students set out on a determined campaign to convince the non-political students to join their movement. They set up stations at major intersections where students passed by, for example in front of the dining hall, often using bullhorns. They also maneuvered in small groups in dormitory rooms where they applied enormous pressure on wavering students. In the process they took over student government and even dormitories, most notably the Second Men's where they unfurled red banners that reflected their increasing power and influence on campus, as well as their political orientation.

Within this setting, the following account traces the unforgettable adventure of one ICU faculty member during one of the most turbulent periods of the decade of campus turmoil, as recalled over forty years later. It may vary slightly from the recollections of my colleagues. Nevertheless, and in spite of the split that developed among the faculty in reaction to the student turmoil, the experience left an indelible mark on everyone of us. To this day it's painful to be reminded of that decade of campus turmoil when the vision of ICU painted so vividly by Dr. Yuasa, the charismatic first president, was shattered requiring years to be restored inevitably in a modified version.

On a cold overcast February 10th, 1967, when I parked my bike at the little used east entrance of the Honkan where my office was located, I sensed there was something amiss. As I reached out to open the door, I spotted a strange site through the window. Student lockers, chairs, and desks were stacked up against the inside of the door from floor to ceiling. The door was locked shut.

At that moment two grounds staff went hustling by. I asked what was going on. They replied that a large group of students had occupied the building. They would allow no one in or out. Classes had been suspended. Return home and wait for further instructions.

I was stunned. Perhaps I should have expected something like this. After all, the campus had been in a state of confusion for months with protesting students making public speeches, conducting tense sessions in dormitories, and posting signs in conspicuous locations.

The particular issue that became the focal point of the ICU student movement against the university in 1967 was the proposal presented by the administration at the faculty meeting in May 1966. It called for the adoption of a new national achievement examination named Noken as a first-stage experimental screening in the 1967 entrance examination procedure. Faculty from the psychology department in my division involved in preparing the annual entrance examination argued persuasively that ICU could not compare the graduates from one high school to the other since standards among high schools differed considerably. In addition we could not always rely on the high school grades as an initial standard for the initial screening. The competition for high schools to place their graduates in the best universities had become so extreme that our officials suspected that grades were purposely altered by some high school administrators to increase their schools success rates.

Documentation was presented to the faculty showing that, for example, on a number of occasions an applicant's high school grades were markedly higher on official transcripts the second year one applied upon failing the exam the first year. In order to have a national standard to compare each applicant's high school achievement, our educational psychologists concluded that ICU should adopt the newly-designed Noken Test prepared by the Ministry of Education as an initial instrument to test scholastic ability for applicants to national universities. The faculty became convinced of the necessity of the exam purely on academic grounds which, notably, placed ICU as the only private university to adopt the new government examination.

The Japan Teachers Union under leftwing leadership with close ties to the Japan Communist Party had taken an official position opposing the Noken Test. In its publications the union argued that the government would bias the examination questions in the Noken Test toward a conservative stance on world affairs. That, in turn, would compel teachers to orient their lessons accordingly to prepare their students to pass the exam. It was rumored that the Union had contacts with ICU student leaders who charged that the university was aiding and abetting the government's conservative political bias by adopting the Noken Test considered as a political instrument.

I must confess that when I personally voted for the original proposal at the faculty meeting in May 1966 to adopt the Noken Test on a trial basis as part of the first screening in the 1967 entrance examination, I did not appreciate the degree of opposition that protesting students could achieve. My decision was based solely on academic factors. That was the basis for a consensus among the faculty to initially approve the test.

By January of 1967, amidst the mushrooming campaign by the Hantaisha Domei, the Opposition League of students, opposing the use of the Noken Test at ICU, the faculty reconsidered its original decision to use the test. By then a large number of applicants had already followed ICU's instruction to take the test at government-designated centers for the 1967 entrance exam The question now was whether to use the available test scores along with high school transcripts in the selection of those to proceed to the second stage involving ICU's internal examination.

It was extremely difficult amidst strongly held opinions on both sides to reach a consensus at the faculty meeting. Finally a vote to recommend that the Noken Test scores not be used for the 1967 first stage selection process only, and that further study be made whether to use it for the 1968 entrance examination passed. It was a compromise that did not suit either side in a growing division among us.

The next step that remains delicate to this day is somewhat vague in my mind. As I understood it, President Ukai Nobushige, brother-in-law of Dr. Yuasa succeeding him upon retirement, made a difficult and controversial decision. Under the prevailing circumstances, and based on the faculty decision, he agreed to both of the student demands stating that ICU would not use the Noken test in the future, and the increase in the examination fee would be reduced. At the following faculty meeting the president's declaration was discussed at great length, mostly in critical terms over his unilateral decision to concede to the student demands unconditionally. It provoked further friction among us that would widen as the dispute continued.

When Dr. Ukai held an open meeting to explain his position on February 9th, he came under heavy criticism from the audience made up mostly of activist students. I found that meeting exceedingly disturbing. Dr. Ukai in his quiet scholarly manner answered the questions, clearly intended to intimidate him, in the usual manner of Japanese scholars. When students demanded to know why ICU decided to use the Noken Test in the first place, he began with a background analysis of the underlying conditions at the time of the decision. The students were in no mood for rational discourse demanding that the president answer their questions directly. They became frustrated with his careful analysis refusing to allow him off the stage until his answers were acceptable. It was an impossible situation that ended in a stalemate.

The following day, February 10, 1967, sixty students physically occupied the Main Building barricading the entrances. Their action effectively closed the university since the vast majority of classrooms were located in the huge Honkan building, as well as most faculty and all administrative offices. The struggle for control of the university had taken a radical direction. The students settled down for a blockade of unknown duration. They ordered in food delivered by vendors at a rear door, and kept warm at night with heaters plugged in to electrical outlets that the university allowed to be kept on, apparently for humanitarian purposes.

On March 1st classes were resumed in other buildings mostly in Science Hall and in faculty homes where possible. They lasted exactly one week marked by student disturbances such as the encounter I had with the activists who attempted to disrupt my general education class, and the surrounding of Ted Kidder's home where his class was held, described above.

On March 15, the Vice President for Academic Affairs, Dr. Everett Kleinjans, convened a special faculty meeting to consider disciplinary action against the students occupying the Honkan. Since the regular faculty meeting room was located in the barricaded Honkan, the meeting was held in the small three-cornered Seabury Chapel located about thirty meters from the end of the huge Main Building occupied by the students. They had already hung large banners from the roof against Noken, clearly visible from the Chapel. It was, without doubt, the most memorable meeting I ever attended at ICU.

We faculty members were filled with anticipation as the chairman called the meeting to order at 10 o'clock. He began with an overview of the tense situation on campus. The police had been notified of the illegal occupation of the Main Building, advising ICU authorities to handle the situation as an internal university matter. The legal implications were also being explored. Various questions were raised.

After about twenty minutes of the meeting carried on in a matter-of-fact atmosphere, we were suddenly aware of a commotion outside the Chapel that had large windows running around the building on all three sides. The radical students barricaded inside the Main Building somehow became aware of the faculty meeting underway within thirty meters of their, so to speak, fortress. Unbeknownst to us, they had come poring out of the Honkan to take up a position around the chapel, at the same time wiring the doors shut in the single entrance. Suddenly we were confined by our own students.

As we became cognizant of our predicament the chairman counseled everyone to remain calm. The meeting would continue. The students had a different plan. Incensed that the faculty had ignored their demands on the use of the Noken Test in the first place, they were now demanding that no student be punished for participating in the occupation of the Main Building. They chanted the usual slogans and criticisms over their ever-present bullhorns pressed up against the windows. The noise was deafening. The chairman, realizing that the meeting could not possibly continue under such circumstances, stopped the procedure. We simply sat there suffering under a barrage of demands that gradually diminished in volume as a stalemate set in.

A division among the faculty concerning the response by the university to the student behavior, both in the Honkan barricade and the siege of the faculty in Seabury Chapel, grew more intense that day. Should ICU call in the famed Kidotai, riot police, to forcefully evacuate the barricading students from the Honkan, or should patient negotiations be continued in an attempt to reason with the students to arrive at an amicable solution? After all, some argued, we were dealing with adolescents for whom we accepted responsibility to educate based on Christian principles of love, forgiveness, etc. Several senior Japanese scholars who experienced suppression as Christians by the notorious wartime secret police expressed some reluctance to call police to the campus. There were also a few faculty who held a sympathetic view of the argument that ICU was, in fact, complicit with government policy.

In my simplistic way of thinking, and as an American with no wartime memories, although I sympathized with those who had unpleasant experiences with wartime police, I was ready to call in the

Kidotai and retake control of the university. I assumed that it would be carried out expeditiously without serious injury, as it was being done up to that time on several other university campuses. I had no religious scruples against police force.

About an hour after the siege of the Chapel began, as we chatted in small groups trying to figure out what to do, one of the American professors in science, my dear friend Don Worth who arrived late for the meeting and could not get in once the doors had been wired shut, unexpectedly appeared outside the window where I was seated. At well over six feet tall and weighing over 200 pounds, he forced his way through the student cordon to reach the chapel window surrounded by several angry students. I opened the window. Speaking rapid-fire English far too fast for the Japanese students to understand, he said, "Ben, I have wire cutters in my pocket. Ask Ets (Kleinjans) what I should do." The agitated students yelled at him, "What did you say? What did you say?"

I immediately went to the chairman who was on the phone with the ICU president who also could not get to the meeting before the blockade and was handling matters from his office. It was through this line of communication that we learned that plainclothes Mitaka police were in the growing crowd outside the chapel observing developments. Ets' reply, "Tell Don not to do a thing. The students are wild with rage. If they find out that he has wire cutters to open the doors, there is no predicting what they'll do."

I returned to the window and as rapidly as I could speak I told Don, "Don't do anything!" He nodded and walked away as the students yelled, "What did he say? What did he say?" Fortunately they had no idea what had just transpired. The deadlock continued.

Meanwhile, by early afternoon with no solution evident, several wives of faculty who lived on campus thoughtfully made sandwiches for those of us confined inside the small chapel for several hours with only water fountains, bathrooms, and a telephone. We learned that they would shortly appear to appeal to the students, and hopefully be allowed to hand several boxes of sandwiches in through one of the windows. The students reluctantly agreed and we ate lunch in confinement, thanks to the wives.

The siege of Seabury Chapel continued into the evening with the wives returning once again with boxes of sandwiches and some drinks for our evening meal. At around eight o'clock Dr. Richard Miller, noted scholar on Japanese history, slumped in his chair, his face ashen white. I asked Dick what was wrong. He said that he had a heart condition and that his pulse was dangerously low. Please call his wife, a nurse, to take him to the hospital. The president's office was called to relay the message.

Miriam arrived within a short time driving up to the Chapel followed by an ambulance with blinking lights and blaring sirens forcing their way through the cordon of students. Taken by surprise the leaders reluctantly removed the wire. Miriam and two emergency personnel entered the Chapel and carried Dick out on a stretcher through the students who ridiculed the 'weak foreigner' on his way to the hospital. The image of that dramatic moment as the kyukyusha, the ambulance, pulled away from the chapel into the darkness with sirens blaring and lights flashing remains clearly in my mind.

Several hours later Dr. Kleinjans opened up a direct line of communication with a student leader through a crack in the front door. It was a rather comical site to see the six-foot-four American kneeling down to negotiate with the five-foot-five Japanese student through a crack in the door as the wire was loosened for the negotiations. The student leader was backed by about ten students surrounding him making it impossible, and inadvisable, to attempt to break the blockade through the front door.

Unable to meet the impossible demands of the radical students, a compromise was reached at around 11 PM. After being confined by our own students since 10 o'clock that morning, the chairman of the faculty agreed that he and several other administrative officers would meet the student leaders to continue the negotiations in an open forum in the university auditorium the following morning at 10 o'clock, with as many faculty members present as possible. With that, the wire was removed from the entrance to the chapel as the students quietly withdrew to their nearby fortress, the Main Building. I returned home before midnight totally exhausted. It was quite an adventure to be confined by our own students.

The following morning I went to the auditorium that had been physically taken over by the radical students. They stationed male students at each of the several entrances so that once inside, no one was allowed to leave. The auditorium was crowded overwhelmingly with students since many faculty refused to submit themselves to such an artificially imposed confrontation. It was a kangaroo court from the very opening with students yelling out their demands, heckling ICU officials when they attempted to explain the university position. The meeting was getting out of hand.

Finally, in desperation the student leaders themselves stopped the meeting with a warning that their movement and the occupation of the Honkan would continue until their demands were met. The students set the conditions to end the meeting. University authorities must agree to another meeting the following day at the same site. At that meeting they should be properly prepared to respond to student demands. The conditions were accepted. We were allowed to leave.

That evening it was agreed that no one from the administration or the faculty would show up for the next meeting, ending direct negotiations. We simply could not face such an ordeal again. The students came out from the Honkan that night angrily demonstrating around the campus because we called off the meeting. They marched past our house deep within the wooded campus in formation chanting slogans and blowing whistles in cadence. We remember our daughter, Noriko Susan then three years old, when hearing the whistles approaching the house in darkness since we turned off all lights when the sound of whistles was first detected, telling June that, "The noisy students are coming again." They were intent on intimidating faculty who lived on campus.

In response ICU hired twenty professional guardsmen in part to protect faculty families living on campus, which further provoked the students. They claimed that the hired guards were trained to maim their victims. They did present an intimidating presence on campus as they openly practiced their skills to overcome resistance. By employing them, the students charged, ICU revealed the real intent of the university that made a mockery of the purposes of a Christian institution.

In order to secure the other academic buildings on campus, the library and science hall, faculty members were then asked to take turns standing guard in them overnight. I volunteered for library duty reporting at six in the evening until six in the morning every few days. I walked around and around the second floor looking out the window for suspicious activity that would warrant calling the professional guards into action. I often fell asleep in a chair around 3 or 4 AM to be awakened from a deep sleep when the hired guards appeared for the day shift. It was all in the line of duty of an ICU faculty member.

As long as the student occupation continued, classes could not be resumed under any circumstance since the vast number of classes was scheduled in the huge Main Building then under student control. The group of sixty radical students had effectively shut down the International Christian University, as did radical students at many other Japanese institutions from the most prestigious national Tokyo University through the most distinguished private Keio and Waseda universities. Japan's higher education had essentially been closed by students.

Without any forewarning, on March 26 I received a cryptic handwritten note from Dr. Harashima Akira, surely the most polite and reticent member of the faculty, who was appointed chairman of a special committee on the student problem. Curiously he had been given the authority to end the Honkan occupation, a most unlikely candidate for such an assignment as senior officials one by one resigned out of exhaustion. Some, including President Ukai, were hospitalized. I still have my copy of Professor Harashima's appeal that I knew would set off another adventure in the student uprising when, upon handing it to me at our doorstep in the dark of night, he, in his usual manner, politely asked me to bring June along to a special event planned for Monday.

> To all the members of ICU   March 26, 1967
> Dear Friends,
> I would like to take the leadership in physically re-opening the Main Building on Monday, March 27 at 10:30 o'clock in the morning. Mrs. Harashima will be with me representing the students. Your spiritual cooperation, or physical presence in front of the Main Building, will be very much appreciated.
>   Respectfully Yours,
>   Akira Harashima
>   Chairman, Special Committee

When June and I showed up in front of the Honkan before 10 o'clock on Monday along with about fifty other faculty and staff, some also with wives, we were divided into two groups. One was led to the north entrance and the other to the south entrance of the 100-meter long Main Building. The purpose was to tear down the barricade inside each entrance led by ground staff equipped with wire cutters. The main entrance in the center was apparently considered too heavily barricaded to attempt to remove. Females were stationed shortly behind the males in the line of attack. I was uncomfortable with the plan but assumed that a great deal of thought had been put into it by Dr. Harashima and staff or our wives would not have been invited to participate in a potentially dangerous operation.

By the time our unit approached the north entrance of the Honkan, the occupying students realized that an invasion was about to be launched on their fortress. Just before the staff with wire cutters reached the door, the window on the second floor directly above us suddenly opened. A helmeted masked student with a fire hose in his hand pointed it directly down at us, none of whom were helmeted. I cringed waiting for a heavy stream of water to strike my bare head. Just as the hose was turned on, the stream turned into a dribble. Fortunately the main water valve to the Honkan had been shut off that very instant. But I knew we were headed for trouble.

As we struggled to remove the chairs and desks from the north entrance the students went wild with rage. They had stacked a big supply in the hallway reinforcing the blockade from within as we chipped away at it from the outside. Amidst great confusion faculty and students began to push and shove each other with the defenders screaming in our ears to get out. Amazingly fists were not used. It was one of the most incredible sights in the history of ICU as the faculty literally fought our students for control of the Main Building.

Amidst the pushing and shoving between faculty and students, a young physical education faculty member tapped me on the shoulder to follow him. "Where are we going?" "We're going inside. Follow me!" He led three of us around the end extension of the Honkan to the toilet were he broke a window allowing easy access to the side hallway. That led to the long central hallway which traversed the entire first floor where the battle for control raged at each end.

We climbed into the large bathroom and on through the door to the side hallway. We had penetrated the student castle without detection as the defenders needed all available hands to repel the faculty at the north and south entrances. It was a peculiar feeling to be inside the Honkan under siege conditions even though my office for seven years was located on the third floor directly above me.

Suddenly one of the student leaders, infamous for his rousing speeches attacking ICU, spotted the four of us approaching from the side hallway. In disbelief he and a buddy rushed toward us highly agitated ordering us to get out. He claimed we had no right to be there. We didn't know quite what to do under the circumstances as the student grew increasingly frustrated with our penetration of his stronghold. A scenario then unfolded that will forever remain in my mind. The young activist could not contain his feelings any longer and began to cry with tears streaming down his checks as he ordered us out. I must confess that a sudden sense of sympathy struck me as I thought to myself that we're really dealing with immature students.

At that very instant another faculty member came around the back of the Honkan and motioned to us through the window to come out. He explained in a loud voice that Dr. Harashima had called off the attack fearing that it would lead to serious injury as faculty and students continued to scuffle for control of the entrances. The attack had not gone as he planned. We immediately turned around, went back to the bathroom and climbed out the window to rejoin June and our colleagues then retreating from the north entrance as they were from the south entrance. By then students were throwing pint-sized milk bottles filled with dirt from the roof of the Honkan on to the hastily retreating faculty and wives. The battle for control of the Main Building had ended. ICU lost.

The students immediately closed the two entrances quickly rewiring the doors shut. Some of them then came running out the back entrance approaching our two faculty groups, one at each end of the long building. They warned us not to try that again. If so, blood will be spilled. We returned home unnerved by the harrowing experience of attacking our own students, and to await the next episode in the student struggle to control ICU as the barricades were reinforced for a long siege.

However, after two more weeks of stalemate with the radical students maintaining their occupation of the Main Building, bold action was finally taken. After the occupation began, a series of administrative turnovers took place as Dr. Ukai entered the hospital followed by short-lived successors. Finally, faculty chairmen of the four divisions were authorized by the Board of Trustees to take charge of the university's response to the stalemate. They conducted a series of secret meetings off campus in the absence of full faculty meetings to avoid student disruption. They carried out a detailed investigation in so far as possible of the activities of many of the barricading students for purposes of punishment, beginning with the first group of ten being expelled in mid-March. In the process a legal maneuver was also set in motion that proved productive.

ICU brought charges against the occupying students for illegally occupying the Main Building rendering it impossible to gain access to the documents necessary to prepare for the second step in the 1967 entrance examination procedure. It was also charged that ten of the students were guilty of assault and battery in connection with their activities as leaders in the violent resistance to the attempt by faculty members to take control of the Main Building in order to secure official documents. The district court agreed with the charges and ordered the evacuation of the Honkan by the students on April 10.

For me, the last act of the 1967 student uprising opened on the evening of April 9 when I received a phone call from Vice President Kleinjans instructing me to come to a small building near the back gate at 6 AM the next morning. Twenty-five younger faculty members were being organized by ICU to assist in forcibly entering the Honkan led by over two hundred riot police, the well-known Kidotai, at 7 AM. It was a secret operation. I could only tell my wife of the plan.

I showed up at the small building at 6 the next morning with great anxiety. VPAA Kleinjans explained to us that a court order had been obtained to evict the students for illegally occupying the Honkan. In addition, the court order contained arrest warrants for assault and battery, stemming from the faculty attack on the Honkan, of ten leaders, five males and five females. Technically the riot police had been ordered to campus to carry out the orders of the court to secure official documents led by a bailiff. Since arrest warrants had been issued, the operation was planned in secrecy for the early morning hours in order to arrest the students by surprise after a period of inactivity.

The operation had been carefully planned with the first phase already carried out by ICU grounds personnel. In the hour before daybreak they had quietly encircled the entire Honkan with a heavy rope held in place by stakes in the ground about thirty meters from the building. Do-not-enter signs were posted at short intervals. The twenty-five faculty members wearing ICU armbands, of which I was one, were to be stationed at appropriate intervals all the way around the building inside the roped-in area. Our role was to show the ICU presence and witness the operation from beginning to end. I was assigned to stand on the small mound directly in front of the main entrance, the so-called bakayama (crazy mountain), providing me with a perfect location to watch the famed riot police in action.

The plan took me by surprise. In one sense I was pleased that bold action was finally underway. On the other hand, being involved in a police action against our own students that could become violent before my eyes was not a pleasant thought. Nevertheless we all accepted it as our duty to follow directions. We were told to walk or ride our bicycles to the Honkan area by different paths so that we did not attract attention. I hopped on my bike with great anxiety.

This is what I personally witnessed from the top of bakayama on February 10, 1967, as I reconstruct it in my mind over forty years later. Precisely at 7 AM, two hundred forty riot police carrying long shields marched in perfect formation to the front of the main entrance of the Honkan. At that moment the bailiff from the court read the eviction notice over a loudspeaker followed by a brief pause. Assuming the students had not yet been aroused from sleep, the court's workmen began cutting the wires on the door to remove the barricade to enter the building in order to arrest the ten students who were identified as leaders. It was raining slightly to make it more dramatic.

Within a moment or two after they began tearing down the barricade, a large classroom window on the first floor nearest the barricaded entrance opened wide. To my astonishment the barricading students came pouring out of the window jumping the three feet off the windowsill to the ground. They were fully dressed carrying handbags and chanting slogans against the Noken Test.

They were quickly surrounded by about a hundred riot police and confined to the immediate area. I have a collection of pictures carried in major newspapers that day and the next of the very scene that I personally witnessed of either the barricade being torn down or the students engulfed by the police in front of the Honkan.

We were later told that a leftwing newspaper reporter assigned to cover police activities visited the police headquarters the previous evening. He incidentally discovered a great deal of activity underway as hundreds of police were preparing their gear for an early morning assignment. The reporter somehow learned that they were planning the ICU assault on the Honkan at 7 AM and informed the occupying students by phone. Consequently, rather than being a surprise assault designed to capture the leaders without a struggle, the students were up bright and early, had packed their personal belongings, and were waiting inside the classroom next to the main entrance when the court-ordered workers began to dismantle the barricade at the main entrance.

As I looked down upon the amorphous mass of riot police in full gear and the radical ICU students shuffling around in the center of them, I could not discern what was happening. Suddenly I saw two police in regular uniforms seize a student and pull him through the cordon of riot police to the outer edge of the mass. One officer held the student while the other read from a clipboard, immediately hauling the captive student away. As it turned out, there were five teams of two officers each, with each team assigned to identify and arrest two of the ten leaders after reading their rights to them.

When six student leaders were arrested with the other four being absent that morning, the police opened their ranks and the remaining students promptly formed into lines of four. They marched through the opening of the roped-in area to freedom. The police immediately reformed their ranks just outside the opening to prevent the students from approaching the Honkan again.

Then, surely as a final act of defiance, two students in front of the chanting column led their faithful followers in a slow trotting cadence back toward the riot police standing in formation with shields planted on the ground before them. The students purposely swept by the police nearly grazing them seemingly daring a reaction. For the next fifteen minutes they weaved back and forth taunting the famed riot police to react as they swept by. Finally the students trotted off toward the front gate and disappeared.

Immediately after the students paraded off the campus, the front entrance of the Honkan was cleared of debris. Wearing my official ICU armband I was one of the first from ICU allowed in by the police. I found that the faculty offices and classrooms were not seriously damaged and nothing was destroyed. However the building was filthy with litter throughout, including piles of desks, chairs, and tables used in the barricades, not a few broken from the struggles with the faculty to remove them.

This episode in the struggle for control of the university was finalized with the expulsion of twelve students, thirty-two indefinitely suspended, and ten reprimanded. Classes remained in suspension for the main body of students until September, seven months after the student occupation of the Honkan began on February 10. The struggle at ICU in 1967 for control of the university over the Noken Test had come to a bitter end.

In retrospect, the Noken controversy was just one chapter in the student uprising for control of the university. Precisely two years later student activists occupied the Main Building once again which resulted in the use of the Kidotai leading to the closure of the university for a prolonged period. It was another adventure at ICU in the struggle for control of the university during the decade of campus turmoil that I do not care to recall in my memoirs. As Dr. Harashima wrote in his note of appreciation to the faculty members when he was released from the position as Chairman of the Committee Concerning the Student problem in 1967,

> To remember for years
> To remember with tears

MEMOIR 14

THE SECOND PH.D. – AT THE UNIVERSITY OF LONDON

- DEAN HIDAKA VERSUS THE JAPAN TEACHERS UNION -

In the mid 1960s I experienced an unusual adventure in Tokyo that unexpectedly led to a second doctorate, this time at the University of London. During the spring holiday season in 1965 I was invited to attend the General Assembly of Nikkyoso, the Japan Teachers Union, at a convention hall in Tokyo as a guest of the President. Upon exiting the nearest subway station I immediately became aware of Japanese martial music blaring from a loudspeaker down the road. As I approached the hall I found that the entire complex was surrounded by a line of Kidotai, the Japanese riot police. And circling around the hall was a line of six trucks with anti-communist and anti-Nikkyoso slogans blaring traditional Japanese military tunes. It was a bizarre scene.

The police in full riot gear had opened their lines at the entrance forming a narrow corridor for union members and guests to enter the building. Producing my guest invitation I was allowed through the line and, to my surprise, quickly ushered on to the stage to sit among special guests. They included the head of Sohyo, the General Labor Union, two other high labor union officials, a representative from the teacher's association of the Soviet Union, and myself.

As I sat on the stage at Nikkyoso's annual convention that unusual morning in 1965, I found it astounding that the largest union of teachers in Japan had to conduct their meeting under such conditions. The delegates were literally surrounded by a cordon of riot police that enabled them to carry out their activities without interruption. And the riot police were faced toward trucks driving around the hall with powerful loudspeakers demanding the destruction of Nikkyoso. Although somewhat muted inside the hall, the vocal demands and music were loud enough to be heard by the delegates for over an hour. I never imagined that the event would provide reference material for a doctoral thesis at the University of London four years later.

The origin of the thesis on the Japan Teacher's Union at the University of London can be traced back to my first course at ICU in 1959 in the Graduate School of Education. The Dean and founder of ICU's graduate school two years previously was the elderly and most distinguished Hidaka Daiishiro. Dean Hidaka was distinguished in a variety of ways. First of all he was the former Vice Minister of Education. In the educational bureaucracy of Japan, that placed him in the senior administrative position responsible for the nation's schools. Noted previously, under the structure of the Japanese government, the Minister of Education is a political appointee from the ruling party who is frequently replaced when the Prime Minister shuffles the cabinet. The Vice Minister remains in place.

Dean Hidaka

As Vice Minister of Education, Dean Hidaka held enormous influence over Japanese educational policy since the administrative structure of Japanese education is centrally controlled under the Ministry of Education. Every educational institution in the land must receive Ministry approval for many aspects of the program from the curricula to the textbooks depending on their status as private or public. The Vice Minister of Education in Japan is accordingly a powerful institution in itself.

Dean Hidaka distinguished himself in other ways as well. First of all he was a Christian, a rarity in the higher echelons of Japanese bureaucracy. It was his religious convictions that motivated him to retire from government service to join the faculty of ICU as a new Christian institution in 1952 following the war. Dean Hidaka also stood out among the senior ICU Japanese faculty in dress. On occasion during his later years he wore the Japanese hakata or kimono attire to class with the unique sandals on his feet that go with it. As an elderly gentleman, and former Vice Minister of Education, Dean Hidaka commanded immense respect and admiration from his peers, his students, and his young American protégé.

As a non-Japanese on the faculty of Dean Hidaka's Graduate School of Education, whose experience in the educational field consisted of a two-year stint as a public school teacher in Hershey, I must have been an oddity to the Dean. Nevertheless he took an immediate interest in his young colleague from America. Stern and upright for his advanced age, he devoted considerable time to explain the intricacies of Japanese education to me for which I will always be grateful.

The topic that Dean Hidaka was most interested in discussing was the Japan Teachers Union, better known as Nikkyoso. He knew that I had no knowledge of the Union when I joined the ICU faculty in 1959. But since the Union had become one of the most powerful institutions in the Japanese educational as well as political world, Dean Hidaka also realized that a faculty member in his Graduate School of Education at a Japanese university had to become familiar with the Union and its activities. Dean Hidaka early on become my mentor on the Japan Teachers Union. No one could have been better prepared to enlighten me about Nikkyoso than my Dean.

The first factor that became immediately apparent from our tutorials was the emotional feeling Dean Hidaka held toward the Union. He would begin his comments calmly but soon his lower lip began to quiver as he invariably became agitated the further he proceeded. As I learned from him and others, the Ministry of Education and the Teachers Union, representing the two most powerful institutions in public education, had clashed bitterly over virtually every aspect of postwar Japanese education. Their widely heralded confrontation, a topic frequently analyzed in the press, had reached the stage where senior Ministry officials refused to meet with union officials.

The confrontation between the Union and the Ministry was based on one overriding question: Who shall have the power to determine what is taught in the nation's public schools – the teachers, the locally elected school boards instituted by the American military occupation forces after the war, or the government, that is, the Ministry of Education? Every nation, of course, faces the same question. In Japan it takes on a special connotation since the problem that inevitably arises relates primarily to the social studies and history courses.

The fundamental issue of contention concerned what every Japanese child should be taught about Japan's long history shrouded in ancient mystical beliefs, and Japan's responsibility for, and conduct in, the Pacific War. That includes the very sensitive issue of Emperor Hirohito's role in the war's beginning and ending, and the fundamental question never fully addressed by the government. Could he have either averted the outbreak of war or brought it to a conclusion much earlier than he did?

Union representatives vigorously argued that social studies teachers who are trained and certified as professionals to teach the subject should have the right to determine what and how to teach their courses in the public schools under supervision of the locally elected school boards. Under that interpretation the Teachers Union supported the new school board system that was launched under the democratic reforms of Japanese education carried out by the Americans during the occupation. The school board was intended as a fundamental instrument of democracy whereby the locally elected lay school board determines educational policy reflecting the will of the community. If the board did not, it would be replaced by the voters at the next election based on the American model.

Union spokesmen defended the school boards as grassroots democratic institutions conforming to the reforms of Japanese education carried out by the Americans. Consequently the Union and its supporters, mainly members of other unions and leftwing intellectuals, then set out to influence the election results for the school boards. The Union not only campaigned for candidates who sympathized with Union demands, it encouraged and supported activist Union members to run as candidates themselves. In other words, teachers became members of school boards making policy for teachers.

Dean Hidaka, as Vice Minister of Education legally responsible for the nation's schools, adamantly rejected that interpretation. He based his objection partly on the ideological position that the Teachers Union had embraced that grew out of the general labor movement. Leaders of the immediate postwar Japanese labor movement had formed an ideological position opposed to government policy in general that mirrored that of the Soviet Union, hence the criticism that it was communist-oriented. Central to their anti-government rhetoric was the opposition to the power and influence of a reviving business complex that formed a close relationship with the ruling conservative political party, and, of great significance, opposition to American military bases in Japan that the conservative government had endorsed.

I learned early on from Dean Hidaka that the struggle for control of Japanese education originated from the controversy over textbook content in the history and social studies courses shortly after the end of World War II, and involved a much broader topic than textbooks. The Union and the Ministry conflict grew out of a major political and ideological confrontation between conservative and socialist-communist political parties in their divergent interpretations of who was responsible for World War II in which millions of lives were lost on both sides. That naturally involved the role of the Emperor.

Right wing elements supporting the ruling conservative political party adamantly opposed any interpretation of the Emperor's activities prior to and during World War II. These groups provided the funds, personnel, and trucks to mount the noisy opposition to Nikkyoso's annual conventions like the one I attended. Leftwing political parties included the Socialist and Communist Parties which had come under the influence of the Soviet Union that championed their anti-government policies of the ruling conservative party.

Under these conditions Dean Hidaka had come to the conclusion that the Ministry of Education under his direction as the Vice Minister had the mandate to preserve the political neutrality of the classroom from the leftwing teachers committed to the Union. The only way to achieve the principle of democratic education was to empower the Ministry, under the direction of the political party in power that appoints the Minister of Education which had been held by the conservative party ever since the end of the war, to set a national curriculum.

The Ministry established a system to approve textbooks through a series of committees including scholars and teachers. Their mandate was to screen textbooks for political and ideological content authorizing a list of approved texts. Local school boards had to choose one of the approved texts for their district.

Within this context, I decided that I should gain some perspective of Nikkyoso's position since I had become so close to Dean Hidaka as a member of his Graduate School of Education. I was able to schedule a meeting with Nikkyoso's well-known President, Miyanohara Sadamitsu. A rather quiet reserved man, he was delighted to tell his side of the story to someone in Dean Hidaka's graduate school. He outlined it as I briefly described it above. At that meeting he invited me to attend the forthcoming annual convention of the Union, which is how I got invited to the event where I experienced the conditions under which the union conducted its annual conventions.

One of the results of my meeting with President Miyanohara of the Japan Teachers Union was an awareness of the delicacy of my personal position in the Japanese world of education and business. Miyanohara specifically criticized the emerging influence over the ruling conservative political party, the Jiminto, by Keidanren, the Federation of Japanese Industries. He made the point that with the rebirth of Japanese businesses following the devastation during World War II, their expanded economic power enabled them to provide much of the funding through Keidanren for the Jiminto. In turn the government inexorably reflected big business interests often at the expense of the workers with which Nikkyoso identified.

When Miyanohara criticized Keidanren's growing influence and power with the ruling political party, I could not reveal my relationship with Keidanren. As described in an earlier memoir, by the time I met Miyanohara I had already been holding a Keidanren Seminar of leading Japanese businessmen for several years in the Industrial Club in downtown Tokyo. Union President Miyanohara would have been shocked if he knew that the head of my seminar was no other than Hanamura Nihachiro, the Executive Director of Keidanren and my dear friend. I was well aware of Keidanren's enormous influence with politicians of the ruling party through Hanamura's fascinating revelations as described in the earlier memoir.

Around this time we arranged a trip to America for the following summer by traveling eastward stopping in India and London on the way. I took the opportunity to visit my graduate advisor at the University of London. When I spent a year's study there in the doctoral program, Dr. Joseph Lauwerys, Director of the Comparative and International Education Faculty at the University's Institute for Education, was appointed as my advisor. I still had the requirement of a publishable thesis to complete the Ph.D.

Upon my visit to Dr. Lauwerys' office in Bedford Square, I told him of my growing interest in the confrontation between the Japan Teachers Union and Dean Hidaka, who he met many years previously in Japan. Dr. Lauwerys found the topic of such interest that he encouraged me to analyze the issues between the Union and the Ministry in a thesis on the postwar history of the Japan Teachers Union to complete the doctorate under his supervision. The main requirement that the thesis be publishable could be met since the confrontation between the Japan Teachers Union and the Japanese Government had never been covered in print in English by that time.

I accepted the challenge. Upon returning to ICU I devoted as much time as possible to collecting the necessary data for the thesis. I then applied for a leave for the following year, 1968-9, to complete the second Ph.D., this time at London University. Finally, in 1969, precisely ten years after earning the first doctorate from Penn State, I was awarded the Ph.D. from the University of London. My doctoral thesis entitled The History of Nikkyoso, the Japan Teachers Union, was approved after an exhaustive oral defense under my professor, Dr. Brian Holmes, who had by then succeeded Dr. Lauwerys upon his retirement. It was also approved by my external examiner, and Britain's leading scholar on Japan, Dr. Ronald Dore from the London School of Economics. He was chosen as the external examiner in part because of his classic book on Education in Tokugawa Japan.

One year later the doctoral thesis on Nikkyoso was slightly revised for publication in the United States by Praeger Press. It was given the title of Japan's Militant Teachers: A History of the Left Wing Teachers Movement in Japan. During the year of its publication, it became Praeger Press' number one seller in the field of education.

Dean Hidaka would have been proud of his American protégé when Japan's Militant Teachers was translated into Japanese and published in Japan several years later. The United States Ambassador to Japan, Dr. Edwin Reischauer, America's leading scholar on Japan, kindly wrote an introduction for the Japanese reader. Unfortunately Dean Hidaka died before its publication.

MEMOIR 15

AN INTRODUCTION TO COMMUNIST EDUCATION

- WITH THE BRITISH-SOVIET UNION STUDENT FRIENDSHIP SOCIETY IN THE USSR –

During my two years as a doctoral student at the University of London, one of my tutors, Professor Brian Holmes, was famous among his students for leading comparative education tours to Europe and the Soviet Union. During my first year I joined the tour visiting schools in Germany, France, and Spain. It was a very enjoyable and informative opportunity to gain a perspective of the differences and similarities between continental education and British education. From my perspective, it was even more instructive in comparing continental education with Japanese and American education with which I was most familiar.

When the announcement was made during my second year at the University of London in 1968 that Dr. Holmes had scheduled a comparative education tour to the Soviet Union under the auspices of the British-Soviet Union Student Friendship Society, I immediately signed up for it. As a full-time graduate student under Dr. Holmes, who lectured on Soviet Education that I found fascinating, I automatically qualified as a delegate from Britain with the British-Soviet Union Student Friendship Society.

During Dr. Holmes' lectures on Education in the Soviet Union, the particular topic that interested me, and which rendered education in a communist country distinctly different from that in non-communist societies, was the role of the communist party in the schools. I decided to use the opportunity whenever possible during the tour to pursue that issue. If I could gain a reasonable understanding of it I would be in a position to make it the central focus of a new section in one of my courses at ICU under the title of The Role of the Communist Party in Education in Communist Societies.

Upon our arrival in Moscow representatives of the British-Soviet Union Student Friendship Society met us at the airport. They were all acquainted with Dr. Holmes who had conducted an annual tour to the Soviet Union for a number of years. They informed us that a welcoming party had been planned for that evening at the apartment of the President of the Society in the Soviet Union. Several members of the Moscow branch would escort us from our hotel to the party.

That evening the fifteen-member student delegation from Britain plus Dr. Holmes were taken by subway to the suburbs of Moscow where the Society President lived in a surprisingly luxurious apartment on the top floor of an apartment building overlooking Moscow. The sight of the city from the balcony in the evening was magnificent. And the elaborate display of chocolate candies upon entering the apartment curiously remains in my mind to this very day.

Clearly the President of the Soviet chapter of the British-Soviet Union Student Friendship Society was not an ordinary student. Indeed she was not. She was in fact a fairly high-ranking member of the Communist Party in her fifties who spoke elegant English and dressed as elegantly befitting her luxurious apartment with the magnificent view of Moscow. Moreover she was introduced to me by her old friend, Dr. Holmes, as

Mrs. Bernie Cooper. I was baffled to be welcomed to the Soviet Union by someone with an American name.

Mrs. Cooper, on detecting my American accent that set me apart from my fellow student delegates from Britain, as did my age, explained that her husband Bernie would be delighted to meet me since he was born and brought up in Brooklyn. He would be arriving home shortly after a meeting at the office. By that time I was understandably mystified by the situation as well as anxious to meet her American husband, Bernie.

Bernie Cooper turned out to a very friendly fellow who had all the positive attributes of an American. He spoke English with native fluency. We hit it off from the moment we met in his magnificent apartment in the suburbs of Moscow. He was intrigued to learn of my background as an American professor at a university in Tokyo visiting the Soviet Union as a student from a British university. I found his background as intriguing as he found mine.

Bernie Cooper had a fascinating career. Brought up in Brooklyn as the son of Russian immigrants, he served in the United States Army during World War II and as an American translator (Russian) at the Nuremberg trials after the war. During the so-called honeymoon period in relationships between the Soviet Union and the United States just prior to the Cold War that soured that relationship from 1949, Bernie's parents returned with him to the Soviet Union settling down in Moscow. Because Bernie was bilingual with an interest in politics, he was hired by Radio Moscow as an announcer in the North American bureau. He joined the Communist Party cell at the station and eventually became chairman of the cell itself.

Bernie was not only friendly but quite objective about communism, and open about the internal workings of the Communist Party both at the station level and above. He turned out to be a treasure of information about the role of the Communist Party particularly at the local level about which we talked for hours. One evening at his Moscow apartment we continued the discussion until midnight. During our short walk to the nearest subway station, he pointed out a little old man walking his dog across the street as Nikita Khrushchev. The famous leader of the Soviet Union had been unceremoniously removed as head of the Communist Party some time before and retired in Bernie's neighborhood.

From Bernie's detailed and frank explanation about the structure and operations about the Communist Party in the Soviet Union, he made it clear that the Party was the 'backbone' that kept the vast conglomerates of peoples in the many republics together under one government. Perpetuating a common interpretation of communist ideology, the Communist Party chapter in each school served as an overseer of political ideology from one end of the mammoth country to the other. It superseded local traditions, customs, religious diversity, and local languages of which there were many in the USSR. Consequently the Communist Party played a fundamental role in education ensuring stability and social cohesiveness amidst great diversity, as well as the perpetuation of communist hegemony utilizing the local school as an instrument to achieve that goal.

When I respectfully brought up a common criticism that some members of the Communist Party took advantage of their positions as an elite sector of the society for personal gain, Bernie accepted it as a legitimate concern that was on occasion addressed by party leaders at all levels. I chose not to mention that his luxurious apartment with its splendid view of Moscow could be interpreted as an example of that. He noted that he and his wife have indeed benefited by their loyalty to the Party.

Bernie was clearly pleased to help arrange visits to a variety of schools in Moscow and to meet the heads of the Communist Party cells in each one. His analysis proved true. Each head of the party chapter reinforced the others. They all gave me similar answers to the same questions. Their solidarity was reflected in the similarities of the room set aside in each school for political teachings always dominated by a statue of Lenin. The social events as well as summer activities of each school were planned under the guidance of the Party to conform and reinforce the teachings of Communism.

The tour to the Soviet Union led by Dr. Holmes included two stops for comparative purposes. The first was Moscow dominated by Russians. The other was Riga, the capital of the Soviet Republic of Latvia, an example of the many Soviet Republics whose people were non-Russians and whose native language differed from the Russian language. By now I had gained a fair understanding of the role of the Communist Party at the local school level through the classroom visits in Moscow sufficient to ask critical questions of teachers in Latvian schools. I wanted to compare the differences and similarities from the perspective of a non-Russian republic.

On the first school visit at a secondary school in Riga near the fine beaches on the Baltic Sea, I was introduced to a female English language teacher assigned to me for the day as a guide and translator. When I described my background as an American on the faculty of a university in Japan, she found that to be of considerable interest as well as a curiosity, especially when I explained that I wanted to teach my students at ICU about the role of the Communist Party in the USSR. With that she began to reveal a completely different perspective on the topic from what I had gained in Moscow. My background and purpose disarmed her somewhat and she became more open and animated on the topic. And the longer we were together that day the more detailed she became in her desire to make certain that I understood the primary role of the Communist Party in Latvian schools.

As it turned out she was a proud Latvian who deeply resented not only the domination of Latvia by Russians, but by the Communist Party influence in her school profoundly influenced by Russian teachers that perpetuated what she called the myth of Soviet solidarity and the supremacy of communist ideology in the USSR. My new Latvian friend, a practicing Christian, was particularly unhappy with the composition of the Communist Party chapter in her school. She claimed that it was dominated by teachers from the Russian community in Riga which had significantly grown in size and influence after World War II.

In her opinion, the increase in Russian immigrants into most of the Russian Republics that were independent before World War II reflected the policy of the Russian-dominated Central Committee of the Communist Party in Moscow. The ultimate goal was to assure communist hegemony, and thereby Russian hegemony, over all of the non-Russian republics in the Soviet Union. The primary purpose of the Communist Party in Latvia, according to my guide and interpreter, was to suppress Latvian culture with the long-range goal of superceding it with Russian culture and ultimately the Russian language. To her, the Communist Party in her school was an instrument of Russian colonialism. It would, she assured me, never accomplish its mission.

I was deeply impressed not only by the frankness and openness of the English teacher in that school, but by the vastly different interpretation of the role of the Communist Party in education from that as interpreted by the teachers I met in Moscow several days previously. From then on during the four-day tour of Latvian schools, I questioned many Latvian teachers and learned that the first teacher I met was not alone in her criticisms of the political structure of her native Latvia as well as that of the USSR. It was widespread among her fellow countrymen and women who entered the teaching profession.

When we left the Soviet Union to return to Britain and the continuation of my graduate studies, I had gained a perspective of the role of the Communist Party in the schools of the USSR that was most revealing. Manifestly the interpretation of the Communist Party as the backbone of Soviet society as explained by Bernie Cooper differed in fundamental ways from that as interpreted by the Latvian teachers I met.

After receiving the doctorate from the University of London in 1969 to return to Japan, I felt well enough informed on the issue to include it in my comparative education classes at ICU based on my visit to the USSR with the British-Soviet Student Friendship Society. My students found the topic of special interest since they had never been introduced to the role of the Communist Party in communist societies. When the

Soviet Union collapsed in the late 1980s and the Communist Party was disbanded as many of the soviet republics became independent including Latvia, students in my ICU classes had some understanding of the causes as a result of my graduate studies at the University of London.

MEMOIR 16

INTRODUCING THE OXFORD-CAMBRIDGE TUTORIAL TO ICU

- AN UNFORGETTABLE EXPERIENCE FOR MY STUDENTS -

Beginning with my first course at ICU in 1959, I was concerned about the lack of student participation in my classes. Since few non-Japanese students enrolled in our Education Division having come to ICU to learn Japanese, my classes were overwhelmingly made up of Japanese students. And they came out of an educational culture that discouraged active student participation either through asking questions or responding freely to questions during class.

The tradition of the passive student in Japan was based on several factors. The well-known adage that the nail that sticks out gets knocked down stemmed in part from the fear of embarrassment or shame that pervades this ancient culture embedded in Chinese traditions. However it has been further ingrained with the emergence of the supreme role of the university entrance examinations from which the phrase examination hell was coined. Virtually every ICU Japanese student went through a rigorous examination preparation in high school classes and private preparatory courses.

By the time our Japanese students entered ICU, they had become accustomed to passing courses by memorizing volumes of information in preparation for an examination, for which their test-taking skills were finely honed. They were not accustomed to actively participate in the learning process by asking questions during class, or entering into a dialogue with the teacher or a fellow student as a routine class activity. I had to adjust to the inevitable. The students who entered my classroom expected me to lecture for note-taking in preparation for an examination.

During the two years as a graduate student at the University of London, I became intrigued with the ancient tutorial system that originated at the medieval universities of Oxford and Cambridge. The tutorial was designed as a one-to-one exchange and dialogue between student and tutor, the professor. It was intended not only to ascertain the student's understanding of the subject, but to motivate the student to search more deeply for the answers to the questions posed by the tutor who directed the student to relevant resources.

Students at those prestigious institutions refer even to this day to their major area of study as 'reading classics' or 'reading economics.' In contrast, American students refer to their main subject of study as 'majoring in economics' or 'taking a history course.' The difference between 'reading a course' and 'taking a course' derives from the tutorial at Cambridge and Oxford where students literally read their way to a degree. Rather than enrolling in a history course offered at 10 o'clock Monday, Wednesday, and Friday as in the typical American college or university, as well as at ICU, the Oxbridge student majoring in history begins his course by meeting with the professor to determine the timing of the first tutorial. The student will be given a tutorial assignment requiring a paper to be based on a set of readings. At the agreed upon date, perhaps two weeks later, the student appears at the office of the professor with paper in hand to read and defend before his 'tutor,' his professor, in a one-to-one dialogue.

During the tutorial the professor as tutor probes the student on the ideas, the analyses, and the conclusions expressed in the paper. The student must defend them in a face-to-face encounter with an authority on the subject. At Oxford and Cambridge this often involves a preeminent scholar in the field who will also expound on the topic. Under a wise and skillful tutor the capable student learns to respond to probing questions in a thoughtful manner that can withstand critical analyses. In such a setting it's difficult to conceal poor preparation. By its very nature, the tutorial is a demanding exercise.

At the end of the tutorial the student will receive the assignment for the next tutorial requiring a more advanced paper based on a set of recommended readings. And so it goes until the end of term at which time the student will have 'read' his or her way through a course in which the professor 'tutored' rather than lectured in a formal classroom atmosphere.

During the term the professor will also schedule a public lecture or two on a specialized topic. The titles and schedules of all the special lectures are published in a program before term, open to anyone who chooses to attend. The student in the professor's tutorial may or may not attend the lecture depending on the precise topic and one's personal inclinations. In contrast, American and ICU students are expected to attend the Monday, Wednesday, Friday lectures at 10 o'clock in order to prepare for a possible midterm and surely a final examination.

Needless to say the tutorial system presents a unique experience for the student. When Oxford and Cambridge were rather small institutions in years gone by, the tutorial consisted of a one-on-one meeting with the professor. As the institutions expanded the number of students in a tutorial increased to two or three, thereby reducing the time that each student had to defend his paper and the ideas incorporated in it. Nevertheless the student 'read' history in its literal meaning.

As a doctoral student at the University of London I experienced a modified tutorial system under my professor, Dr. Brian Holmes. During the first year he assigned papers to be read and defended before him in tutorial sessions one-on-one in his office. One of the unique features of Dr. Holmes' tutorials was the sipping of British

Sherry provided and served by him as we went over my analyses and conclusions which he rigorously questioned. By the time I wrote the doctoral thesis, I knew what was expected. I had also grown rather fond of British Sherry.

When I returned to ICU with my second doctorate in 1969, I was determined to introduce some form of the tutorial in my upper level undergraduate courses with an enrollment usually between ten and fifteen students, as well as with my graduate courses of around five students. Since I had to follow the usual Monday, Wednesday, Friday schedule of lectures, I decided to assign a midterm and final tutorial in lieu of a midterm and final examination. The requirement was that each student would appear with paper in hand for a tutorial at the mid-term and the end on an assigned topic where they would read the paper and then defend it in the Oxbridge style. I began with two or three students per tutorial since I realized how revolutionary the process was at ICU. A one-on-one encounter was too much to ask.

I also decided to add a feature that reflected the ICU tradition. The tutorials were held in our home on campus, three minutes from the Main Building. We were accustomed to having students for open-house for freshmen every April and, as part of the ICU Church program, open house for students at Christmas. During those occasions, June baked cookies which the students greatly appreciated. She agreed to bake cookies during the tutorial season.

When I first explained the tutorial to my students they were, as anticipated, perplexed. They had never heard of such a system. Their reaction was understandable. As mentioned above, Japanese students especially from the high school through the university primarily listen to the teacher lecture. The typical classroom especially in the elite preparatory high schools consists of lecture, memorization, and testing. Seldom are questions asked by students in the Japanese high school and university classroom, and that includes to a great extent the typical ICU classroom. The tutorial was intended as my way to break the tradition of the Japanese teaching-learning process.

Open House at the Dukes

The first semester when I scheduled the tutorials to supplement my lectures, the experience was revealing. To say that my Japanese students were nervous was an understatement. The demands that I placed upon them were to some extent unprecedented. They were compelled to defend their ideas on education in a foreign language in an unusual situation, although I did everything possible to make the atmosphere as comfortable as possible. And June served her chocolate chip cookies with tea as soon as the students got settled in our living room, or on a mild day in the spring or fall on our patio with a breathtaking view of Mt. Fuji in the distance. Even at Oxford and Cambridge it would be difficult to match the setting for a tutorial that I had at ICU.

The tutorials were a learning experience for me as well as the students. They confirmed that a wide discrepancy existed among ICU students from various aspects. First of all, although the majority of our Japanese students came from Tokyo, we also had a significant number of students who originated from remote areas of Japan with considerably different family backgrounds. For example, during our early days at ICU when modern flush toilets were rare in rural Japan, it was necessary to provide instructions on how to use them in the Honkan. Attached to the wall behind the toilet was a sketch showing a stick figure squatting with feet on the toilet seat. A large red X ran through the picture indicating that this was not the proper procedure. Students from Tokyo found the instructions as comical as I did. Those from the rural areas found them instructive as intended. Differences in sophistication among our students were evident in the classroom as well.

Another difference that became obvious from the beginning of the tutorials was the discrepancy in the English speaking ability of our students. Although we took great pride in the bilingual ability of our students, they ranged from very good to very bad. I often began my courses noting that since ICU students, according to the PR brochures, were bilingual, I could expect everyone to readily understand my English. That not only provoked considerable laughter, it reduced the tension of the opening class.

The language reality rendered it especially difficult to conduct the tutorials in English with students who had a limited ability in spoken English, often from rural Japan. I had to make accommodations accordingly. I assured those who had much trouble expressing themselves in English that I was not that concerned about grammar, etc., but in the underlying ideas they were trying to convey. I was able to do that in most cases so that the course grade did not depend on English ability but rather with the ideas and analyses of the students.

Although most students were uncomfortable at the beginning of the first tutorial, they relaxed somewhat as it went along, even more so during the second one. And those students who took several of my courses seemed to really enjoy the tutorials the more they experienced them, as I did. As I improved my tutoring skills, the students responded in ways that were gratifying and impressive. During the tutorials many students expressed profound concern over the inequalities in educational opportunities between advanced nations like Japan and third world countries like Bangladesh, and within democratic societies like Japan between the affluent and the poor. I could not have learned about those attitudes through lectures and examinations. Moreover it was most gratifying when not a few of them upon graduation worked in developing nations in Africa and Asia to help reduce the inequalities in educational opportunities that concerned them as expressed during the tutorials

Regardless of whether it was the first, third, or fifth tutorial, most of my students expressed a deep sense of appreciation for the opportunity to visit the home of a foreign professor and to experience the hospitality they received. I became convinced that the ancient Oxbridge tutorial contributed positively to their educational experience at ICU. I included tutorials in every course I offered, except the large general education SS3 course, until retirement.

Years later after retirement when I meet my former students, they often comment on the tutorials at our home. A typical conversation between former student and tutor follows a remarkably similar format. It runs something like this: "Duke sensei, you may not remember me but I took your course many years ago. How well I remember and appreciate the tutorials at your home. And I also remember Mrs. Duke's chocolate chip cookies. It was an unforgettable experience."

MEMOIR 17

THE EDUCATION OF OUR CHILDREN AT OSAWADAI

- LEARNING TO BE JAPANESE -

One of the most critical decisions we made at ICU was to enroll our first child, Noriko Susan, in the local Japanese public elementary school, Osawadai, from the first grade in 1970. At the time we did not fully appreciate the ramifications that would follow. First of all we accepted the reality that our daughter would receive her basic education in a school system much different from the one her parents experienced in America, and in a foreign language. We also understood that the role of Osawadai was to prepare Japanese children to live successfully in Japanese society, that is, learning to be Japanese. Although we lived in Japan our home life was typical of a middle class American setting. We felt our daughter could adjust to both environments.

What we did not anticipate at the time was the latter addition of two siblings. The decision to send the first child to Osawadai led to sending her younger sister Kimiko, and later an unexpected brother Christopher, to follow her in the Japanese school. In other words, by sending our first child to a Japanese public school, our three children were destined to receive their entire basic education at Osawadai. During Noriko Susan's last year in the sixth grade prior to her entrance to Mitaka Nichu, the Mitaka Middle School, Kim was in the third grade and Chris just entered the first grade.

We could not envision that year, when our whole family was absorbed into the life of Osawadai, that Noriko Susan would eventually become an attorney with the Commonwealth Court of Pennsylvania later to join the police force in Bethesda, Maryland, Kim would become a public school teacher and a registered nurse in Mechanicsburg, Pennsylvania, and that Chris would become a Japanese language teacher in New York City. As it turned out, learning to be Japanese at Osawadai prepared them well for successful careers in America.

There were several other unexpected consequences that grew out of that early decision to send our first child to the Japanese school. It set the stage for a book that I titled simply The Japanese School. It was "Dedicated to Susan, Kim and Chris whose experiences in the Japanese school provided many of the insights for this book." The Foreword, written by a former Minister of Education, Nagai Michio, noted that, "The readers of this book, whether they be Americans or Japanese, or Europeans and Asians as well, will gain important insights into the relationships between the school and modern societies. I appreciate Professor Duke's efforts in preparing this excellent study."

One of the tertiary results of sending our children to Osawadai was to provide me with a firsthand opportunity to discover, and appreciate, the educational foundation of my Japanese students at ICU. In an oversimplified but accurate assessment, the typical ICU student received his or her basic education in an elementary school similar to Osawadai where they learned to be Japanese, forming attitudes toward schooling and many other aspects of life.

It all began when our oldest daughter, Noriko Susan, reached the age of six in 1970. We had to choose which of two routes would be best for her basic education. We could send her to the American School in Japan, an excellent institution from kindergarten to high school. It was located just ten minutes away by bicycle on the extreme side of the ICU campus on land ICU sold to them for their new campus. ASIJ had an outstanding reputation for providing a solid, well-rounded education on the American model completely in English.

We were teaching Noriko Susan to read and write English at home using materials from America. As a native English speaker since we had adopted her shortly after birth, our daughter had reached a sufficient level in English to qualify her for entry into the first grade of ASIJ. Most of the non-Japanese on the ICU faculty sent their children to ASIJ with the tuition paid by our supporting organization in New York, the Japan ICU Foundation. In other words, an English education in a nearby prestigious private school was available tuition-free from the first to the twelfth grade.

The alternative was the local Japanese elementary school, Osawadai Shogakko, located less than ten minutes on foot from the ICU back gate in the opposite direction from ASIJ. Osawadai was a typical public school following the curriculum set by the local Mitaka city school board in conformity to the standardized national curriculum approved by the Ministry of Education. Many of the Japanese faculty who lived on the ICU campus, that is, most of our neighbors, enrolled their children in Osawadai. Others sent their kids to private Japanese schools paying tuition in hopes that the experience would better qualify them to enter select private secondary schools that, in turn, would prepare their offspring for the better university.

Since Noriko Susan was a Japanese child by birth living in Japan, we made a major decision in her life to enroll her in the local Japanese elementary school. The opportunity for her to become fluent in two languages, and to experience the culture of the land of her birth, seemed to us too valuable to pass up. In addition, since she had attended the ICU Church kindergarten on campus conducted in Japanese for two years, she had already become fluent as a six-year old speaking the Japanese language. Although we were not familiar with the demands placed on children in Japanese public schools, we were confident that our daughter could cope with the situation. We were, however, also oblivious to the demands placed upon the parents of children at Japanese public schools.

Noriko Susan (left side leaning on chin) in first grade

The process of beginning the first grade for our daughter proved somewhat exhaustive not only for us but for the parents of all the other children as well. It was a foretaste of what was to follow, and to continue throughout the elementary and junior high school. In a word, the Japanese take the education of their children very seriously, not only by the teachers and the school administrators but by the parents as well. We quickly became aware of a seriousness of purpose among virtually all who were involved in the process.

We also learned early on that, although a public school, it would not necessarily be inexpensive. For example, all children were required to carry their books and school materials to and from school each day in a randoseru, a leather bookbag worn on the back with straps around the shoulders so the arms are free. When we went to the nearest store where they were on display for the new school year beginning in April, 1970, the price ranged from $100 to $200. Fortunately a neighbor's child had completed the elementary school that March and had no further need of one. They kindly gave it to Noriko Susan. Uniforms were not required at the elementary school level.

The entrance ceremony for the first graders was revealing. It was held in the gymnasium with all students and teachers present and the administrators seated on the podium waiting for the grand entrance of each of the first grade classes lead by their respective homeroom teachers. Seated on chairs set up for the occasion was virtually every mother, and many fathers as well, dressed in their finest for the occasion. With appropriate pomp and circumstance music, each first grade class entered in perfect formation following the teacher to take their assigned seats. With the introduction of each class welcomed by great applause, followed by a formal speech by the principal, and a formal departure of each first grade class to great applause by the standing audience, the Japanese education of our daughter had begun.

Immediately after the ceremony and the picture-taking, the first grade parents were expected to return to the respective classrooms to stand in the back of the room for a short session. The teacher introduced herself and invited us to attend the initial PTA meeting after the abbreviated session on the opening day of school had ended. Virtually all did. It was the beginning of countless meetings that June or I attended during the year as a PTA parent.

It was also during the first session that we learned about the custom of katei-homon, the home visit by the teacher. We received a schedule of available hours during the afternoon of the second week of school for the teacher to come, on bicycle no less, to each home for a 20 minute visit. Each parent filled out the most convenient times. Several days later a master schedule was returned and we prepared to host the teacher for the home visit.

As we learned from Japanese friends with children in the first grade, this meeting was considered very important by the parent and teacher providing an opportunity for the teacher to observe the home environment of each of the students. It also provided an opportunity for the parent to get to know the teacher, as well as to present a favorable impression on the teacher. To many mothers, and not a few fathers who stayed home from the office for the visit, it was a stressful occasion for them.

One of our close Japanese friends from the ICU Church, the Kawakamis, he being vice president of Coca Cola Japan, also had a daughter in the same class as ours. They prepped us for the teacher's visit. As it turned out, on the day of the teacher's visit to the Kawakami household scheduled for 2 o'clock, the two of them were hosing down the front steps in boots and work clothes when the teacher rode up on her bicycle for the interview at 1:30. The parents were horrified to greet the teacher of their daughter with boots on through a misunderstanding of the timing. Although we found it amusing, the Kawakamis understandably did not.

We also soon received from the teacher the schedule of studies for each subject that included the pages from each textbook that were being taught that particular week. Parents were urged to spend time with the child by going over the assigned sections before they were taken up at school. That was the initial clue that the teacher expected parents, including the Dukes, to become directly involved in the education of their children from day one not only through the many activities of the PTA, but by personally participating in the subject matter.

Beginning with Noriko Susan and continuing with Kimiko Anne three years later and Christopher Kenji two years after Kim, our children experienced 'how to be Japanese' at Osawadai. And that included cultural patterns that I analyzed in The Japanese School under four themes or goals of Osawadai. They include loyalty, literacy, competency, and diligence.

The chapter on loyalty begins accordingly: "One of the predominant traits of the Japanese – be it at work, school, or play – is loyalty to the group. It transcends all layers of society. It is the stuff of being Japanese It begins in the first grade when each child is assigned to A Kumi, B Kumi, or C Kumi, the child's class under the homeroom teacher. From then on the child identifies himself or herself as in Ichinen B Kumi, first grader in B Kumi, not a student in Kikukawa Sensei's class.

Christopher Kenji at Osawadai

The kumi stays together under the same teacher for two years, that is grade one and two, grade three and four, and grade five and six. The kumi sets the stage for the formal process of group training, developing ties that bind the individual to the group in order to achieve the ultimate goal, group harmony. For two years the children in each kumi study together in the classroom, they eat lunch together in the classroom, they play together on the playground, and they clean up the classroom together after school. Deep bonds of friendship are forged within the kumi that often extend a lifetime.

The role of the group is further enhanced when all teachers divide the kumi of forty or so students into small groups called hans, consisting of four to six students sitting in the same area. The composition of the hans change about three times a year when seat assignments in straight rows are rearranged randomly for new hans to be formed. The word used in English, hancho, comes from han, a small group, and cho, the leader elected by the han members. It is particularly in the han that the role of the leader in Japanese culture is first ingrained. And that role is to achieve group harmony, a consensus, by leading without standing out too much conforming to the cherished adage that 'the nail that stands out gets knocked down.' The kumi mentality with its positive as well as negative influences is one of the most important traits of being a Japanese ingrained from grade one at Osawadai. Our children, as did their classmates, fit into the pattern successfully.

The second goal of Osawadai and every other elementary school is to teach every child to read and write the Japanese language at a national standard set by the Ministry of Education. This is an extraordinary achievement since the written Japanese consists of kanji, adapted from Chinese characters that each range in strokes from one, for the number of one, to well over twenty. Our children had to learn to write our address in Mitaka, a suburb of Tokyo. Mi means three and is written in three simple strokes. Taka which means hawk is written with 24 strokes that must be memorized and written in a precise stroke order. The Japanese learn well over two thousand characters in order to read the daily newspaper by the time they graduate from high school. Over ninety-five percent of the population complete high school with that ability, a remarkable achievement few countries can match.

Learning to read Japanese begins in the first grade at Osawadai with the first full day of school as it does in every public elementary school. Every child including the three Duke children turned to page one of the textbook chosen from a short list approved by the Ministry of Education that conforms to a national standard required by the government. The class was taught as a whole with much choral reading. The teacher made a major effort to keep every child up to the class standard. To those who fall a bit short of that, parents are brought into the effort through encouragement from the kumi (home room) teacher.

As one of the most homogenous societies in the world, the Japanese language, referred to in school as the kokugo, literally the 'national (koku) language (go),' serves as one of the great unifying influences of being Japanese. Few nations have attained the mass standard of literacy that Japan has by virtue of the effectiveness of teaching the kokugo at Osawadai and its counterparts throughout the land. As I state in my book, "Literacy from the first grade is an affair of state in Japan."

The Ministry of Education in this centralized school system has the responsibility to arrange the Japanese language systematically for teaching purposes into a standardized curriculum. Each of our three children brought home their first grade readers, copies of which we still have, that introduced seventy-six written characters (kanji) beginning with the simplest ones gradually proceeding to the more difficult ones. Each year our kids learned a greater number as all Japanese children did. The process began naturally and continued in complexity to include a total of 1,850 by the completion of junior high school, which ends compulsory education. However over 95% of all children continue to the high school where more kanji are taught. The end result is a national literacy standard with a most difficult written language that ranks Japan among the highest in the world.

I posed this question in my book. How does the Japanese classroom teacher accomplish this mass literacy standard? My answer: by sheer diligence, patience, and perseverance. Language teaching at Osawadai is a continual process of memorization, repetition, drilling, and testing. The higher the student goes in school, the more the student, every student, memorizes, repeats, drills, and takes tests. There are no secrets in teaching methodology in Japan. They are the traditional methods.

The third goal of Osawadai that our children experienced was the effort to instill competency in the students, that is, having sufficient power, skill, or resources to accomplish an object. In the book I use mathematics at the elementary school as the subject used to instill a sense of competency among Japanese children. The standard of mathematics at Osawadai from grade one onward is most impressive. It is second only to the level of literacy.

The Japanese maintain one of the highest standards of mathematical achievement in the world. It is attained through the same process that mass literacy is attained under the careful planning of the Minister of Education with approved textbooks setting a national standard of mathematics that the Duke children were subject to. They struggled with the demands as did their classmates, but they, as it were, got swept up in a relentless effort at Osawadai to become competent in mathematical computation.

When Chris was in the fourth grade at Osawadai, we took his textbooks, typical of the approved texts set by the Ministry of Education, to America with us for the summer vacation. Our return to Japan that year was delayed by one week so that we were in the States for the opening of the Pennsylvania school year in September. We spent that week with our parents in our hometown of Berwick. We made arrangements through childhood friends to visit the local elementary school where June and I both attended from grade one to six.

I purposely asked to visit the fourth grade classes so that I could show the three teachers, all female, the mathematics textbook from Osawadai. As they paged through it, they could immediately determine the standard since many pages included mathematical problems to be solved by the student. They included grafts, charts, and figures of increasingly difficulty. The teachers were shocked at the fourth grade level of mathematics at Osawadai.

One comment remains in my mind to this day. One of the teachers concluded that her students could not possibly solve the problems on a particular page that required the calculation of the area of a figure in the shape of a magnet. And, with a sheepish grin on her face, she acknowledged that she couldn't do them either. The other two agreed. It was a testimony to the competency of the students at Osawadai.

The final goal of Osawadai is to instill among the students a sense of perseverance. In Japanese it's the most familiar exhortation of Gambare! Persevere! Don't give up! One hears it everywhere and in any kind of a situation. As I wrote in the book, throughout the lifetime of every Japanese they are surrounded, encouraged, and motivated by the spirit of gambare. It begins in the home. The school takes it up from the first day the child enters the classroom. It continues through graduation. It engulfs every facet of the society. Gambare is integral to being Japanese.

I have come to the conclusion that the sense of gambare that our children experienced at Osawadai derives from the severe geographical limitations of Japan. In a nation the size of the state of Montana with only 15% level enough to live on, and with no natural resources, to survive requires perseverance, gambare, by every member of the society. Otherwise the nation faces a catastrophic future. That state of affairs was true during the agrarian days as it is today during the technological era. For Japan to become a super economic power second only to the United States, with its vast areas and natural resources, the Japanese instinctively recognize the role of perseverance in every endeavor. It is an essential part of being a Japanese.

Learning to be Japanese as students at Osawadai by Susan, Kim and Chris did not come easy. Nor was it easy for us as parents, who did not experience the Japanese school, to play the role of parents who were expected to reinforce the efforts of the teachers to achieve the common goals necessary to live successfully in Japanese society. And yet our children did little complaining during the six years that each spent at Osawadai. On the contrary they enjoyed Osawadai and their Japanese friends.

If we faced the same situation today, as we did in 1970, whether to send our children to the Japanese school, we would make the same decision. Learning to be Japanese has served all three well in their adjustments to, and success in, learning to be an American.

MEMOIR 18

THE GERTRUDE DICKSON SCHOLARSHIPS FOR THIRD WORLD STUDENTS

- ARRIVING ON THE QE 2 TO VISIT THE RECIPIENTS -

W hen I was a student in the junior high school in my hometown of Berwick, Pennsylvania, for some reason long-forgotten I joined the local chapter of the Junior Red Cross Association to be elected the student president. The wife of the most prominent lawyer of the community, Mrs. Gertrude Dickson, was the adult volunteer advisor to the Association. Who could have imagined that that chance association in Berwick in the 1940s would play out through her financial generosity that enabled not a few students from Africa and Asia to study at ICU several decades later.

Gertie, as she was most commonly known in my hometown, was a truly eccentric, although generous, woman with a unique background. First of all she was not from the small town of Berwick. Indeed she was from New York City where her father had been a very successful lawyer. Upon his death in the 1930s her mother and two daughters inherited a multi-million dollar estate.

By the time Gertie graduated from an elite private high school in New York City, her musical talents with the piano were of such a level that she was accepted at one of America's premier musical institutions, the Julliard School of Music in New York City. She was, she hoped, destined for a professional musical career. With financial support from the family estate, and trained at Julliard, her future was bright.

During her first year at Julliard, her mother took her two daughters on vacation to the tiny resort village of Eagles Mere, Pennsylvania, a favorite of the rich from New York City and Philadelphia before World War II. Interestingly this Memoir is being written at our summer home on Lake Mokoma in the Endless Mountains of Pennsylvania exactly six miles from Eagles Mere. We attend the Eagles Mere Presbyterian Church during the summer months.

Less than a mile from our church in Eagles Mere stood a grand old hotel called Crestmont that catered to the rich city folk like Gertie's family. During her first weekend at the Crestmont, a young lawyer from the most prominent family of lawyers from my hometown of Berwick 50 miles away named Conway Dickson was also a guest. A recent graduate of Yale Law School, he spotted Gertie, then age 18, playing tennis, a favorite of the rich in those days. He asked the tennis pro to introduce him to Gertie when he planned to return for the following weekend from Berwick.

According to plan the tennis pro promptly informed Gertie about Con's desire to meet her and agreed to the introduction the following weekend. After the introduction the two played tennis together and enjoyed each other's company during their first two-day acquaintance in spite of the gap in ages and distance between home towns. They agreed to meet again during the following weekend.

The third weekend, when Con drove over to Eagles Mere from Berwick to meet Gertie, turned out to be of great consequence that many years later extended to Japan. Con proposed to the 18-year old wealthy socialite from New York, a first-year student at Julliard

School of Music in New York City. He asked her to withdraw from the music school and move to the tiny town of Berwick, Pennsylvania as the wife of a promising young lawyer in his father's law firm, the most successful in the town. In order to help convince her to accept his proposal, Con promised to buy her a fine Steinway grand piano for their new home.

Gertie's mother was adamantly opposed to the idea of her daughter not only of dropping out of Julliard and thereby giving up any chance of a musical career, but she was especially against the idea of her sophisticated socialite daughter moving from New York to settle down in an obscure Pennsylvania town of 10,000 residents on the Susquehanna River. Infatuated with the handsome erudite young lawyer, Gertie resolutely made up her mind to accept Con's proposal of marriage in spite of her mother's strong opposition. Within six months Gertie was trying to adjust to small town life in America as Mrs. Gertrude Dickson.

About twenty years later when I, at age 14, first met Gertie at a meeting of the Junior Red Cross, I was somewhat overwhelmed by her dominating personality as well as her stylish looks and dress. She had by then become one of the most prominent women of the Berwick community involved in many welfare activities such as the Junior Red Cross. She also took an active role in the First Presbyterian Church donating a huge sum of money for a fine organ. My most memorable association with her was the trip to Cleveland by train, my first ride on a train, to attend the national convention of the Junior Red Cross with two other student officers under her responsibility.

The next time I met Gertie Dickson took place about thirty years later when we were visiting our parents in Berwick during the summer vacation from ICU. I was asked to speak about the Christian movement at ICU during the morning worship service at the First Presbyterian Church as the guest speaker.

Following the usual procedure of the church, I stood with the pastor at the church foyer following the service to greet the parishioners as they filed out. As it turned out, the last person to come by was Gertie Dickson. She introduced herself accordingly: "Ben, you probably don't recognize me. I'm Gertie Dickson. We met at the Junior High Red Cross meetings many years ago." Once she identified herself, I recognized her immediately. Although still quite stylish, she had aged noticeably from how I remembered her as a teenager. But I was then taken by surprise when she expressed a desire to contribute to the Christian activities of ICU. She asked me to develop a proposal for her to consider and to call her when I had one ready.

Without asking how much money she was considering, I came up with the idea of an open-ended proposal entitled the Gertrude Dickson Scholarships for Third World Students. At that time ICU had few students from Asian or African countries primarily because Japan had achieved an economic miracle that brought with it an economy with one of the highest costs of living in the world. Most Asian and African countries were still in the early stages of development. The only way to recruit students to ICU other than from North America or Europe was through scholarships.

Gertie immediately accepted my proposal with two provisions. One was that I would be responsible for determining which students would receive the scholarships in order for her to have confidence in the way her money was being spent. The second condition was that wherever possible and feasible, the recipient would be required to work several hours each week at the university. In other words it was not to be simply a gift. The recipients had to work for the scholarships. She then wrote me an initial check for $15,000, a sum far larger than I anticipated.

Upon returning to ICU in September I immediately began to consider how to implement Gertie's scholarship fund. It so happens that three students from Ghana had been accepted at ICU for the September semester. Unbeknownst to me, in order for ICU to meet its commitment to the I and C in the name International Christian University, tuition was waived for the three applicants who had applied from Ghana through, as I recall, their churches.

The problem these students faced was how to finance their daily costs of living, which was substantial especially for foreign students coming from such an alien culture unaccustomed to Japanese food and customs. I immediately contacted each one and learned that they were very fine young men from Christian families eager to learn the Japanese language and enter fully into student life at ICU. Since English was the language of their home school system in Ghana, they were fluent in the second language of ICU. In desperation they had already found odd jobs off campus that required ten to fifteen hours per week.

I offered each of them a Gertrude Dickson scholarship if they quit their off-campus jobs and devote their full attention to the Intensive Japanese Language Course designed for foreign students to become sufficiently capable to take courses in Japanese during the second year at ICU. Although this did not conform to Gertie's conditions about working several hours per week on campus, I felt it was best for the students since Intensive Japanese was extremely demanding requiring their full efforts.

The following year Gertie's secretary notified me that she was planning an around-the-world trip of eighty days on the QE2. Among the itinerary was an overnight stop at Yokohama arriving at 6 in the morning and departing at 6 the following afternoon. During the two days in Japan Gertie wanted to meet 'her boys,' the recipients of her scholarship.

Through her secretary we invited Gertie to spend her night in Japan with us at ICU where we planned a dinner for her and her boys at our home. On the day of arrival I met her at the dock in Yokohama where the great QE2 berthed. It was an awesome moment to see that famous ship come into port. We returned to ICU by taxi to meet the African boys for dinner. They were awed by her. She enjoyed them immensely. They thanked her profusely for the scholarship which pleased her. They also sang a few songs from their native country which she enjoyed.

Gertie Dickson and 'her students'

Gertie was most appreciative of the way I was handling her scholarship fund and assured me that the fund would be refinanced when the original amount was fully used. But Gertie at age 84 was anxious to get home after living on the QE2 for over seventy days. She was eager to get back to the port for the ship's departure the following day at 6 PM.

It normally takes about one and a half hours by car from ICU to the port at Yokohama. Since the ship was to depart on a Sunday afternoon we ordered a taxi to take Gertie and our family to Yokohama to leave ICU at 3:30. June and our three children wanted to see the great QE2 and send Gertie off at the port. She invited us to come aboard with her to tour the great ship.

As we neared Yokohama around 4:30 a build-up of traffic was noticeable. It seemed natural as we approached the big city. However as we came closer to the downtown through which we had to pass to reach the port, traffic was so heavy that our taxi was barely crawling along by 5:30. We still had two miles to go to reach the harbor. By now Gertie was becoming highly agitated in fear that she might miss her departure. We shared her feelings.

By that time traffic had come to a stop for ten minutes or so every hundred yards. Gertie was becoming distraught. By 5:45 we were still well over a half mile from the dock amidst a solid line of traffic moving a few feet at a time. Without doubt we could not reach the QE2 by the departure time of 6 o'clock. All I could think about was what am I going to do with this distraught eighty-four year old woman who missed her departure on the QE2.

The reason we found ourselves in this predicament became clear. The departure of the QE2 from Japan was treated as a major event attracting thousands of Japanese who came to view the spectacle of the giant ship slowly pulling away from the harbor with horns blowing after a grand farewell. On a Sunday afternoon every road leading to the dock was jammed with cars. The Japanese all wanted to get close enough to the dock for a good view of the departure, an impossibility due to the shear numbers of visitors and the limited space at the dock. We were caught in that mammoth traffic jam with an elderly passenger among us who was distraught as well as angry with me because I had not arranged to leave ICU at least an hour earlier to beat the traffic, about which I had no realization of the magnitude.

We could see the docked ship as my watch showed that it was 6 o'clock. It was over. We missed the departure. However the ship did not move on the dot of 6 as I expected. At 6:15 it was still at the dock and we were still some distance away. I began to think about the possibility that we could still make it. A policeman was directing traffic just ahead of us. We called out to him that we had a passenger with us showing him Gertie's QE2 pass. He took one look and immediately started to clear out the traffic so that we could squeeze through the last section enabling us to arrive at the dock at 6:45.

Much to our surprise a band was playing, followed by a short speech by, as we learned later, the mayor of Yokohama. Beside him on the stand by the gangplank was the captain of the QE2 who was about to make a departing note of thanks to the Japanese for their hospitality. The passengers were lined up on the various decks watching the departing ceremony below delayed by the traffic. We did not know that the car carrying the mayor of Yokohama and the bus bringing the Yokohama City band had also been delayed by the massive traffic jam so that the QE2 had to delay its departure for the mayor and his band.

Amidst the departing ceremony, and in full view of thousands of sightseers and hundreds of QE2 passengers looking down from the decks above us, we got out of the taxi with Gertie's luggage and slowly walked up the gangplank. She literally fell into a seat in the lounge totally exhausted as we said our hasty farewell amidst the splendor of the QE2.

Returning to our taxi we had a grandstand view of the mighty QE2 slowly pulling away from the dock over an hour late. And what a spectacle it was. The distinctive horns periodically blared from the moment the ship began to move until it reached open waters. It was an unforgettable moment not only because of the majesty of it all but because Gertie Dickson was aboard.

And now the rest of the story . . .

Gertie Dickson's boys from Ghana received her scholarships for the four years they studied at ICU. Without her financial support it's doubtful whether they could have completed their course of study in Japan. During the four years we became very close to them having them over for dinner on many an occasion. One of them became particularly active in our ICU Church. He joined the choir taking a leadership role in the student life of the church. He made one of the most important contributions to the religious life of ICU of any student in the history of the university.

Upon graduation from ICU the three went their separate ways. One, Kweku Ampiah, eventually earned a Ph.D. in Britain and joined the faculty of the Scottish Centre for Japanese Studies at the University of Stirling in Scotland. Another entered government service in his home country rising, as I recall, to the rank of Vice Minister of Agriculture. When I later launched the ICU International Forest, the topic of another memoir, I contacted him requesting trees from Ghana. Within a month the trees arrived at the Ghanaian Embassy in Tokyo. When I went down to pick them up, I was met by the third Ghanaian student, the one who sang in the ICU church choir, then an official at the Embassy. How appropriate it was that the two of us opened the box that had been sent from the office of another of Gertie's boys then in Ghana.

Gertie was delighted to learn about their activities. She continued the Gertrude Dickson Scholarships until her death at age ninety, providing financial support for over a dozen students from four countries. She included the scholarship fund in her will to continue the program after her death. One recipient, my advisee, the ex-marine graduate student from Korea, Byung-Yul Yoon, is the topic of the next memoir.

MEMOIR 19

YOON SAN: MY KOREAN EX-MARINE GRADUATE STUDENT

- THE DR. DUKE – DR. YOON SCHOLARSHIP FUND THIRTY YEARS LATER -

I n 1975 a 27-year old ex-Marine from Korea walked into my office to schedule his courses for the ICU Graduate School. As Chairman of the Graduate School Division of Education, my responsibility was to provide guidance for his first semester majoring in psychology. His background was impressive as a graduate of one of the leading private Korean universities, Yonsei, which I had first visited many years ago during military duty in Korea, covered in an earlier memoir. After receiving his undergraduate degree, he was required to spend three years in one of the Korean armed forces. He chose the Marines.

Upon discharge Yoon entered the Yonsei Graduate School where he was chosen as an exchange student from Yonsei University to the ICU Graduate School. Ironically I was among the promoters of the first student exchange program between ICU and Yonsei in the early 1960s, considered in a previous memoir.

Yoon san was a very affable young man with reasonable English. His professional goal was to eventually earn a doctorate in America to become a child psychologist working with disturbed Korean children. While a student at Yonsei, he had learned about the exchange program between ICU and Yonsei University. He also read the English edition of the ICU Graduate School catalog and took an immediate interest in the Department of Psychology. With little knowledge or understanding of the ICU Graduate School, Yoon san applied and was accepted. I was his first academic contact after the entrance procedure had been completed.

At our initial meeting it became immediately apparent that my new advisee had a major misunderstanding of our program. He assumed that he could earn a masters degree in child psychology primarily through courses taught in English. When we began to select his first semester courses, he learned that there were no graduate courses in his area of interest offered in English. The realization that he would have to take intensive Japanese in order to take most of his major courses that were only taught in Japanese overwhelmed him. We finally designed his first semester of courses with two undergraduate courses in psychology taught in English that would qualify among ten units acceptable from the undergraduate level, as well as my graduate course in education and a beginning course in Japanese.

Yoon san faced an additional problem at the outset. At that time the Korean economy had not yet taken off. Coming from a poor family, Yoon faced a greater financial burden than he expected when he came face to face with the high cost of living in Japan. The monthly payment for a tiny room off campus was considerably more than he had prepared for. He had already cut down on his eating habits due to the high cost of meals even in the ICU dining room, which were, in contrast, reasonable for Japanese students.

It just so happens that a rather wealthy woman from my hometown had set up the Gertrude Dickson Scholarship Fund For Third World Students, the subject of the previous memoir. As described, I was authorized by Gertie to distribute the funds at my discretion with one stipulation. She wanted the recipients of her scholarships to work in some constructive manner each week for a few hours so that they did not feel that they were receiving financial assistance without some meaningful act in return. I was to determine the type of work and the number of hours devoted to it each week.

I offered a scholarship to Yoon san to cover his meals and incidentals and part of his room rent. In return he was to devote five hours per week helping me around the house with chores such as cutting wood for the fireplace and raking leaves in the fall. He was pleased with the stipulation as his first semester began in September. Although he was not keenly interested in learning Japanese, he looked forward to his courses in psychology.

Since the cost of kerosene for heating our rather large house on campus was egregiously high, we burned a great amount of wood in our fireplace to supplement the small kerosene heaters we had placed one per room. An indication of the heavy use of our fireplace occurred one early winter evening when our long-standing neighbors and dear friends, the David Rackhams from Canada, called. They saw fire spitting out our chimney throwing burning ashes into the forest that surrounded our ICU homes. The chimney had caught on fire.

David rushed over to form a bucket brigade. He filled a bucket with water from the outside faucet and carried it to a ladder we stuck up to the roof. I carried it up the ladder where daughter Kim carried it across the roof to throw it on the red-hot chimney. The water puffed into a cloud of vapor. We continued the process for twenty minutes rotating between three buckets before the fire inside the chimney was brought under control. Our chimney fire could have had disastrous consequences if the leaves had caught fire in the great ICU forest.

Living in the woods of the 360-acre campus covered mostly with trees, we had an ample supply of firewood all around us. Each year older trees were blown down with typhoons or strong windstorms. Others had grown old and were eligible for cutting by age and deterioration. The problem was that the trees had to be cut down and split in pieces small enough for the fireplace. They then had to be brought to the house from around the campus on a wheelbarrow or a two-wheel cart borrowed from the grounds office. The whole process required a considerable effort to adequately supply us for the cold winter months when we turned off the kerosene heaters late each evening as the temperature dropped sharply inside the house with no insulation. I typically stacked firewood five feet high all across the back of our 28-foot wide house by the end of September each year to prepare for the winter.

The first week Yoon san came to the house for work we went out to cut up a good-sized locust tree that had been blown down. Since he had never cut wood before I demonstrated the process. He then followed suit with unusual vigor. He soon got the hang of it cutting up a wheelbarrow full in a short time. We put a rope around the load and pushed it through the woods to stack it behind the house. We repeated the process several times to cut up the entire tree. Yoon san clearly enjoyed the physical labor and I realized that he was a good worker. It was a win-win situation since it provided him with an opportunity to improve his English as well. He cut up a good amount of wood during his first month at school.

The next month when he came to the house for work I had him rake up the leaves around the house and place them in a large pit I had dug by the side of the house for burning leaves. Although these were the first to fall, we were soon overwhelmed with leaves since our campus house was located in the middle of the woods surrounded mainly by maple and locust trees. At that time our three children were all out playing in the leaves when Yoon san came on a Saturday to begin the seemingly never-ending process of raking them up.

Within an hour Yoon had gathered quite a pile of leaves in the pit when I looked out to see our three kids romping in the pile throwing leaves over each other in great delight. I looked closer to find Yoon in the pile with them, covering the kids with leaves while also rolling around the pile. They then climbed into the wheelbarrow with Yoon pushing them to the next area to be raked, the four laughing all the way. I grabbed my video camera and got it all on film.

I realized early on that this ex-Korean Marine was really a child at heart. He loved children and our kids grew to enjoy him. He found it liberating to play with them. By that time, however, he was having much trouble with his Japanese language course, in part because he wasn't interested in it. He found it distracting from his goal of becoming a child psychologist. By that time we were also inviting him for dinner after he completed the work assignment. He enjoyed sitting around the table with the five of us. June soon found that he had an enormous appetite especially for rice that we used as a staple. The kids were amazed at the amount Yoon san ate at each meal with us.

As the year passed we became attached to Yoon and he became attached to us. Unfortunately he fell further and further behind in his Japanese language course. As the academic year neared an end, I felt that Yoon's chances of learning Japanese sufficiently to complete a master's degree in psychology taught in Japanese were nil. Something drastic had to be done or his future was in serious doubt. His goal of earning a doctorate in child psychology in America seemed beyond the realm of possibility.

It so happened that a Visiting Professor from Brigham Young University in Utah happened to be on the faculty of ICU that year in the field of science. I contacted him and asked him if he thought it possible to get a scholarship at Brigham Young for Yoon in the field of psychology. He appreciated the situation and immediately looked into the possibility. Within two weeks he had the forms necessary to apply for a graduate scholarship. I then had a long talk with Yoon about his future and recommended that he apply for the Brigham Young scholarship and, if accepted, withdraw from the ICU Graduate School. I promised that we would buy a plane ticket to America for him, and that he would be eligible for a work assignment with the university to finance his life as a student.

Weeks later Yoon was accepted as a scholarship student in psychology at Brigham Young University, withdrew from ICU, and departed for America to begin the long path to become a child psychologist. Although our family was very sorry to see him off, we felt that it was surely in his best interest. And I was satisfied that Gertie Dickson's scholarship had been wisely used with Yoon even though he did not earn a master's degree from ICU. At least it had played an important role enabling him to pursue his life's ambition to work with needy Korean children.

And now the rest of the story . . .

For the next thirty years or so we never heard a word from Yoon san except one Christmas card that arrived about ten years after he departed. It included a picture with the simple inscription Dr. and Mrs. Byung-Yul Yoon. Standing beside him in the picture was a woman clearly of Asian descent, presumably Korean. There was no return address although the postmark was from Los Angeles. Regardless, I took considerable pride in learning that my Korean graduate student had earned his doctorate, hopefully in child psychology, and that he had married. Mrs. Dickson's scholarship had borne fruit.

One summer day in 2005, after I had retired from ICU and settled down near Harrisburg, Pennsylvania, I was mowing the lawn when June came out of the house with the phone in her hand and an unusual look on her face. I shut the lawnmower off and took the phone. "Duke sensei. This is Yoon. Do you remember me?" In astonishment I replied, "Yoon san. How could I ever forget you?" I asked him where he was living. He replied that he was calling from Los Angeles. He then took me by complete surprise. "I think of you and Mrs. Duke every day of my life. You are my models. I try to live my life like you and Mrs. Duke. I have even adopted two girls and have a biological son, just like you and Mrs. Duke did." I was puzzled about that wondering how he managed to arrange his family so precisely.

I asked what had happened to him after he left ICU for Brigham Young University over thirty years ago. This was his story. Six months after he entered Brigham Young University he withdrew primarily because he felt that the restrictions on students were too strict for him to follow. He was able to get a scholarship at the University of California through Korean friends in the area. He did indeed complete the doctoral program in child psychology and opened a counseling office for needy children of Korean descent living in the Los Angeles area who were unable to adjust to school. He had also married a woman of Korean descent that he met at the local Korean Christian church, and had three children, two adopted girls of Korean descent and a biological son.

It proved to be difficult for Yoon to make a living as a private counselor for needy Korean children in the Los Angeles area. After many years he decided that he must make a major effort to stabilize his financial situation. He was able to borrow a very large amount of money from a local bank through Korean friends to purchase the second largest Korean restaurant in Los Angeles. It turned out to be so prosperous that he was able to invest the income in other businesses that also prospered. He had, in fact, become a very successful businessman. Yoon explained that once he became prosperous he founded The Korean Needy Children Supporters' Association of Southern California to gather funds to send to Korea to carry out its purpose.

Having heard Yoon's very impressive and successful story of his life in America after ICU, I wondered why he was calling me at this time after thirty years of no communication. He then revealed the primary purpose of the call. He attributed much of his success in life to his experiences at ICU. Consequently he wanted to use his wealth to benefit Korean students at ICU as he was by Mrs. Dickson's Scholarship that he received from me. I commended him for his proposal but noted that he didn't need my approval for it.

He then explained that he wanted to call the scholarship The Dr. Duke-Dr. Yoon Scholarship for Korean Students. He was calling to get my approval for the use of my name. I was naturally honored but suggested that the names be reversed. He replied that it was through our kindness toward him that he got the idea and therefore my name should be first. With that understanding the first conversation with Yoon san in over thirty years ended on a very positive note.

A week later a check for $10,000 arrived from Yoon for the first year of the scholarship. In addition, there was a check for $1,000 made out to June in appreciation for the many meals she had made for him while he was a student at ICU. As a Trustee of the Japan ICU Foundation in New York, I redirected the $10,000 check to the Foundation to begin the Dr. Duke-Dr. Yoon Scholarship for Korean Students.

The following spring when June and I spent a month at ICU, we had the opportunity to meet the first recipient of the Duke-Yoon scholarship, a Korean girl enrolled in doctoral studies named Yeon Ju Hong from Pusan. She had been privately teaching Korean to Japanese in the evening to finance her living expenses as a student and was delighted to receive the scholarship. It enabled her to give up the evening teaching and devote fulltime to her studies. She was also very pleased to learn who Dr. Yoon was and how and why he set up the Duke-Yoon scholarship for Korean students.

Ironically Ms. Hong's academic advisor at ICU who recommended her for the first Duke-Yoon Scholarship, Dr. Hirose Masayoshi, was my advisee when he entered ICU. Little could he have imagined as an ICU student in the 1960s that he would be writing a letter of recommendation in 2005 as Director of the Japanese Language Programs at ICU for a Korean student to receive a Duke-Yoon scholarship. He included the following comment about Ms. Hong.

Ms. Hong is in the Ph.D. program in the Graduate School of Comparative Culture. Financially she has been supporting herself by teaching Korean at a language school in Tokyo. Her lifestyle seems very modest. She has been living in Kokubunji until recently from where she was commuting to ICU by bicycle. I was told by one of her friends recently that the apartment she was in was so poor that her friends worried about her. I learned that she has moved to a better apartment. This should give her a better living and studying environment. I consider that Ms. Hong qualifies to become the first recipient of the new Duke-

Yoon Scholarship for students from Korea and hereby recommend her most strongly.

June and I decided to use the $1000 that she received from Yoon toward a fiftieth wedding anniversary trip to the Riviera Maya in the Caribbean. We had traveled throughout Asia and Europe but had never been to the Caribbean. We had a wonderful week at a resort from where we sent Yoon a postcard noting that we had used his gift to celebrate our wedding anniversary and thanked him for his generosity. We felt confident that he would be pleased that his gift was used for such an occasion.

When Yoon san made the second contribution of $10,000 for the Dr. Duke-Dr. Yoon scholarship, he noted in an accompanying letter that during the past twenty years his Korean Needy Children's Association had sent ten million dollars to Korea to help the suffering children. He was at that time planning to purchase an adult day care facility for 2.5 million dollars in the "hope that this new business will produce better income that will be shared with beloved friends." Shortly thereafter he was recognized for his charitable work as an Outstanding Alumni of Yonsei University by the President, who had come from Korea to attend an alumni meeting attended by 500 graduates from the Los Angeles area.

MEMOIR 20

BACKYARD BARBECUE AT ICU FOR THE UNITED STATES SENATE MAJORITY LEADER

- SENATOR HUGH SCOTT PAYS A VISIT TO 'HIS GIRLS' NORIKO SUSAN AND KIMIKO ANNE -

In the spring of 1978 we received a phone call one Saturday evening around nine o'clock from our long-time friend, Mitsuya Goto, senior executive of Nissan Motors and a member of the ICU church. He informed us that he was bringing a friend to the church service the following morning at ten o'clock. Could he invite Senator Hugh Scott from our home state of Pennsylvania, then the Majority Leader of the United States Senate, to our home for lunch after the church service? According to Goto san, Senator Scott specifically wanted to meet, as he put it, 'his girls,' that is, our two daughters Noriko Susan and Kimiko Anne.

We were, of course, taken by surprise by the request, not because Senator Scott wanted to meet our daughters. Rather we were unprepared to have the highest-ranking politician in the United States Senate visit us for lunch on such short notice. Nevertheless we readily agreed to host Senator Scott for lunch the following day.

The reason why this most powerful political figure wanted to meet our daughters while on an official visit to Japan requires an explanation. It all began when the legal requirements of the Japanese Family Court were completed for the adoption of our first daughter, Noriko Susan, born as a Japanese citizen in 1964. About a year later we began to investigate the process for obtaining American citizenship for her. We learned that it required a two-year period of residency in America before the naturalization process could be completed for citizenship. Since I was contractually employed by a university in Japan, there was no way we could meet the U. S. residency qualification.

We then discovered that there was an alternate route for citizenship called a Private Member's Bill. When proposed by a member of the United States Congress it would, in effect, override residency requirements. We sent a letter of explanation and an appeal to Hugh Scott, United States Senator who represented our home state of Pennsylvania. He graciously agreed to support our case. Following due process he submitted a Private Member's Bill to the United States Senate granting citizenship to our daughter, Noriko Susan Duke. It passed the Senate, a formality especially when sponsored by the Senate Majority Leader.

We searched for the United States Federal Court nearest to our hometown of Berwick, Pennsylvania, scheduled to hold a citizenship ceremony the following year during our summer vacation in America. The closest site happened to be in Wilmington, Delaware. On the scheduled day we left early in the morning for the three hour drive to Wilmington to make the ten o'clock ceremony. Unfortunately several days prior to the ceremony, four-year-old Noriko Susan came down with a severe case of oozing chicken pox. Since we had waited nearly two years for this event, we did not want to postpone the ceremony for the following summer, the next time that we could return to the States.

When we arrived at the Federal Court House in Wilmington we explained our predicament to an aide of the court. He advised us to keep our daughter in the car until the last minute when he would come out and escort us into the courtroom just before the ceremony was scheduled to begin. In fact he had reserved three seats in the front row of the courtroom where we were escorted in front of an audience of over one hundred foreigners waiting to be naturalized. Thanks to the Private Member's Bill submitted by Senator Scott, Noriko Susan Duke, oozing with chicken pox, became a citizen of the United States. In his reply to our letter of deep appreciation, the Majority Leader of the United States Senate, Hugh Scott, referred to our daughter as 'his girl.'

Three years later we followed the same procedure with our second daughter, Kimiko Anne, who was born in the same Tokyo Red Cross Maternity Hospital as was her older sister. We also faced the same problem of citizenship for Kim since she, too, was born a Japanese citizen. Once again we contacted Senator Scott to request his assistance with a Private Member's Bill granting American citizenship for Kim. He graciously consented and the process got underway. A year later during the next summer vacation, Kim appeared with one other foreigner before a federal judge in Scranton, Pennsylvania, to receive American citizenship. This time Senator Scott referred to 'his girls' in response to our letter of deep appreciation.

Five years later when Senator Scott attended the ICU Church service, Susan was a student in the local Japanese junior high school, Mitaka Nichu. Since it was Sunday she was home to greet the Senator. However Kim, a fourth grader at Osawadai, the local public elementary school, was at school for the annual sports day. This is a major event of the year for every Japanese elementary school in which nearly all parents attend for the entire day of games, races, and various events held on the school playground. It's frequently held on Sundays so fathers, many who worked on Saturdays in the 1970s, could attend.

Since we received a last-minute notice of Senator Scott's plans to visit ICU, we decided to hold a barbecue after church in our backyard. Guests enjoy the atmosphere of our backyard since Mt. Fuji is visible in all its splendor from that vantage point. We met Senator Scott for the first time immediately after the church service and walked home through the campus woods with him and Goto san. He was enchanted with the glorious view of Mt. Fuji from our backyard. We apologized for Kim's absence at school but Susan's presence made up for it. The Senator had never met either daughter.

As we sat around the grill in our backyard with the most powerful United States Senator as our guest, I suddenly got an idea. I asked him if he would like to meet Kim personally by going to the Sports Day event ourselves. I explained that it was a unique opportunity to see a local school activity which all Japanese experience. He reacted in a most positive manner. "Let's go!"

Senator Scott, Goto san, Noriko Susan, June and I got into the U. S. Embassy Cadillac that brought the Senator to church, and which looked out of place on the narrow streets of suburban Tokyo. When we pulled up to the playground on a small side street by the school, everyone in sight turned in amazement as our mixed party got out and walked into the crowd of parents seated all the way around the playground. Among our party, Senator Scott really stood out. At 6 foot four inches tall weighing well over 200 pounds, he did indeed attract attention from the Japanese since he towered over everyone.

Kim was dressed in her shorts with a tiny red cap sitting down in front with her fourth grade class joining in each competitive event with her classmates. We finally got her attention and waved to her to come up through the chairs to the top of a low bank behind the seats where we were standing. One can imagine the surprise of the parents, teachers, and students when this little Japanese fourth grader came running through the crowd to where we were standing. And when the huge American bent over and hugged her, and then posed with his arm around Kim for pictures for our cameras, the Japanese were amazed at the spectacle.

Kim with the U.S. Senate Majority Leader at Osawadai

They would have been even further shocked if they knew that the tall American was the most powerful senator in the United States Congress. It was indeed one of the most memorable moments of our forty years in Japan when the United States Senate Majority Leader posed for pictures with 'his girls,' our daughters, during a sports day at Osawadai Elementary School on a Sunday afternoon in the spring of 1978.

MEMOIR 21

'THE FINEST TROMBONIST IN THE WORLD' FROM THE PHILADELPHIA ORCHESTRA VISITS ICU

- REMINISCING ABOUT OUR HIGH SCHOOL JAZZ BAND -

When the Philadelphia Orchestra, one of the premier classical orchestras in the world, first performed in Japan under Eugene Ormandy and later under Riccardo Muti, the principal trombone position was held by Glenn Dodson who occupied that prestigious post for thirty seven years. On both occasions Glenn visited our campus home at ICU to renew a special relationship. He, June, and I were brought up in the tiny town of Berwick, Pennsylvania, and graduated in the Berwick High School Class of 1949.

Glenn and I, however, had another unique relationship that began even before our high school days. When we were in the junior high school Glenn organized a jazz combo of our classmates who were just learning to play musical instruments, in my case a trumpet. That small group developed into The Glenn Dodson Orchestra, one of the finest high school jazz outfits in America during the 'big band era' of the 1940s just after World War II. It also launched the musical career of the orchestra's teenage founder and leader destined to become, according to Eugene Ormandy, the 'finest trombonist in the world.' When I switched from trumpet to piano during our first year of high school, I had the memorable opportunity to accompany Glenn when we played the theme song of America's most popular trombonist of the day, Tommy Dorsey.

The Glenn Dodson Orchestra

When Glenn visited us at ICU on the two occasions, we reminisced about the beginning of our childhood relationship over sixty years ago. One Sunday afternoon in 1946, six of us in the ninth grade met in the tiny front room at the Dodson home in Berwick. Glenn had invited us to bring our musical instruments. By that time he had already become a respectable trombone player. Several years earlier he found an old trombone in his uncle's attic. Upon the urging of his mother, who was the organist at the local Methodist church, he began taking trombone lessons. It was a natural fit. By the ninth grade he was already quite good.

I, in contrast, grew up in Berwick spending many hours at the local baseball field. I had little interest in music although my parents made me take piano lessons during elementary school. I hated it and quit after six months. During the 8th grade I learned that you could rent an instrument from the Berwick School District and receive free lessons from the director of music, 'Prof.' Llewellyn, to join the Berwick High School Band. From some unexplained motivation, I took six months of lessons and joined the band as the bottom player in the third trumpet section. It was at this time that I met Glenn who was already in the band. Interestingly, my future wife, June Smith, was a twirler with the band to become the drum majorette in her junior year.

Big dance bands such as the Tommy Dorsey, Harry James, and Stan Kenton bands were very popular at that time. Glenn had somehow obtained copies of some of the famous pieces by these big bands arranged for small combos and passed out the music to us on that first Sunday at his home. None of us had ever seen music like that before. We played it all afternoon. We sounded badly but it was fun. We decided to meet again the following Sunday and continued to practice gradually improving with each session.

At that time, the Berwick Junior High School Student Council planned a school dance but had no budget. Members heard about our group and asked us to play for the dance without pay. We jumped at the chance. We played poorly but the kids didn't mind. The word was out. We got other requests and began playing free dance jobs for other school groups. Our female pianist dropped out and I switched to piano. With Glenn's constant encouragement we not only added a few players but markedly improved looking for paying dance jobs outside of our hometown. During our junior year we signed a contract to play for a dance at Hotel Altamont in Hazleton, a small nearby city, in itself recognition that we had become a first-rate orchestra in the Susquehanna Valley.

During our senior year at Berwick High School we had grown to ten members and were playing at well-known hotels throughout the area. By now Glenn played the Tommy Dorsey theme song, the famous trombone solo Getting Sentimental Over You, just as well as Dorsey himself. Glenn was also taking lessons every other Saturday in Philadelphia with the principal trombonist of the great Philadelphia Orchestra, one of the six major American classical orchestras, and I was accompanying him with the great jazz tunes for local dances.

Upon graduation from Berwick High School in 1949, the Glenn Dodson Orchestra disbanded as we all went our separate ways. Glenn entered the Curtis Institute of Music in Philadelphia, one of America's premier schools of music. I entered a local state college, the only school I could afford earning enough from tips as a desk clerk at a resort hotel in the nearby Pocono Mountains for three summers to pay the tuition.

The draft was in effect as a result of the Korean War so upon graduation from college, many of us were drafted into the United States Army. Glenn, however, went directly from Curtis to the United States Marine Corps Band, known as the President's Band, in Washington. He became an instant Marine sergeant and solo performer for the famed Marine Corps Band.

After military service, noted previously, I became a public school teacher in Hershey and then entered the graduate school at Pennsylvania State University, and from there moved to Japan to join the faculty at ICU. Meanwhile Glenn was discharged from the Marines and joined the New Orleans Symphony Orchestra. He later transferred to the fourth trombone position at the Cleveland Orchestra, one of America's leading orchestra, under director George Szell.

Several years later when Eugene Ormandy, arguably the most famous musical director in America at the great Philadelphia Orchestra, auditioned for the principal trombonist position, over one hundred leading musicians tried out for that most prestigious position. Glenn was among them. After a rigorous competition, Ormandy personally chose Glenn as the principal trombonist at Philadelphia, a post he held until retirement. It was during Glenn's long reign with the Philadelphia Orchestra under Eugene Ormandy that the great maestro referred to Glenn as 'the finest trombonist in the world' upon his 60th birthday. Only someone like Eugene Ormandy was in a position to make such a remarkable judgment.

During Glenn's tenure with the Philadelphia Orchestra, he performed at the national concert hall in Ueno, Tokyo, on two occasions. Before his departure from America for the first concert in Tokyo, he invited June and me to attend the concert assuring us he could get complimentary tickets after arriving in Japan. We were not able to buy tickets in advance. After having dinner with Glenn at a Tokyo restaurant, we arrived at the hall to learn that every seat had been sold. However one ticket holder returned a ticket that we bought for June. Glenn then came up with the idea for me to accompany him backstage through the musician's entrance on the assumption that the attendant at the entrance would assume that as a foreigner I was a member of the Philadelphia Orchestra. It worked.

The site of a huge classical orchestra backstage preparing for a major concert was an unforgettable moment. Each member had two large boxes that contained the instruments and attire for the concert. It was a cacophony of sounds as each musician warmed up before walking out on stage. The question that concerned Glenn was where I would sit for the concert. He spotted a small chair at a side opening to the stage where the musicians filed in from the huge adjoining preparation room. We realized that anyone seated there could not be seen by the audience but who had a direct view of the rear half of the orchestra including the trombone section. The French horn players were only about four feet from my chair.

It was from that very unique position just offstage at Ueno Hall that I had the glorious opportunity to hear the Philadelphia Orchestra perform in Japan. Moreover, since Glenn could easily see me from his position, he would occasionally give me a nod after a section of the piece that included trombones. I would nod in approval. No one in the audience, of course, had any idea that two members of the Glenn Dodson Orchestra of the 1940s from the Berwick High School in Pennsylvania were nodding to each other during the concert.

During Glenn's second concert in Japan we had dinner together at a Japanese restaurant in Shinjuku, Tokyo, on the 42nd floor with a magnificent view of Mt. Fuji covered with snow. Displaying Glenn's sense of humor, he looked out the window and wistfully commented, "Wouldn't our fathers, who both spent their entire working lives at the Berwick AC&F, (Note: A factory that made subway cars.) be pleased to see us here today, you teaching at a Japanese university in Tokyo and I being paid far too much to blow air through a metal tube." That provoked a great belly laughter for which all who knew Glenn remember him. And, as always, we reminisced about our high school orchestra. He remarked that it was such a pity there were no tape recorders at that time to record our orchestra because he personally believed that we were surely one of the finest high school jazz bands in America in 1949.

And now the rest of the story . . .

When we met again in our hometown of Berwick for a class reunion after our retirements, Glenn expressed a wish to get together for a music session. I welcomed the idea since I continued to play the piano everyday enjoying the sound of the Kawai grand piano we shipped from our home at ICU to our new home in America. Several weeks later I received in the mail thirty-eight pages of etudes to accompany trombone, and a note from Glenn that after I had a chance to practice them, he would come with his wife from Philadelphia to our home near Harrisburg to play them with me. I was of course excited about the great opportunity to once again accompany the finest trombonist in the world, and in my home on my own grand piano.

Fortunately the etudes were not too difficult for the piano. My concern was the tempo. If Glenn played them at a fast tempo, I was in trouble. In February he and his wife came to our home with his trombone. As he was setting up, he began with the explanation that

these etudes were meant to be played at a very slow tempo. What a
relief. We spent hours together playing those pieces. It was a thrill. It
took me back to our high school days when I first had the pleasure
of hearing that magnificent sound of the trombone in the hands of a
master musician. We agreed to do it again at his home in Philadelphia
the following spring.

Glenn Dodson at our home in Pennsylvania

One month after our home concert, Glenn's wife called in tears.
While showing a friend his new Porsche, Glenn suddenly collapsed and
died on the way to the hospital of a heart attack. That not only ended
the career of the 'finest trombonist in the world,' it also brought back
the wonderful memories of one of the finest high school orchestras in
America and our reminisces about it at ICU.

MEMOIR 22

SUMMERS AT LAKE MOKOMA IN THE ENDLESS MOUNTAINS OF PENNSYLVANIA

- THE TRANS-SIBERIAN RAILROAD – THE HIMALAYAS – THE GREAT WALL OF CHINA – THE LONDON MUSICALS -

Every year since 1964 when we adopted our first child, until retirement, we returned to America for a vacation at our family summer home on Lake Mokoma in the Endless Mountains of Pennsylvania. One of the main reasons we faithfully followed this routine was to provide an opportunity for our families in America to become familiar with our daughter, and later her two siblings as well, and for our children to feel part of an extended family. Another reason was to enable our children to play with American children becoming directly involved in American culture at the basic level since they were surrounded by Japanese children during the rest of the year. This became particularly important when each child at age four entered the ICU church kindergarten that prepared them to enter the local Japanese public elementary school at age six. A final factor concerned the oppressive heat that engulfs Tokyo in the summer. It was a relief to leave the city and head for the mountains.

The problem we faced each year was how to plan the route to and from Japan to the mountains in Pennsylvania where our families annually rendezvoused on beautiful Lake Mokoma. During the first ten summers when all three children were quite young we flew directly from Tokyo to New York via Anchorage. As they became old enough to appreciate the great sites of the world, we flew on around the world via Singapore, or Bangkok, or India, etc., and on to London and New York.

Among the various stopovers during the summer vacations on the way to Lake Mokoma, four stand out: riding across Siberia on the Trans-Siberian Railroad during the Communist era of the Soviet Union, trekking in the Himalayan Mountains in the volatile Indian state of Kashmir, climbing the steep sections of the Great Wall of China near Beijing, and enjoying the popular musicals of the West End theatrical district of London.

The first time we stopped on our way to London and New York we rented one of the famous houseboats for a week on Dal Lake in Srinagar, the summer capital of the Indian state of Kashmir deep in the Himalayan Mountains. Upon arrival at New Delhi, we first toured that city and immediately headed south to Agra to visit the magnificent Taj Mahal. We then flew northward to Srinagar well aware of the dispute between India and Pakistan over India's claim to sovereign control over the mostly Muslim area. We were assured that it was safe for tourists.

What we didn't know upon arrival is that the Kashmir houseboats are elegant vessels of a standard reminiscent of old-world European hotels for the rich. And like a hotel that never moves, they're tethered in long rows on a lake at the edge of Srinagar. To get to them we took a decorated rowboat with a quaint roof from the shore. Every time we went somewhere, we took the rowboat to the shore to get a taxi.

Each houseboat has three or four splendid bedrooms, a dining room and a living room all finished with dark rich-looking wooden walls and ceilings. Our family occupied one boat with a manager, a chef, and a houseboy to take care of all our needs. The meals were prepared at near gourmet levels and delicately arranged. From the open deck the views of the surrounding Himalayan Mountains were breathtaking. It was as if living in a bygone era.

We arranged to go trekking in the magnificent snow-covered Himalayan Mountains that surround Srinagar. We first took the rowboat to the shore to be picked up by a small taxicab for the ride on winding dirt roads to a trekking path that leads to the nearest village three hours by foot. Trekking in the Himalayas is vastly different from climbing them. Trekking is the local terminology for walking along paths often by streams that flow through the valleys that wind among the towering peaks. Not only are you surrounded on all sides by the incredible scenery, you often encounter locals walking from one village to another in native attire, with some on horseback carrying all sorts of goods for sale. Not only was it an unforgettable experience amidst the towering Himalayan Mountains, it was a most pleasant walk on a summer day in Kashmir.

One of the highlights of our adventure in Kashmir was a day's visit to a local public elementary school, the leading one in Srinagar, an opportunity that I could not pass up. The headmaster, an Indian Hindu, was pleased to welcome us to the school of which he was proud and rightly so. It was simple but neat and orderly. The teachers were mostly from the local area, meaning Muslims. They were all eager to have us visit their classrooms with simple chairs and desks and one blackboard each.

The most fascinating aspect of the school was that, although a public elementary school, it was essentially a language school. The local children spoke Urdu, one of the major languages of nearby Pakistan, and were learning to read and write the peculiar script used with Urdu. In addition, since Kashmir is controlled by India, the two national languages of India, Hindi and English, were also required. Since the written script of both Hindi and English are completely different from each other and from Urdu script, all children in the school were being taught how to read and write three different languages, each with a distinct script. It was an enormous burden on peasant children many of whom, we were told, came from families whose parents were illiterate.

What made the visit to the school in Srinagar so memorable to this day transpired about six weeks later when we were enjoying the Endless Mountains of Pennsylvania. We learned that Srinagar had been ravaged by militant Muslims attempting to end Indian control of Kashmir supported and encouraged by Pakistan and the Pakistan Army. It was reported that the schools were badly damaged and that Indian headmasters, including our host at the leading elementary school, had been killed. Surely plans for the violent uprising were being hatched while we were visiting the school.

During another summer vacation on our way to Lake Mokoma, we had the opportunity to visit the Great Wall of China open to the public not that far from Beijing. After solemnly viewing the body of Mao Tse Tung on display at his mausoleum at one end of Tiananmen Square, similar to Lenin's Tomb in Red Square of Moscow, we traveled to the Great Wall by taxi. Of all the impressive features about the Great Wall that is visible far into the distant mountains are the portions that were built up steep slopes. In those sections one doesn't walk on the wall, you climb it. There are steps and railings to help you get up from one watchtower to the next.

Another notable feature, in addition to its length of nearly four thousand miles, is the width of the wall. It is so wide, over four yards in some sections, that large numbers of sightseers walk up and down it comfortably passing those going the other way. It becomes a social event as visitors enjoy an afternoon in the sun, as we did, when Chinese tourists greeted us with smiles and handshakes. There were quite a few Chinese soldiers in uniform with wives and children dressed in colorful clothing pleased to welcome foreigners to their country.

We then flew south to Guilin where the famous ornately shaped mountains are located that are often included in Chinese landscape paintings. They deserve the recognition. Flowing through the picturesque mountains is the Li River. One of our lasting images of China is the five-hour cruise down the Li River in a procession of six tourist boats each with about fifty passengers quietly floating under the shadow of the peaks. We ate dinner cooked in front of us and basked in the open lounge enjoying the river scenes. From there we flew on to Hong Kong headed for London and New York.

In the summer of 1980 when Susan was 16, Kim 13 and Chris 11 years old, we began the summer trip to Lake Mokoma via the USSR on the Trans-Siberian Railroad. Reservations were made on a small Soviet passenger ship that traveled between Yokohama and Nakhodka, an inconsequential seaport near the great far eastern Soviet naval base of Vladivostok, officially closed to commercial travel. From there we traveled by overnight train to transfer to the famous Trans-Siberian Railroad that originated in Kharbarovsk headed for Moscow. Train reservations were then made from Moscow to Holland where we took a ferry across the English Channel to London. After a week in London we flew to New York to be met by a relative who took us to Lake Mokoma. It was quite a schedule.

During the Soviet era of communist government a major challenge was to obtain the approval of the official travel agency Intourist to travel through Siberia where Americans were not allowed to travel independently. A certified guide and translator had to be assigned to the tourist during this period of the Cold War. After dutifully submitting the proper documents, approval of our itinerary was received. Notice was also sent that we would meet out Intourist guide at Kharbarovsk rather than Nakhodka where we would be directed to the train from the boat by local travel officials.

Twelve years earlier, June and I traveled by boat from Yokohama to Nakhodka and on to Kharbarovsk by overnight train to catch a plane to Moscow for an extended visit to the western regions of the Soviet Union. On that occasion we particularly noticed how poor the Siberian villages appeared. The streets were invariably unpaved and the houses tiny and bleak. But what impressed us most were the many tiny houses with attached sheds where animals including a horse and a cow or so were stabled. The animals looked as if they were living in the houses. Twelve years later with our three children, the bleak houses with the animals looking out the windows of what appeared to be the living rooms were still there. The scene, repeated many times as we passed by countless tiny villages, proved fascinating to Susan, Kim and Chris on their first venture into the Soviet Union.

When we arrived in Kharbarovsk we were met by our official guide, his wife, and four-year old daughter. After the initial introductions our guide in his late 20s explained that he was an English school teacher in a small Siberian village not far from Kharbarovsk. He worked as an English-speaking guide during his summer vacations not only to earn money to supplement his very meager salary, but to meet foreigners to improve his English by speaking with native English-speaking tourists like we were. Since he would be away from home for about two weeks on the Trans-Siberian Railroad, his wife and daughter came to the train station to see him off.

From the moment we met our guide, we liked him. He was a bit awkward but personable, friendly, and concerned about our well-being. And with his very shy but pleasant wife and cute daughter beside him, our family felt an immediate attraction to them all. When he asked me to help him with his English during the long train ride, I was pleased to do so if he agreed to answer my questions about the Soviet Union, which he did. I realized that it was a golden opportunity to further my research in comparative and international education for my courses at ICU.

During the first day of our train trip our guide and I stood in the aisle outside our compartments for several hours looking out at the magnificent Siberian mountain ranges that reminded us of the Susquehanna Valley in Pennsylvania where June and I were brought up. I began our conversation asking simple questions about his English classes to establish a relationship of mutual understanding and acceptance. His English was quite good. He had little trouble responding to my questions.

On the second day I asked a few general questions about Soviet society. For example, I asked him to explain how the election system worked. I noted that statistics from throughout the Soviet Union at election time always showed that nearly 99% of all eligible voters had voted in favor of the single candidate approved by the Communist Party for each position. For the first time he hesitated. He apologized and said he would give me the answer the following day. When I reminded him that he agreed to answer every one of my questions, his face showed some embarrassment. I said tomorrow would be fine.

The next morning he immediately began our conversation explaining that in his Siberian village, a member of the Communist Party in charge of elections personally visited every household strongly urging every eligible adult to vote on election day. On that day those who failed to show up by mid-afternoon received a visit by the election officer who now castigated the non-voter to get to the election site to vote yes to the one approved candidate for each position. At the end of the voting day, the election officer checked the roll of voters. For those who did not vote, the officer filled out a ballot for every one of them and placed it in the ballet box so that he could report to his superiors that 100% of eligible voters voted.

When I asked him why he didn't explain the system to me the previous day, he was a bit reticent. Nevertheless he explained that he didn't know how the system worked since he had never voted in his life. He thought it was a useless system and went hunting on election day when the schools were closed. I asked him how he found out how the system worked since yesterday. Again with some embarrassment he explained that he had to ask one of the other guides on the train who described how the communist voting system functioned in their area.

From that moment onward I realized that our guide was as honest, and naïve, as he could be. We hit it off wonderfully. Our three kids recognized his simple ways and took an instant liking to him as well, as he did with us. I spent hours talking about Soviet education and the role of the Communist Party in it. Although he didn't know precisely how the Communist Party cell in his school worked, he said he was typical of the large majority of his fellow teachers who had little interest in the Communist Party. That, in itself, was most revealing.

The Trans-Siberian train was primitive at best. Few passengers ate in the dining car, and for good reason. The food was terrible. After two days we stopped eating there in part because of the foul odor coming from the kitchen that took away our appetite. Fortunately June had brought two large carryall bags of snacks including cheese and crackers and other kinds of goodies. When the train made scheduled stops most passengers rushed to small stalls where women sold boiled eggs, cooked chicken, bottled drinks, etc. When the train whistle blew we all rushed back to the train not to be left behind in some distant Siberian town.

On the Trans-Siberian Railroad with guide

The toilets were as primitive as could be. Tiny sinks had cold water only. The commode opened up to the train tracks below. The toilets were apparently not cleaned once during the trip as the floor became increasingly slippery by the day. There were no provisions for bathing. Daughter Kim became a celebrity when word got around among the few foreign travelers that she somehow managed to shampoo her hair in the sink. She never revealed how she did it.

The Siberian scenery more than made up for the poor accommodations. The mountain ranges covered by forests were crisscrossed with streams that turned into rushing rivers flowing along side the train tracks for great distances. We passed by countless towns and villages with small cottage-like homes on dirt lanes centered around a church with spires that stood out from the surroundings. On occasion the train stopped long enough for the passengers to walk through the town where we spotted flowers in the windows of the quaint houses.

The most memorable part of the trip through Siberia was a stopover at Irkutsk near Lake Baikal, the Pearl of Siberia, the largest and deepest fresh water lake in the world. The lake is famous for its pristine waters which breed the renown Baikal sturgeon. We took a boat across Lake Baikal to a distant shore from where we had a spectacular view of the lake. It was worth the trip on the Trans-Siberian Railroad by itself.

All of our initial stopovers on the way to America each summer proceeded on to London to catch a plane to New York. During our two years in London when I was completing graduate work at the University of London, we had become attached to the city attending on occasion plays at West End, the famous theatrical district of London. It was during this period when we saw the original cast in Fiddler on the Roof. We were determined to take our children to the great London musicals when they were old enough to appreciate them.

During the first summer on our stopover in London on the way to Lake Mokoma with our three children, the youngest being Chris at age 8, we found an inexpensive bed and breakfast hotel and headed for Piccadilly Circus. We knew of a kiosk that sold tickets for that day's performances hopefully for Oliver. We were able to get five tickets during a weekday performance. Oliver was the introduction of London musicals to our children who loved it. I bought the original piano score that we took back to Japan with us where Chris memorized the complete score singing Oliver's part around our Kawai grand piano. Susan and Kim learned the songs as well. We sang them over and over again.

Oliver set the scene, so to speak, for our children to enjoy the leading musicals of the London stage on our annual stopovers during the summer vacations from ICU on our way to the mountains of Pennsylvania. They included a rerun of Fiddler on the Roof so the kids could see one of the most popular musicals ever, Les Miserables, Phantom of the Opera, Cats, Pirates of Penzance, South Pacific, and Oliver.

The month or more at Lake Mokoma every summer followed a most enjoyable pattern. Susan, Kimiko, and Chris each spent their first summers on a blanket on the beach, then played in the sand box followed by wading in the roped-in shallow area learning to swim short distances. Later they moved to a deeper area for longer swims, and finally to the dock out in the lake where they jumped off the diving board. After that they participated in the annual swim across the lake. It all led to them becoming first class swimmers with Kim and Chris certified to teach swimming later at the American School in Japan, where Susan was a member of the swim team during her high school days.

When they each reached four or five years old, they joined me on a fiberglass rowboat that June's father, an old-line fisherman, built by hand many years ago for bass fishing in the Susquehanna River. It was so heavy that the kids could walk around in it without fear of overturning. I taught each of them how to cast for bass. They picked it up quickly and in the process became avid and highly skilled at bass fishing as the lake produced near trophy specimens, one of which was mounted to hang over our large cottage fireplace.

A good catch at Lake Mokoma

They also became skilled rowers since motors were not allowed on the lake. Each had to take turns rowing us up and down the lake moving from one spot to another in search of the elusive bass. The four of us went fishing in the late afternoon not infrequently returning across the lake under the stars or a full moon with a nice catch.

We all remember particularly exciting days in the boat when powerful thunderstorms suddenly appeared over the mountain by the lake sending lightening bolts across the lake that frightened us. When we were alerted to the sound of the thunder behind the mountain, we headed for home as fast as we could row. One unforgettable afternoon we hesitated before making the dash to our side of the lake when lightning bolts were suddenly upon us. We were terrified as we reached the shore just as a bolt struck very close to us. We ran as fast as we could through a downpour to reach the safety of the beach house where we realized how lucky we were, and how dangerous it was by not getting off the lake sooner.

The adventures at Lake Mokoma during the summer vacations from ICU will always remain as wonderful memories to the Duke family.

The picnics with relatives, the three-mile walks around the lake, the picking of huckleberries that grow all around the shore, the frequent sightings of deer and the occasional bear right behind the cottage, were all captured on film. They're repeated every summer to this day when our family reunites at our summer home in the Endless Mountains of Pennsylvania where we reminisce about spending every summer at Lake Mokoma while we lived on the ICU campus in Japan.

A day on the beach at Lake Mokoma

MEMOIR 23

ENCOUNTERING JAPAN'S PAST IN MALAYA

- MR. DOI: THE KIND JAPANESE ARMY
OFFICER AND MY DEAR FRIEND -

D uring the many years on the faculty of ICU, I had various opportunities to travel throughout Asia. On one occasion in the mid 1960s I was invited by a Christian organization to participate as a speaker at a convention of Asian youth held in Port Dickson, Malaysia, formerly Malaya. Since I had become fascinated with Malaya during my research travels in 1961-2, the topic of an earlier memoir, I readily accepted the invitation. Port Dickson is located on the Straits of Malacca facing Indonesia not that many miles across the water. The coast is beautiful, the sea is calm, and the setting is idyllic. Upon my departure I was determined to bring the family back for a vacation.

Two years later the opportunity arose when I was assigned to teach a new course at ICU on Education in Developing Nations. Since Malaysia was a developing country I decided to undertake a field trip there to visit schools and interview administrators, teachers, and students about the issues of education in a developing country. Since Malaysian society consisted of about 40% Malays, 40% Chinese, and 10% Indians, all receiving much of their education at the time in their native languages plus English, it was an ideal country to use as an example of a multi-ethnic, multi-lingual, multi-religious developing Asian society to contrast with Japan which is exactly the opposite.

I naturally decided to visit Port Dickson on the trip, the very center of the Indian community ever since the colonial period under the British. They brought in tens of thousands of Hindus from south India to work on the rubber plantations in that area. This was the opportunity to take my wife and our three children along to enjoy the Straits of Malacca.

We rented a car upon arrival at the capital city of Kuala Lumpur and headed for Port Dickson. Driving down the coastal highway we looked for a hotel from where I could visit local Indian schools. We stopped at the Hari Hotel on the beach and found that accommodations were available. That evening after dinner in a unique dining room that reached out over the crystal clear water, I met the hotel manager to ask for assistance in arranging a visit to the nearby Indian school located in the middle of the rubber plantation area. It turned out that the manager was the head of the school council, a type of school board. He would be delighted to personally take me to the school the next morning. He also invited my family to go along in his Mercedes.

When he asked where we came from, my answer of Japan took him by surprise. But his response took me by even greater surprise. He replied that, "I'm half Japanese." That was startling. Standing before me was a tall Indian man with the skin color of a very dark Indian typical of the Tamils of South Indian. Not a trace of Japanese was evident. He then pointed to a little old wizened lady behind the cash register who he identified as his Japanese mother, Haruko. She had come to Malaysia, that is, Malaya prior to independence from the British, before World War II with her husband, a Japanese businessman.

After several years Haruko's husband died. However she loved the country and stayed on. Sometime afterwards she married a business acquaintance of her husband, an Indian man who owned the hotel where we were staying. The manager then pointed to a tall elderly Indian man wearing a turban talking to friends in the lobby and identified him as his father. He explained that as a result of the intercultural marriage he spoke native Japanese since his mother spoke only her language to him as a child. He also spoke Hindi, the major language of south India which his father spoke to him as a child, as well as Malay, the language of the country and many of his childhood friends, and English, the mandatory language of the school system under British occupation when he went through his early schooling. He also explained that he was given the name of Haru after his Japanese mother Haruko. Haru became Harry to his English-speaking friends which he used most of the time.

Harry then proceeded to tell me a wartime story that he thought I would enjoy since I had been living in Japan for many years. In 1941 when the Japanese army invaded Malaya, he was twelve years old. His family experienced a difficult existence when food shortages became widespread. In order to ease their plight, his father came up with the idea that his only son could possibly find a translation job with the local Japanese army officer. With his mother's approval, he went to the nearest Japanese post and, in native Japanese, asked for a translation job.

Harry was immediately escorted to the local commander's office, a captain in the army. In disbelief, the Japanese officer questioned him in Japanese and then in his limited English. Apparently satisfied with the replies, and assuming the boy could speak Malay, the captain decided to hire him as a translator since he was particularly in need of someone who could communicate in Malay, the language of the native Malay people, and Japanese.

After several weeks of daily contact between the young Japanese army captain and the 12-year old Indian-Japanese boy from Malaya, a unique relationship developed between the two. They got along very well indeed. The captain was obviously not a typical military officer since he had his men locate a piano in the town placing it in the house confiscated for their headquarters. Every evening he played western classical music for hours, especially Beethoven compositions.

After a month the Japanese unit was ordered south as the British defense began to collapse. The captain had by now become not only dependent on the young Indian boy for translation needs but a mutual sense of trust was emerging. The captain personally went to Harry's parents and asked them if he could take their son south with him explaining that he was the commander of the railroad troops who entered an area after the frontline troops had secured the area. Their responsibility was to repair the railroads and keep the trains running to supply the front troops. The area in which the railroad troops operated was secure and peaceful. Under the financial conditions they faced, Harry's parents consented.

For the next several months Harry remained with the Japanese captain as the invading army moved south to occupy the entire Malay Peninsula. The relationship between the two unlikely friends grew even stronger as the captain, according to Harry, treated him as his own son. When they finally reached Singapore, the railroad unit boarded a Japanese transport headed for Thailand as Japanese forces expanded their sphere of control across southeast Asia. Harry and the Japanese captain parted in an emotional farewell. To Harry he was saying farewell to a Japanese soldier he came to love, and who he would probably never see again. As they waved goodbye at the port, Harry headed home with nothing but fond memories of, as he described him, 'the kind Japanese Army officer."

A week later we returned to Tokyo after a memorable trip to Malaysia. I was anxious to tell my story to my Thursday evening businessmen's seminar at Keidanren, the Federation of Japanese Industries. Since they were all prewar men, and several had served in the Japanese military forces, I knew they would appreciate the story of Harry and the kind Japanese army officer.

During the following Thursday evening Keidanren seminar at the Industrial Club, I got right to the story. As I reached the part where Harry was escorted into the Japanese captain's office, Mr. Doi, Managing Director of the Tohoku Paper and Pulp Company, interrupted me. In his quiet demeanor Mr. Doi recalled one day while serving with the Japanese army in Malaya that his aide brought a young Indian boy into his office who spoke native Japanese. He was startled. He was so impressed with his language skills that he hired him on the spot to translate for him with the local people. During their time together he developed a great admiration and fondness for the boy keeping him with him all the way to Singapore when he said goodbye as he left on a troop transport for Thailand.

We were all stunned by the revelation. The 'kind Japanese army officer' was, in fact, my own dear friend and longtime member of my weekly businessmen's seminar in downtown Tokyo, Mr. Doi. I was well aware of his great love of western music and broad knowledge about all the major western composers and orchestras. He could listen to about five bars of many western classics and tell you the name of the piece and the composer, a rare ability for a Japanese businessman. He attended classical concerts in Tokyo every week. And he loved to play the piano. It all fit into place.

Mr. Doi (far left) at the Keidanren Seminar

But Doi san had another unusual interest. He loved birds and made a very serious study of birds in Japan becoming quite an expert on the subject. He carried his expertise on birds in Japan to an unusual extent. It seems that Mrs. Doi was a Christian although Mr. Doi was not. Nevertheless he read the Christian Bible at his wife's insistence. When he came across the Japanese translation of birds in several chapters, he checked them with the names in the English Bible and found that some of the translations were incorrect. He notified the Bible publishers who revised the next edition to include Doi's translation.

Because of his expertise on birds in Japan, I invited him to come to the 350 acre wooded campus of ICU to survey the birds which had never been done. He also agreed to make a presentation later at a weekly convocation hour on the subject of Birds on the ICU Campus. Since I was to accompany my dear friend on the survey, he came to our house set deep in the middle of the wooded campus. He brought an English translation of a book entitled Birds in Japan. Since the leaves were still on the trees, Doi san knew that it would be difficult to see the birds although we could hear their unique warbling.

As we quietly walked through the ICU forests, when the sound of a bird was heard, Doi san would direct me to a certain page in the bird book. There was a picture of the bird we had just heard but could not see. I wrote down the name on a list. We spent the day in that manner surveying the campus bird population. Several weeks later Doi san made an interesting presentation to the student body at an open convocation on Birds on the ICU Campus. No one in the audience knew that they were listening to a former Japanese officer during the occupation of Malaya.

And now for the rest of the story . . .

Several years later Doi san died. On behalf of his wife, his son called me to ask if I would give a eulogy at his funeral to be held in the nearby Kichijoji Church. She recalled that since her husband enjoyed my Keidanren Seminar so much and loved to speak English, she thought it would be appropriate to have a eulogy for her husband in English. Since Doi san had been baptized on his death bed, a Christian service had been planned. Based on Mr. Doi's twenty years as a faithful member of my Keidanren seminar each week, and a personal friend with a deep interest in ICU, I couldn't refuse his wife's request. I was honored.

I had to quickly prepare my remarks for the funeral scheduled for three days later. An idea came to me. Why not tell the story of the kind Japanese army officer of World War II? I was well aware that the war remains a sensitive issue in Japan, particularly among the older generation of veterans. As an American, I would be taking a risk by bringing up the topic at a funeral of a Japanese veteran of the war especially during the Japanese invasion of an Asian country. I decided to chance it.

I wrote out the full story and asked my trusted Japanese assistant, Hayakawa Eichi, now the head of the English Department at the ICU High School, to translate the story into Japanese sentence by sentence appropriate for a funeral service. When I approached the church on foot for the funeral from the Kichijoji train station, I encountered a traffic jam. Walking through the lines of cars barely moving, I realized that most of them were driven by chauffeurs. They contained businessmen heading for Doi san's funeral in the Kichijoji Church located on a small side road.

When I arrived at the church I asked to meet Mr. Doi's son, a businessman, who was expecting me. I explained my plan to read my eulogy in English one sentence at a time. I asked the son to stand next to me and read the translation of my remarks sentence by sentence following my lead. He readily agreed.

The son then ushered me to the front of the church, which was rapidly filling up with Mr. Doi's many friends in the business world, to a chair facing a bank of flowers. In the middle of the flowers rested a picture of Doi san, following Japanese style. The body, by law, had already been cremated. I noticed that there was only one other chair next to mine at the front of the church. It was occupied by an elderly Japanese man. Suddenly I realized that there would only be two eulogists at this well known Japanese businessman's funeral. And I was one of them. I assumed that the elderly gentleman next to me would be giving the main eulogy.

The service followed the Christian style of funerals with the preacher reading the history of Doi's long life concentrating on his business accomplishments. His wartime experiences were not mentioned. Finally it was time for the two guest speakers to make their presentations. The elderly man next to me was introduced first and began by facing the picture of Mr. Doi addressing him in the familiar tense as if he were talking directly to him. He recalled their experiences as teammates on the 1921 baseball team at Keio University when they beat their archrivals, Waseda University. It was quite touching, and quite short, no longer than five minutes.

It suddenly dawned on me that I was the main eulogist, something I could not have imagined when asked to participate. Upon being introduced as an ICU faculty member and the teacher of a Keidanren English seminar which Mr. Doi faithfully attended for twenty years, I was joined by Mr. Doi's son. Facing the audience, not Mr Doi's picture, I began my remarks with this introductory sentence in slow and precise English. "I would like to tell you the story of a kind Japanese Army officer in Malaya during World War II, my dear friend Mr. Doi." When his son read the opening sentence in Japanese, a hush came over the audience. There was no doubt that I was treading on a very sensitive topic.

It was truly an unusual scene with an American professor at a university in Japan relating a heartwarming story about the kindness of a Japanese army officer at his funeral in front of an audience of senior Japanese businessmen, many of whom also served in the Japanese military during World War II. But that is exactly what I did. I slowly unveiled the dramatic story of Mr. Doi's experiences in occupied Malaya with Harry, the young Indian boy befriended by him, precisely as Harry told it to me. I ended my eulogy quoting Harry's very words. When the ship pulled away from Singapore with Captain Doi on board waving goodbye to his young friend, Harry's last memory of him was as "the kind Japanese army officer."

The next day Doi's son called me to once again offer the family's appreciation for my eulogy. But in particular he wanted me to know that his mother was overwhelmed with my story about her husband. It was an episode in her husband's military career that she had never heard before. She felt that it was the most meaningful part of the funeral service. I was very pleased to have honored my dear friend in my eulogy to him as the kind Japanese army officer.

MEMOIR 24

THE DR. CAROL BROWNING STORY
- CELINE BROWNING SCHOLARSHIPS FOR CHINESE WOMEN -

During the summer of 1988 I received a curious telephone call while on summer vacation at Lake Mokoma in the Endless Mountains of Pennsylvania. A woman who identified herself as Carol Browning from Ogden, Utah, had just read my book, The Japanese School. She began the conversation by telling me how much she appreciated it. In fact, when she noticed that it was "Dedicated to Susan, Kim, and Chris, whose experiences in the Japanese school provided many of the insights for this book," it further motivated her to contact me. She had made a special effort to find our telephone number in the tiny county seat of Laporte in rural Sullivan County where Lake Mokoma is located.

Mrs. Browning explained that she had two children of pre-school age, a son and daughter separated by several years in age. Upon reading my book she began to ponder the possibility of moving to Japan in order to enroll them in a Japanese school. The goal was to provide an opportunity for both of them to receive a basic education similar to the one that our three children experienced as I described it in the book. She wanted to know what I thought about that idea.

I was somewhat perplexed with such a consequential question from someone I did not know. My immediate reaction was that the idea seemed beyond comprehension. For an American woman, presumably with no relationship to Japan, to move to that country to bring up her two very young Caucasian children like Japanese children was surely unprecedented. I cautiously began my reply with an explanation that I thought would bring into perspective why we put our three children through the Japanese elementary school with two going on to the middle school. It had no relationship to her situation.

Assuming that the caller was unaware of our family makeup, I informed Mrs. Browning that the two oldest, Noriko Susan and Kimiko Anne, were adopted Japanese daughters. Since we lived in Japan we felt that our first daughter should have the experience of learning the language and customs of Japan. Moreover, many of my fellow ICU faculty members who lived on campus as neighbors, and who had children who played with our kids, sent their children to the local public elementary school located just ten minutes from ICU. Under our circumstances it seemed appropriate to send Noriko Susan to the same school where her friends were enrolled.

Since our first child's experience in the Japanese school was so successful, we entered her younger sister Kimiko in the same school when the time came, which proved equally successful. With the unexpected birth of a son, Christopher Kenji, only two years after adopting the second Japanese baby girl, it was reasonable at age six to send him to the same school where both of his older sisters were then enrolled. In other words, the decision to send our three children to a Japanese school followed a natural progression.

Mrs. Browning thanked me for my reaction. Before the summer was out she called several more times about the same issue. We were now addressing each other as Carol and Ben. During our lengthy conversations I learned that Carol had earned a doctorate at Teachers College, Columbia University, studying with Dr. George Bereday in comparative and international education. Ironically I had taken courses with Dr. Bereday at Columbia in the 1960s. I had also invited him to ICU where he spent several weeks lecturing to my students in comparative education. I was even more impressed to learn that Carol had served as his assistant during her graduate studies. By this time I was well aware that I was dealing with a sophisticated woman with a broad background in the field of education who could fully appreciate the consequences of her decisions.

Carol continued to probe about the experiences our children underwent in the Japanese school as I described them in the book. They were without question positive, which was one of the main reasons I wrote the book. Her most provocative question that brought our summer conversation to a close was, as usual, to the point. Would we make the same decision based on the current situation of our children? In hindsight, was it the right thing to do?

At that time in 1988 Susan was completing the law degree from Dickinson Law School in Pennsylvania after graduating from ICU, and had received the award as the best legal writer, in English, of course, in her class. She had just been hired as an attorney on the staff of a judge in the Pennsylvania Commonwealth Court. Kim was in the third year at Elizabethtown College, a private liberal arts college near Harrisburg, preparing to become a teacher. She was also interested in becoming a nurse, which she did several years later. Chris was a student at Dickinson College, a prestigious liberal arts school also located near Harrisburg, majoring in Asian studies.

I told Carol that we were very pleased with the Japanese school that had given our children a solid foundation to further their education in America with bright prospects of a successful career in life. If we had to do it over again, without doubt we would enroll them in the Japanese school for their basic education. With that unequivocal assessment, the telephone calls with Carol ended and we returned to ICU for the September semester putting the matter aside.

Several years later during the fall semester at ICU, as I remember the sequence of events, I received an unexpected call from Carol. She began with, "Hello Ben. It's Carol. We're here." I was startled. "Carol, you're where?" "We're here in Sapporo." She explained that her son Rete was enrolled in a private Japanese elementary school and daughter Celine in a private kindergarten to receive a basic Japanese education just like the Duke children. Carol had found a position teaching English at a college in Sapporo located in the far northern island of Hokkaido. She wanted me to know how appreciative she was of my help in her decision to move to Japan to enroll her children in the Japanese school. It was one of the decisive factors.

My immediate reaction was one of incredulity. How did she do it? I should note that by this time we had not yet met Dr. Carol Browning in person. Things were going well at school for the children. They were enjoying the Japanese school and Carol was enjoying English teaching. She had also started a private advanced English class for adults using my book, The Japanese School, as a text for discussion enabling her to learn more about Japanese education from Japanese adults.

From that moment onward Carol called from time to time, usually about issues relating to her teaching and the normal problems one has in an educational institution. She particularly wanted my advice in dealing with Japanese administrators. But there were also calls of more profound consequences, some of which impacted on our lives at ICU and into retirement in America. We never knew what to expect when Carol Browning called from Sapporo.

For example, one day Carol called about an outstanding Hungarian musician, Endre Hegedus, and wife, also a musician, who was teaching piano at a Japanese university in Sapporo. He was on leave as Professor of Piano from the distinguished Liszt Institute in Budapest, Hungary. He wanted to perform in Tokyo. Since she was deeply interested in music having studied piano for years, and was aware of my interest in music, Carol thought that I might be helpful in arranging a concert in Tokyo for this outstanding artist. She had already hired him to give piano lessons to both of her children and had bought a piano for her apartment in Sapporo. As a result of that conversation, Endre

Hegedus literally became a part of our life for which we will always be grateful. The following memoir, The ICU-Hungarian Piano Fest by Endre Hegedus, concerns the outcome of that telephone call that extended into America.

Many months later I received another call from Carol on an unexpected topic. She was planning to conduct a comparative education study involving students at four middle schools in Japan and four in the United States. This grew out of her work in comparative education at Columbia University under George Bereday. Carol asked if I could find a middle school in Tokyo for her research comparable to the one she had selected in Washington, D.C.

It so happens that my dear friend and colleague, Niwa Yoshio, was a member of our local Mitaka School Board. I knew he would be able to arrange for a Mitaka Junior High School to participate in her research project, perhaps the same one that Noriko Susan and Kimiko Anne had attended. I asked Carol what other schools in Japan she was using for the study. She mentioned one in Sapporo, another in Matsumoto where, she noted, she was taking her two children once a month for special piano lessons at the famed Suzuki school, and one in Kochi.

The mention of Kochi struck me as odd. Kochi is a remote city located in the distant island of Shikoku. My instant reaction was how could Carol make that arrangement from the far northern city of Sapporo on the island of Hokkaido. Her reply: "That's where the Browning Gun Company makes the sporting rifles." She explained that her husband John was president of the company and had moved its production facilities to Japan after the war, which he sold some years later. Although the Browning family had no relationship to the company any longer, Carol was still acquainted with the staff of the Japanese factory which helped her locate a local school for her research. She also mentioned that John remained in Ogden to oversee family investments traveling to Sapporo to pick up the family for Christmas holidays in warmer climates. Carol returned to Utah every summer and on extended holidays with the kids bringing the family together.

Upon learning about the family background of Carol Browning, I thought of the irony in our relationship with her. Browning guns played an important role in the Pacific War bringing the brutal Japanese war machine to a bitter end. Years later I unexpectedly played a part in the process, however indirectly, which led to the children of John and Carol Browning being educated as Japanese children in the Japanese school, as were the Duke children. If there ever was an example of swords being turned into plowshares, the relationship between the Browning family and Japan fits the adage nicely.

Carol then invited June and me to Sapporo to visit her and the children for our first opportunity to meet face to face. She also wanted to introduce me to her English class as the author of the book, The Japanese School, which she used for discussion purposes. It proved to be a very interesting and unusual visit. We found the children to be adorable kids who spoke Japanese to each other and English to Carol and us. They were constantly moving from one language to the other effortlessly. They were obviously enjoying life in the Japanese school having made many friends.

We also drew closer to Carol since we had much in common with many topics to talk about that included our children's education in the Japanese school, our common interests in comparative education with personal stories about the controversial George Bereday at Teachers College, and our musical interests that included the concerts by Endre Hegedus. Carol proved to be a gracious host taking us to the most unusual restaurants in the greater Sapporo area that we never imagined were available in Japan, indicative of her unique life style she had carved out in the northern island of Japan known for its bitter winters. We also learned that Carol had traveled the world, as we had, including some of the most unique places that we had not visited such as Bhutan. We had a wonderful time with the Brownings in Sapporo for our first meeting. There would be many more to follow, including her visit to ICU to attend a Duke Home Concert by Endre Hegedus.

Among the many intriguing calls from Carol Browning from Sapporo, one involved a Prime Minister of Japan. Her dear friend from

Utah had called about her son who had recently graduated from college and was now in Japan for a year's study of Japanese. He had informed his mother several months previously that he was planning to propose to the daughter of the Prime Minister. The mother was concerned about his intentions and wanted Carol, who knew the boy from childhood, to meet with him to dissuade him from taking such action without more consideration of the consequences. Carol was flying down to Tokyo to meet him over dinner. She invited June and me to join them and if possible help her to dissuade the boy from proposing to the daughter of the Prime Minister. It was a curious request to the parents of two daughters of Japanese ancestry.

We arrived at the hotel at the appointed hour and called Carol's room. She had just arrived from the airport and suggested that we look for the boy waiting in the lobby to introduce ourselves before she came down. We found him in casual dress and introduced ourselves. I had to ask the burning question. "Is it true that you're planning to propose to the Prime Minister's daughter?" He smiled and said no, that it wasn't the current Prime Minister's daughter but the daughter of former Prime Minister Hosokawa.

What a surprise. Prime Minister Hosokawa was a well-known politician from southern Japan, a descendent of a famous family with roots in Japan's past. He was also known for his handsome looks and suave demeanor. The boy explained that he first dated the Hosokawa daughter when they were students at the University of Colorado. She was not only very attractive but sophisticated and fun to be around. They had developed what he thought was a serious relationship when she returned to Japan.

By that time Carol came down and we went to dinner. After family pleasantries, and before Carol could bring up the controversial topic, the boy brought it up by describing his life in Japan. He had spent some time at the Hosokawa family home as a guest of the daughter while studying Japanese. When he came to Japan he was seriously thinking about proposing to her. However he recently had seen her in a different light. She had become quite different from her days at the University of Colorado showing a side of her as frivolous which he did not appreciate. He had decided against proposing to her. That ended the topic without any instigation from Carol or me. We were both relieved.

The years passed successfully for the Browning children in the Japanese school. They quickly adjusted to the demands. They learned how to be Japanese so much so that when Celine graduated from junior high school, she was reluctant to return to America. After all she had received all of her formal education in Japan. Her friends were primarily Japanese. Her interests were Japanese. But Carol by now was becoming concerned about Celine's future education. If, as she hoped, it would be at a prominent American university, her daughter would have to receive an American secondary education in order to take the SAT examinations or their equivalent required by virtually all schools. Her son Rete had already been enrolled in an American preparatory school preparing to enter college.

Carol called for advice. I was not helpful because there was no obvious solution that fit the situation. A temporary compromise evolved since Carol had an interest in China and Celine reacted favorably to the possibility of a year's study in China. With her knowledge of the Japanese written symbols adapted from Chinese characters at the junior high school level, which is significant, she was in a good position to be able to adapt to a Chinese school, as she did so readily to the Japanese school.

I contacted a friend, the president of the Chinese Comparative Education Society, who helped make arrangements for Carol to teach English part-time at a university in Beijing and for Celine to enroll in the attached high school. With that the Browning girls left Japan. It had been quite an adventure for Carol to move to Japan for over a decade in order for her children to receive their basic education in a Japanese school, as the Duke children did. In both cases, it proved to be a rewarding experience.

And now the rest of the story . . .

After a year in China where Celine became interested in Chinese culture and language, Carol made arrangements for her to study at a well-known finishing school in New England. When the time drew near for her to graduate, Carol called again for advice about college. At that time we discussed the possibility of ICU since Celine was fluent in Japanese and English, the two required languages necessary for graduation, and who was more comfortable in Japan than perhaps anywhere else. Carol liked the idea as did Celine. She applied with a letter of recommendation from me to major in international relations. Celine moved back to Japan as a four-year student at ICU. Her junior year abroad from ICU was, appropriately, completed at Nanjing University in China in the exchange program between the two institutions. During her year in China she gathered materials for a senior thesis on Chinese women which was awarded the highest grade possible.

Celine graduated with honors from ICU in the summer of 2009. Carol invited June and me to return to Japan for the summer graduation ceremonies but we had commitments that could not be avoided. However the long relationship between the Dukes and the Brownings and ICU did not end at that time. As a member of the Board of Trustees of the Japan International Christian University Foundation headquartered in New York City, I had become active in soliciting funds for ICU scholarships for needy students in Asia and Africa. In that capacity I asked Carol to consider sponsoring a Celine Browning Scholarship Fund for needy students.

Carol reacted positively and with enthusiasm. The idea challenged her as I hoped it would since I learned many years earlier that when Carol Browning decided to carry out a project, nothing could stop her. Taking her children to Japan to enter them in a Japanese school was proof of that. In consultation with Celine they stipulated that the recipients of the scholarship should be Chinese females from ethnic minorities in far-off western China where Carol had visited with her children to witness how educational opportunities were severely restricted for girls.

Through the efforts of the President of the Japan ICU Foundation, Dr. David Vikner, a Celine Carol Browning Scholarship for Ethnic Minority Women in China was established by the time of this writing. David took a particular interest in the project traveling to Ogden, Utah, to meet with Carol to discuss the provisions of the scholarship. He then carefully designed it based on his broad experiences as the former Director of the United Board for Christian Higher Education in Asia.

According to the plan the scholarships will be available throughout the 21st Century and beyond, a fitting legacy from both Carol and Celine. Following their wishes, the recipients from western China will enter the ICU Graduate School for a master's degree. Those Chinese women who receive the Celine Browning scholarships would surely be amazed to learn that they originated from a telephone call from Carol Browning in Ogden, Utah, to the Dukes at Lake Mokoma in the 1980s.

MEMOIR 25

THE ICU – HUNGARIAN PIANO FEST
BY ENDRE HEDEGUS

- THE DUKE HOME CONCERTS -

In June, 1985, Dr. Carol Browning, the topic of the previous memoir, called from Sapporo in the far northern island of Hokkaido where she was teaching English. A pianist she had met, a professor of piano from the Liszt Institute in Hungary who was teaching music at a nearby university for a year, expressed a strong desire to hold a concert in Tokyo. Since Carol, a pianist herself, was extraordinarily impressed with a concert he performed locally, she had become committed to promote his professional career. She asked if I could arrange a concert for him in Tokyo.

I suggested that she have the pianist, Endre Hegedus, send me a recording of a concert performance if available. Within a week one arrived featuring Endre with the Hungarian Symphony Orchestra. After listening to it I took it to the Chair of the ICU Music Department, Professor Kanazawa Masakata, ICU graduate who is highly regarded in the Japanese world of music with a Ph.D. from Harvard University. I asked him to carefully listen to the entire recording consisting mostly of Liszt and Chopin compositions. I had one question hopefully to be answered with a simple yes or no. Is the level of Endre's performance at an international standard of leading pianists? Professor Kanazawa's reaction was positive.

I then had to figure out how to arrange a concert in Tokyo that would introduce Endre to the Japanese world of classical music, enhance ICU's musical reputation, and provide an opportunity for our students to enjoy fine music performed by a European pianist. I came up with the idea of a concert under the title of The ICU-Hungarian Piano Fest. The program, if possible, would be centered around the great Hungarian pianist and composer Franz Liszt.

By that time I had become acquainted with one of the first ICU graduates in the class of 1957 who was responsible for arranging the annual concerts of the ICU Alumni Glee Club in a concert hall in downtown Tokyo. I called him for advice. Watanabe San responded positively to the situation after listening to the tape. Since he was in retirement, he noted that he had a lot of free time and would welcome the challenge. He offered to assume major responsibility for arranging a concert in Tokyo, after working out the financial details, as a contribution to his beloved alma mater, ICU. Since he was knowledgeable about concert halls in Tokyo, and an ICU graduate involved in staging concerts, I enthusiastically entered into the planning with him.

I then contacted Endre with the plan. Although everything was obviously tentative, he was delighted and gave me a weekend date three months later in September when he was passing through Tokyo on his way to Budapest from Sapporo for a concert. I agreed to search for a suitable concert hall for that date.

The next step involved a meeting with the ICU president, Oguchi Kunio, who has a passion for music, and the Hungarian Ambassador at the Embassy and asked them to officially sponsor the concert as the ICU-Hungarian Piano Fest. Both agreed upon the condition that there would be no financial obligation which I agreed to. The Hungarian Ambassador also offered to provide the finest Hungarian wine for a reception after the concert if one could be arranged.

Watanabe and I discussed how to finance the concert hall rental fees and other costs. Based on his many years of involvement in arranging ICU alumni glee club concerts through ticket sales and sales of publicity in the program, he was supremely confident that we could finance the concert. With that he began the search for an appropriate concert hall for the third Saturday in the following September, less than three months away.

Much to our surprise, not one concert hall in Tokyo on that specific Saturday evening was available. And that brought our plans for a concert to an abrupt end. Exactly two weeks later, however, the manager of one of the largest and most famous concert halls in Tokyo called Watanabe. The concert scheduled for the third Saturday in September had been suddenly cancelled. Would we be interested in booking Endre's concert for that date? Watanabe San knew the hall well, although it was never used for the ICU Glee Club concerts because of its immense size. He urgently recommended that we meet with the manager as soon as possible, look the hall over, and make a decision.

The following week we did just that. And what a truly magnificent hall it was with 1500 seats on the main floor and 700 on the second floor. But what impressed me more were the large pictures in the huge lobby of the outstanding artists who had performed in that hall. The first one, that of Artur Rubinstein, convinced me that we were at the right place.

The next issue was the cost. The rental fee for one concert, including the piano and tuning, came to $20,000. I was shocked. Since we had agreed that no financial support from ICU or the Hungarian Embassy would be provided, I was solely responsible for arranging the financing of the concert. But by now Watanabe San had become so engrossed in the project that he assured me we could manage the finances based on his experiences with the Glee Club concerts through ticket sales and advertisements in the program.

The manager of the hall then offered the services of their caterer who could provide a full course buffet dinner reception on the lower floor of the great hall for 60 people after the concert. The cost would be $3000 extra. I became so carried away with the hall, Watanabe san's confidence, and the prospect of a gala concert, that I signed a contract for $23,000 and booked the hall for the third Saturday of September, to include a dinner-reception for sixty people following the concert.

Shortly after the signing, Watanabe san came up with ideas about financing contrary to our original understanding. The major point was that he thought ICU should take responsibility for part of the immense costs for the concert. Since I had given President Oguchi my word that there would be no financial involvement for ICU, I could not agree. When Watanabe san remained adamant about this as precious time was passing by, I finally decided to move ahead without him.

I then asked an ICU colleague, Professor Onishi Naoki, longtime associate in the American Studies Program at ICU which I then chaired, and who played piano himself, to help me arrange the concert. He agreed. We then decided that it was too late to begin advertising for ticket sales. Rather, we would give free tickets to ICU students, faculty, staff, and friends, as well as anyone else interested with 2,200 seats available, and try and sell advertisements to cover the costs at $4,000 a page. The target would be mainly American companies in Japan starting with Coca Cola, whose Vice President was a member of the ICU Church and close friend, and American Express, both of which took out full page advertisements.

After several weeks of frantic activity, and reducing full-page advertisements to half- and even quarter-page size with the great help of Professor Onishi, we were able to sell $20,000 worth of advertisements. There was no other recourse to cover the final $3,000 but for me to contribute $3,000 to the cause. During this period we distributed over a thousand free tickets on campus at noon hour as well as at the ICU Church after Sunday services, and at the nearby American School in Japan.

Endre arrived at ICU to stay at the Maple Grove Guest House the day before the concert. It was our first meeting. He turned out to be very affable and friendly. We hit it off from the first moment. He wanted to practice so I invited him to our home to use our Kawai grand piano recently tuned. What a thrill that was. Endre is a powerful player who made our house reverberate with the great Liszt and Chopin classics chosen for the concert. I knew he was perfect for the great hall we reserved.

The ICU-Hungarian Piano Fest by Endre Hegedus turned out to be a resounding success. The audience of close to one thousand responded with standing ovations. Endre responded in kind with four encores. The final one in a 'tribute to the Dukes' was taken from Gershwin's Rhapsody in Blue. It ended the concert on a light note.

We then proceeded to the reception on a lower floor with guests from ICU and the Hungarian Embassy, and my Keidanren seminar of businessmen with their wives. Both ICU President Oguchi and the Hungarian Ambassador gave introductory comments with the Ambassador giving the toast over splendid Hungarian wine. Endre responded with a heart-warming thank you that endeared him to all. The reception brought the ICU-Hungarian Piano Fest to a memorable conclusion.

And now the rest of the story . . .

The following spring when I learned from Carol Browning that Endre was again passing through Tokyo on his way to Budapest several weeks later, I called and asked him if he would kindly stop at ICU for two nights and play an informal home concert at our house for ICU faculty. Many who attended the concert down town wanted to hear him again. He was pleased and accepted the invitation. The day before the concert we cleared the furniture out of our large living room and brought in fifty folding chairs from ICU. The first Home Concert at the Dukes by Endre Hegedus for a 'Mostly Chopin' concert was a resounding success.

The enjoyment of holding a home concert motivated us to try it again, and again. The next guest artist for a Home Concert at the Dukes was our own ICU senior student then enrolled in my course, Yoshino Naoko. She was already a celebrated harpist with her own public concerts and CDs. She had also performed in America and Europe with excellent reviews. We arranged the chairs around her and the harp providing a unique setting at a campus home never experienced in the history of ICU. She enjoyed the opportunity to perform her musical artistry before her professors who responded with great enthusiasm.

The following Home Concert at the Dukes was also given by an ICU student who had just graduated from the Humanities Division in philosophy. Ueda Satoshi was delighted to play before his professors and gave a magnificent concert. It was during our obento (box lunch) together before the faculty guests arrived that I asked him if he would consider the possibility of studying piano at the Liszt Institute in Budapest under Endre Hegedus. He was startled with the idea. But he explained that since he did not come from a well-to-do family, he could not afford to study abroad. I suggested that perhaps we could find funds to cover his expenses. He responded that if that were possible, he would love to study piano in Hungary.

The following spring Ueda san flew off to Hungary where he spent the next three years studying piano with Endre. A group of his former classmates, then employed, collected funds supplemented by contributions from us and other faculty members that enabled him to concentrate on his studies without financial concerns. Fortunately the cost of living was exceptionally inexpensive in Budapest. When he returned to Tokyo he became a successful piano teacher that he continues to enjoy as his life's work, in addition to the occasional public concert.

We continued the Home Concerts at the Dukes on the ICU campus with a variety of performers. We also sponsored several concerts at the ICU Church featuring Endre on his way through Tokyo to and from Hokkaido. We paid him a fee for those concerts. The 700 seat-church was always filled. We invited all students and faculty to attend the open concerts that had their origin with the ICU-Hungarian Piano Fest in one of the great concert halls in Tokyo.

The final concert by Endre Hegedus sponsored by the Dukes did not take place in Japan. Rather it was held at the magnificent Market Square Presbyterian Church in Harrisburg, Pennsylvania. In 2004 after our retirement in the greater Harrisburg area, we learned that Endre was scheduled to give a concert at Wheaton College in Chicago. We asked him if he would perform in Harrisburg following the Chicago performance at a charity concert if we bought his plane ticket and paid him a fee. He agreed.

Through our local Presbyterian minister we were introduced to the musical director at the large Market Square Presbyterian Church where concerts are regularly performed by visiting artists. He took an immediate interest in the proposal when he listened to a tape of one of Endre's concerts with the Hungarian Philharmonic. He agreed to provide the church for a charity concert at no cost. He even agreed to introduce Endre at the concert.

The next issue was selecting the charity and planning the publicity. I learned from the musical director that their church sponsored a so-called soup kitchen every Friday evening in which dinner was provided for the homeless of Harrisburg. Since the concert would be held in that church, it seemed appropriate to donate half of the proceeds of the concert to one of its most worthy programs.

However I had another recipient in mind for the other half of the proceeds. Daughter Kim worked as a Registered Nurse every summer, while on vacation from her teaching post at a nearby public elementary school, at a free clinic for the poor in downtown Harrisburg run by the Holy Spirit Hospital. I had visited it and observed how the destitute people flocked to an old school building used to house the clinic located on the second floor. A soup kitchen sponsored by the local Catholic Church was located on the first floor open everyday with free meals. Kim enjoyed the work dealing with the American underclass but found it frustrating with every 'client' either a drug addict and/or infected with aids. It was a daily challenge. They always needed more funds. It was a perfect match with the Presbyterian soup kitchen. Fortunately for us, the Holy Spirit Hospital had an active PR office and agreed to handle all the publicity for the concert.

Endre flew in from Chicago. We took him to our home where he practiced for the concert on our Kawai grand piano brought from Japan, the same one he played for the Duke Home Concerts at ICU. We reminisced about the many concerts we sponsored for him in Japan. Daughter Kim and husband agreed to serve as ushers at the church along with June and me. On a beautiful Sunday afternoon three hundred fifty people attended the concert where a goodwill offering was taken for the two charities.

Endre played a 'mostly Chopin' concert magnificently and powerfully on a large 1924 Steinway piano carefully preserved by the church that he was thrilled to play. It was appropriate since he was, and is, one of the one-hundred pianists designated as 'Steinway artists.' The musical director was pleased to introduce him accordingly. Following his custom, Endre played four encores ending the concert with a part of Gershwin's Rhapsody in Blue. He announced that it was 'in honor of the Dukes.'

MEMOIR 26

THE MIKE WALLACE INTERVIEW FOR SIXTY MINUTES ON MY BOOK THE JAPANESE SCHOOL -

- AROUND OUR DINING ROOM TABLE -

In 1986 my manuscript entitled THE JAPANESE SCHOOL: LESSONS FOR INDUSTRIAL AMERICA was published in America by Praeger Press, their number one seller on education for that year. Based on the education of our three children then enrolled at Osawadai, the nearby Japanese public elementary school, the book analyzed the role of education in Japan's economic miracle well underway. At that time Japan was perceived by many Americans as a threat to the industrial supremacy that the United States achieved following World War II.

Six months after the book was published a call came from the Tokyo office of CBS. The most popular TV program in America, Sixty Minutes, was planning to devote a segment to the Japanese economic miracle. They wanted to send a CBS reporter for Sixty Minutes to interview me on my book The Japanese School at my home at the earliest convenience.

We scheduled a CBS interview a week later on Monday evening at 6:30. Careful instructions were given to our house on the 360 acre wooded campus of the International Christian University at the edge of Tokyo. That was essential since our home was located deep within the campus on a bluff facing Mount Fuji with a dirt lane leading through the woods to our front door. It was common for off-campus friends to lose their way trying to find our house for the first time.

On that Monday afternoon at 5 o'clock I went for my usual swim at the ICU pool after class. With no particular concern about the CBS interview at 6:30 I then had a bite to eat with the family at home and decided at the last minute to put on a decent sport shirt for the interview. At about 6:40 a van pulled up out front under the trees. When I went to the door, much to my amazement I immediately recognized Mike Wallace getting out. His name had never been mentioned in the phone call from CBS who simply asked me to meet with a CBS reporter. Recalling how provocative Mike Wallace's interviews could be, my first reaction was that this could be unpleasant. I cautiously opened the door with considerable reservation and some anxiety to meet arguably the most famous reporter on American TV.

"Good evening Professor Duke. I'm Mike Wallace from Sixty Minutes. Thank you for allowing us to come to your home for the interview. I brought a crew of two plus the director who will set up the lights and camera for the interview, if you don't mind." Lights? Cameras? No one mentioned lights and cameras. I had assumed that the interview would be conducted by a local CBS reporter, perhaps Japanese, with pencil and notebook in hand.

Mike Wallace's first impression upon entering our home was one of awe with the magnificent view of Mt. Fuji from our living room window, as described in the Introduction. Not only was he subdued but very friendly as he reacted to the brilliant scene of the setting sun behind the great mountain. He then suggested that we conduct the interview around our dining room table at the far end of the long living room with Mt. Fuji in full view. I immediately told our son Chris, then age 16, to get our video camera ready for him to film the once-in-a-lifetime interview with one of most renown TV personalities for our family records.

During the 20 minutes or so that it took for the CBS crew to rearrange our furniture and set up the lights and camera around the dining room table, Mike and I went out on the porch to view the setting sun and chat a bit. By this time we're calling each other Mike and Ben. We exchanged bits of information such as the fact that we both had sons named Chris. Nowadays every time I see Chris Wallace on Fox Network, I think of that conversation with his father many years ago. I also learned that Mike had been in Israel for interviews for other Sixty Minute topics. He was scheduled to return directly to New York when he was unexpectedly reassigned to return via Tokyo for interviews on Japanese education.

The Sixty Minutes director then called us back into the living room-dining room area where he had placed a chair for Mike on one side of the table and one for me opposite him. My book, The Japanese School, was opened on the table in front of Mike with 24 questions typed on a paper placed on the opened pages. The director then explained that they only had one camera which would be focused on me from behind Mike's shoulder until all the questioning was completed. At the end of that period, the camera would be repositioned behind my shoulder focused only on Mike's face while he posed all 24 questions over again in the same order with a brief pause between each. I was simply to sit quietly during that period while looking straight into Mike's face. In other words during the actual interview itself, Mike Wallace's face was never on camera.

Mike began with a relatively simple question followed by increasingly provocative questions, such as, "Professor Duke. Do you really expect the American public to believe that this nation has virtually eliminated illiteracy and poverty among the Japanese people?" This was one of the major conclusions in the book in which I argued that the Japanese elementary school, where our three children received all of their basic education, taught virtually every Japanese child to read and write and add and subtract, well prepared to enter the work force. From the American perspective, as Mike implied with his question, such an accomplishment of the public schools in America seemed an impossibility.

Although it appeared that Mike was baiting me from the tone of his voice and the content of some of his questions, his facial expression, which were not being recorded during the main part of the interview, were friendly if not encouraging. After an hour or so when the director called for a break, Mike responded with, "Ben. That was great!" I was taken by surprise since I had never before been interviewed on TV and could not evaluate how things were going. But with such an accolade by Mike Wallace, I was ready and confident to continue for the second part of the interview.

By nine o'clock both Mike and I were exhausted. I never imagined that the interview would continue for two hours. When the director called 'cut' to end the interview itself, Mike spontaneously called out to him, "I hope we use more than thirty seconds of this." After two hours of intensive questioning by Mike Wallace for Sixty Minutes around our dining room table at ICU, it seemed inconceivable that only thirty seconds would be included in the final program on Japan. I thought of the time and trouble CBS went to, including flying Mike Wallace from Israel to Tokyo for the interview. What a strange way of doing business.

By the time Mike Wallace and his Sixty Minute crew left our home that unforgettable evening in Tokyo, we had become very friendly toward each other. After expressions of profound appreciation, he assured me that his office would notify me well in advance of the exact date when the segment on Japan would be carried on Sixty Minutes so that our friends and families in America would be sure to watch the program. At that moment he had no idea of the scheduling since he had been unexpectedly assigned to the project when he was in Israel just a few days previously.

I assumed that some part of my interview with Mike Wallace around our living room table in Tokyo, no matter how many seconds long, would be broadcast on Sixty Minutes within a month or two at the earliest. So our family settled in to wait for the notification by CBS. It turned out to be a very long wait indeed. Six months passed without any word when a call came from the NBC office in Tokyo asking for an interview on my book The Japanese School for the Tom Brokow 6:30 Evening News.

My immediate question was whether Tom Brokow himself would be doing the interview. I was informed that Tom was not coming to Japan. Rather, with my permission a local reporter would come to my home for the interview scheduled for the following week during the afternoon.

When the NBC crew arrived with a young female American reporter I had never head of, the director decided to hold the interview in our back yard using the sun for the lighting. They quickly arranged our back yard bench accordingly with panels set up to direct the sunlight toward the bench. The NBC reporter and I then sat on the bench facing each other for the questioning. She posed similar questions as Mike Wallace did in his interview but they were shorter and simpler. We were finished in a half hour. She told me that the segment would be carried on the Evening News precisely ten days later.

Since the Sixty Minute interview had not yet been carried, I immediately contacted Mike Wallace to inquire about the timing of the Sixty Minute segment on Japan. I sent off an airmail letter to him during the pre-email era explaining that Tom Brokow's Evening News had conducted an interview on my book which would be carried in ten days. However it was superficial at best. When, I asked, would the Sixty Minute segment on Japan be broadcast.

Within a week I received a call from CBS Tokyo that the segment on Japan would be broadcast one month later with the exact date provided. That gave us an opportunity to contact many relatives and friends in America to encourage them to watch that particular segment of Sixty Minutes on Japan which would carry part of an interview of me by Mike Wallace that took place in our home. They were also advised to look for our new Kawai grand piano that should appear behind my shoulder.

Since Sixty Minutes is not carried on Japanese television, I would not have the opportunity to see it. Therefore when I contacted daughter Kim, then a student at Elizabethtown College in Pennsylvania, about the program, I told her to make sure the TV in her dormitory lounge was tuned in to the right channel so she could give me a report on my interview with Mike Wallace.

Kim was quite excited about the opportunity to see her father on television, and particularly on the famous Sixty Minutes program with Mike Wallace sitting around our dining room table with which she was most familiar. Also, since the interview was devoted to my book on The Japanese School based on her Japanese elementary school, she looked forward to the program with great anticipation. She notified every student in the dorm about the forthcoming event and invited them to watch the program with her in the lounge. There were no TV sets in student rooms in those days. When the appointed hour arrived, the lounge was full of Kim's friends.

Due to the time differential between Tokyo and the American east coast, when Sixty Minutes was aired in New York it was already 8 AM the following morning Japanese time. Shortly after the program ended, I called Kim in her dorm room to get her reaction. Her unexpected reply in a most excited voice: "Dad! You weren't on the program. Neither was Mike Wallace! What happened?"

According to a letter from Mike Wallace in response to my letter shortly thereafter asking him what happened to our interview, with great regret he explained that the segment on the Japanese economic miracle had to be edited to keep within the usual 20-minute limit for Sixty Minutes including commercials. The director decided to concentrate on issues related directly to the economy and industry such as manufacturing methods, the cooperative role of labor unions, the commitment to life-long employment practices, etc. In the process there simply was no time left for 'peripheral issues' such as the Japanese school.

My reaction was, of course, one of great disappointment not only because it was of some embarrassment not to appear on TV when we had notified so many relatives and friends to tune in to Sixty Minutes for my interview by Mike Wallace. It was also a lost opportunity for Americans to learn about the critical role of education in Japan's economic miracle, the central theme of my book on The Japanese School. Unfortunately the subtitle of the book, Lessons for North America, was ignored in the final editing by the director for the Sixty Minutes segment on the Japanese economic miracle. It's a pity that he did not read the Foreword to the book written by Dr. Nagai Michio, former Minister of Education in Japan, who summed it up succinctly.

Professor Duke's detailed study of The Japanese School, which belongs to a new category, is based on the conviction that the economic growth of modern Japan has depended extensively on the role of the school. The ethical teachings and the basic subject matter of mathematics, reading, and writing, all reflecting the cultural traditions of Japan, are analyzed as major contributing factors in Japan's economic miracle.

MEMOIR 27

U.S. AMBASSADOR MIKE MANSFIELD DEDICATES THE ICU INTERNATIONAL FOREST

- INTRODUCING THE MIGHTY CALIFORNIA SEQUOIA TO THE CAMPUS -

O n a beautiful fall afternoon in 1988, the United States Ambassador to Japan Mike Mansfield and wife came to ICU to dedicate the ICU International Forest. After a luncheon in his honor by President Oguchi Kunio, our party walked across the campus through the woods to the site of the International Forest where he was to dedicate the opening with a tree-planting ceremony of a sequoia tree from California. A large white tent had been set up next to the tree especially chosen for the event with rows of chairs under the tent for faculty, students, friends of ICU, and the media including a television channel.

Before placing a spade of dirt on the roots, Ambassador Mansfield gave brief but moving remarks appropriate for the occasion. His most memorable comment remains in my mind to this day. "Picture this mighty American sequoia from California, the oldest and tallest tree in the world today, towering over the ICU campus a hundred years later."

Unbeknownst to the Ambassador, former leader of the United States Senate, the tree he dedicated that afternoon was not an American sequoia. In fact, twenty tiny sequoia saplings from California about 16 inches tall that arrived a week previously were being held in the ICU greenhouse for later planting. Chosen for the ceremony was a perfectly shaped six-foot tall meta-sequoia purchased for the event at the Mitaka Greenery Center.

When told of the plans to use a similar tree much larger than the tiny saplings from California for the event to be covered by a well-known TV channel, fearing that a spade of dirt would knock the little sapling over, the Agricultural Attache at the American Embassy was understanding. As the official with whom I worked in making the arrangements for the Ambassador's participation, he was also surprisingly nonchalant. His reaction: I don't think I'll bother the Ambassador about the switch. He won't know the difference."

The adventure of the ICU International Forest originated about six months before the grand opening. As long-time Chairman of the ICU Campus Environment Committee, I was constantly searching for ideas to enhance the magnificent 360 acre wooded campus within the city limits of Tokyo. Among them was the proposal to establish an ICU International Forest by inviting nations throughout the world to contribute trees to the forest. I had no idea whether such a proposal could be carried out but I was determined to make the effort.

My first thought was to begin with American trees. I assumed that if the project had any chance of success, it could be determined by working with my own embassy in Tokyo. I then came up with a somewhat novel plan, a deviation on the original idea. A Visiting Professor from the Soviet Union during the communist era, Dr. Grant Pogosyan, had recently joined the ICU faculty on leave from a university in Armenia. Since I had traveled in the Soviet Union undertaking research on education in communist societies for my course on international and comparative education, I had invited Grant to lecture on the topic in my graduate classes. Through that association we became close friends. I knew I could count on Grant.

During Grant's tenure as a Visiting Professor, relationships between the United States and the Soviet Union were tense as usual. Under these circumstances, and pitting one against the other, I asked Grant to cooperate with me in launching the ICU International Forest. He agreed with enthusiasm. Little could I have imagined that upon the breakup of the Soviet Union Grant would return to ICU eventually becoming Dean of the Graduate School.

The plan called for me as an American to approach appropriate officials at the American Embassy in Tokyo and Grant to approach their counterparts at the Soviet Embassy to request trees for the ICU International Forest from our respective countries. Each of us was to imply but not declare outright that we expected trees from the other country to launch the project. The hope was that that would serve as a motivation or a challenge for each country to participate. We also planned to invite the respective ambassadors to dedicate the trees in a formal ceremony at the site of the International Forest on the ICU campus to be given wide publicity.

I then met with the Agricultural Attaché at the American Embassy in Tokyo to present my case. He listened carefully to the plan and asked me what other countries were participating. With a straight face I simply noted with conviction that we expected the Soviet Union to send trees. His immediate reply: "Count us in." It was that simple. His next question, however, stumped me. He asked what species of trees we would like. I actually hadn't thought that far ahead. Rather, I was hoping that knowledgeable American officials at the Embassy would decide on the appropriate species for the Japanese climate.

Without thinking through the consequences, I suddenly had an idea. I had once taken the family to see the famous giant American sequoia trees in California, certainly one of the most impressive sites in the American west, with several hundred-year-old trees towering a hundred meters or so into the sky. "How about California sequoia trees?" His instant reply: "Let me look into it."

I then explained our plan to invite United States Ambassador Mike Mansfield to come to the campus for a luncheon in his honor, and afterwards to dedicate the American trees at the site of the International Forest in a tree-planting ceremony. The ICU President would introduce the American Ambassador. Wide publicity would be given to the event including TV coverage.

I asked the Embassy official if he thought the Ambassador would agree to the plan. He assured me that if he could arrange for sequoia trees to be sent from California, he would be able to convince the amiable Ambassador Mansfield to dedicate them with a short speech. I was delighted. A week later the Attaché called with the exciting news that we should make final plans. He could get the trees within a month, and Ambassador Mansfield readily agreed to participate.

During the same week Grant Pogosyan visited the Soviet Ambassador in Tokyo and received the same positive response when he casually noted that the Americans were planning to send trees. In this case it was decided that relevant Soviet officials would look into the possibility of obtaining white birch trees for the International Forest as symbolic of the Soviet Union. The Ambassador agreed to dedicate the 'communist trees' if arrangements could be made to secure them.

Tentative plans were quickly put in motion to launch the ICU International Forest. The ICU President arranged to host a luncheon separately for each of the two ambassadors from the two most powerful countries in the world when the trees arrived from their respective countries, beginning with the American Ambassador. One of the major TV companies agreed to cover the initial dedication ceremony for their evening news program since Ambassador Mansfield was well known in Japan. And the Japan Times planned to send a reporter to cover the unusual event.

Several weeks later the ICU President's office received a call from Japanese Agriculture and Quarantine officials at the Tokyo Narita

International Airport. Twenty sequoia trees had arrived from the United States. They were simply addressed to the International Christian University. All had survived and had been processed with no dirt on the roots, a prerequisite. They were ready to be picked up.

The next morning we sent a medium sized truck with two grounds keepers to the airport to pick up the great sequoia trees. We also sent a backhoe to the site chosen for the International Forest to clear out a substantial area in preparation for the arrival of the twenty trees, far more than we expected. Several hours later the two grounds keepers called from the airport to report that they had picked up two small cardboard boxes each containing ten sequoia saplings less than a half meter tall (about fifteen inches). They noted that there was no need to prepare a large area to plant them. This came as a complete surprise. We had no forewarning about the size of the trees and assumed as sequoia they would be substantial.

When we received the two boxes later that day, we were immediately concerned that the tiny saplings no thicker than one's little finger would barely show up on the TV screen. We were also afraid that it could be an embarrassment to Ambassador Mansfield if he knocked the little sapling over as he ceremoniously shoveled a spade of dirt on it before the TV camera.

After much discussion, and upon the recommendation of our Japanese professor of biology, we decided to buy a Japanese meta-sequoia about two meters tall (6 feet) from a local nursery for the ceremony, and replace it with the real California sequoia after the event. I had no idea you could buy such a tree in Japan. When I consulted with the Agricultural Attaché at the American Embassy of the plan, he advised us to go ahead with it. As noted above, he concluded that there would be no need to inform Ambassador Mansfield since he wouldn't know the difference anyway. In the meantime the small sequoia saplings from California were carefully placed in the university greenhouse for later planting.

On the appointed day, Ambassador and Mrs. Mansfield along with several Embassy officials arrived for the presidential luncheon.

He brought with him a copy of my recent book, The Japanese School: Lessons for North America. It seems that former American Ambassador to Japan Edwin Reischauer, who kindly wrote the Preface for the book, had recommended it to Ambassador Mansfield. He noted that in fact he had read it completely through and appreciated it so much that he wanted me to sign it for him. Since this brief but unexpected encounter took place in the office of the President before all the guests just prior to the luncheon, I was to say the least honored.

Following lunch on a beautiful sunny day, rather than driving to the International Forest located on the edge of the campus, our party walked to the selected site. I well remember the elderly Ambassador remarking to his wife, as we leisurely strolled through the trees which dominate the ICU campus, that he couldn't imagine they were in Tokyo. A white tent had been set up to accommodate about thirty chairs. Students and faculty also stood in the rear. The TV network had sent a cameraman. In front of the audience but under the tent the two-meter meta-sequoia tree from the local nursery had been planted. A small pile of dirt was placed beside it with several shovels on the ground for the tree-planting ceremony.

The ICU President welcomed the guests and introduced Ambassador Mansfield who then gave a short dedication speech. Exuding great pride he characterized the great California Sequoia trees as part of the historical tradition of America. With true dedication he called everyone's attention to the future in dramatic terms. "Picture this mighty American sequoia from California, the oldest and tallest tree in the world today, towering over the ICU campus a hundred years later." With a few shovels of dirt on the Japanese meta-sequoia by the American Ambassador and the ICU President, the ICU International Forest was formally dedicated.

And now the rest of the story . . .

Three weeks later five white birch trees from the Soviet Union arrived via Siberia. Like their sequoia counterparts, they were tiny saplings that fit into a small cardboard box. And like their counterparts from America, they passed through Japanese Quarantine by having no soil on the roots. Facing the same problem as we did with the American ceremony, we decided on the same solution. We purchased a two-meter tall Japanese white birch from the same Mitaka greenhouse for the ceremony to be dedicated by the USSR Ambassador to Japan. Similar to his counterpart from America, the Soviet Ambassador alluded to the special feeling that his people feel toward their white birch trees. He expressed his gratitude for the opportunity to dedicate the trees from the great Soviet Union.

Several months after the two tree-planting ceremonies, we removed both the Japanese meta-sequoia and the Japanese white birch from the ICU International Forest. In their place we then planted the American sequoia and the Soviet white birch saplings directly across from each other. The remaining ones were planted in a different area. Although several have died over the years, the surviving trees from the United States and the USSR, now Russia, are growing nicely as the centerpiece of the ICU International Forest.

When I retired from ICU at the turn of the century, over twenty countries from Iran to Korea had contributed more than one hundred trees from thirty species. Indeed, as Ambassador Mansfield predicted, one hundred years later the mighty American sequoia will tower over the ICU campus. ICU students of the 22nd Century will look up with awe at the giant sequoia trees from America, and probably wonder how they ever got there.

MEMOIR 28

OBSERVING THE EDUCATION OF FUTURE LEADERS IN JAPAN, AMERICA, AND BRITAIN

- AT ETON, CHOATE, AND KAISEI GAKKO -

I n 1991 my manuscript on Education and Leadership for the Twenty-First Century: Japan, America, and Britain was published by Praeger Press. It was the product of a fascinating adventure in comparative education. It was also a challenge to my ingenuity to design and conduct an international study of the education of the future leaders in three of the most influential nations in the world in the latter half of the 20th Century. It provided me with a rare opportunity to sit in the classrooms where 21st Century leaders were being educated, including the oldest classroom in the world at Eton dating from the 14th Century. It also gave me a chance to interview teenagers some of whom at this writing are the decision-makers of the 21st Century in their respective countries.

By the late 1980s the postwar economic miracle in Japan had reached a level that provoked increasing concern in the United States. Opinions were frequently expressed about the Japanese superceding America as the leading industrial country in the world in the not too distant future. Historical comparisons were made beginning with the 19th Century as the British Century and the 20th as the American Century. The question then was whether the 21st Century was destined to become the Japanese Century in view of the rapidly expanding economy of Japan.

After living in Japan for three decades with three children receiving their basic education in Japanese public schools, and having thousands of Japanese students in my classes at ICU, I began to think about the ramifications of Japan becoming a super-economic power challenging the United States for leadership as the number one nation in the world. Were the ICU students in my classes, for example, prepared to become world leaders in the 21st Century as British leaders did in the 19th Century and the Americans in the 20th Century?

To answer that question, in 1988 I undertook a two-year comparative study of the education of the future leaders of Japan, America, and Britain by visiting ten of the leading secondary schools in each country that consistently produced a disproportionately high number of graduates who become leaders in industry, commerce, and government in their respective countries. The visits included classroom observations, interviews with students, teachers, and administrators, and a written survey of student attitudes toward themselves as leaders, their schools as preparing them for leadership, and the effectiveness of their government leaders.

I received a grant from Keidanren, the Federation of Industries, the leading industrial organization in the nation, where I conducted a weekly seminar of leading businessmen from all major industries, the topic of an earlier memoir. The members of my seminar, all senior company officials and ranking officers of Keidanren, were keen on learning how American and British leaders especially in industry were prepared for leadership in comparison to how the Japanese were. The seminar members eagerly awaited the results of my research.

The intricacies of selecting ten of the leading secondary schools in each nation for the study, which involved the assistance of many knowledgeable individuals in each country, are too detailed for this memoir. The chosen schools included, among others, Kaisei, Lasalle, and Rakusei from the private sector in Japan and Kunitachi, Shuyukan, and

Tsukuba from the public sector. In Britain Eton, Harrow, and Rugby represented the private sector and Blue Coat Comprehensive, Stroke-on-Trent Sixth Form College, and London Oratory Comprehensive represented the public sector. The American private schools included Choate, Andover, and Westminster (Georgia), with New Trier, Palo Alto, and Stuyvesant in New York City representing the public sector.

The results of the study analyzed in the book are as relevant today during the 21st Century as they were when compiled and published in the latter part of the 20th Century. First of all my interviews of the students at these famous schools conducted in all three countries convincingly demonstrated that they were representative of the most outstanding teenagers in America, Britain, and Japan. Their manner, sophistication, and level of awareness confirmed that they were not average high school students from typical families. I found myself encountering an elite group of teenagers, many from families of financial means capable of paying the high tuition charged by famous schools such as Eton and Choate. As one student put it during an interview, "We are all aware of our privileged position."

After visiting ten of the selected schools in each country over a two year period, I made two distinctions among them. First of all I selected Eton from Britain, Choate from the United States, and Kaisei Gakko from Japan as the leading schools in the survey preparing an extraordinarily high number of future leaders in their respective countries. Secondly the difference in physical facilities, relationships between student and teacher in the classroom, and the interpretation of leadership divided east from west. Nevertheless they all had one goal in common. Every effort was made to prepare as many of their students as possible to enter the finest universities in the land, which traditionally led to positions of leadership in all sectors of the society. It is this commonness of purpose that united them. It is in the process of achieving a common goal that divides them, most notably between east and west.

The physical facilities at many of the elite private schools in America and Britain are beyond imagination, not only to the Japanese students in the elite schools in their country, but to the students and teachers in public schools in America and Britain. While walking around the magnificent campuses of Chote, Andover Phillips, Eton, Harrow, Rugby, etc., I thought about my high school in Berwick, Pennsylvania, a simple building with a gymnasium and a small library. In sharp contrast the Eton campus includes many old venerable buildings and broad playing fields including a golf course. Choate in America has dozens of buildings including a hockey rink on a 400 acre campus.

Kaisei Gakko is the leader of both the outstanding private and public secondary schools in Japan most of which are situated amidst bustling cities. Located in several buildings in a heavily populated district of Tokyo, this most elite high school nevertheless attracts the best students since it places well over a hundred graduates in Tokyo University every year in spite of the facilities. Many of the future leaders of Britain and America are studying in extravagant facilities compared to the shabby conditions of Kasei in Japan. In both western countries the exquisite rural sites of many of the elite private schools provide an educational environment so pristine and yet so elaborate that they defy comprehension by the Japanese.

The classroom atmosphere that I personally experienced in these select schools in America, Britain, and Japan reflects this environment. Classes at Eton and Choate often contain 10 to 15 students in an intimate setting. Even at the finest public schools in Britain and America the number of students per class seldom exceeds twenty-five. In contrast, Kaisei Gakko classes routinely contain 50 students in a formal lecture-style classroom setting. To accommodate that many students in a standard classroom, the desks are arranged in an orderly fashion, that is, in straight rows. Although the teacher at Eton wears a formal robe in contrast to the teacher at Kaisei Gakko in regular attire, sleeves rolled up during warm days, the general atmosphere within the two classrooms is distinctly different.

As I described in the book, the consequence of class size in the two western countries compared to that of Japan influences the relationship between student and teacher that assumes a startlingly different character. There is a strong sense of community life with an informal, fairly close relationship between teacher and student in schools with small classes where student-teacher interaction is nurtured. In many of the classes I observed in Britain and America teachers frequently posed questions to the students who were clearly accustomed to the routine. One student revealed his feelings when he noted that, "You never know when you're going to be asked a question. You always have to be ready."

I found the classroom in the western schools in my study to be academically challenging. There was an effort to treat the students as individuals with unique talents, to encourage the students to think independently, to motivate the students to broaden their perspectives and interests, and to encourage each student to develop personal talents outside the classroom in art, music, creative writing, sports, etc. In spite of the rigorous academic demands necessary to enter the prestigious colleges and universities, it is a well-rounded education many of the future leaders of Britain and America were receiving in the 1980s when this study was carried out, as they are today.

The give-and-take, exchange of opinion, discussion, probing, etc. that takes place in many of the western classrooms in this study defy the imagination of the Japanese students in the leading secondary schools like Kaisei, who seldom have to be ready to answer questions during class. Nor are they inclined to ask questions during class. With fifty students in the room, interaction between student and teacher is very difficult to achieve even by the most dedicated teacher. The typical Japanese teacher in both the public and private sector involved in this study, as I witnessed it, formally lectured from prepared notes for the entire period. Few, if any, questions by the teacher or student interrupt the flow of the lecture.

Busily taking notes, the students in Japan's outstanding schools expect nothing less than a teacher most adept at preparing them to pass the entrance examination at the most prestigious universities in the land. If this means the dissemination of factual information most likely to be included on the entrance examination for pure rote memorization, so much the better. Teachers who conduct their classes differently are in a small minority. From this perspective the Japanese classroom is also academically challenging.

With fifty students in the classrooms of Kaisei Gakko, the teachers cannot, nor do they recognize the need to, monitor the individual development of their students except on their progress on the many mock tests administered by the school during the year. Employing computer models, the school can plot the progress of each student throughout the year providing the anxious parents a fairly accurate assessment of the chances the student has in passing the entrance examination at one of the leading universities. It's all part of the intense process of preparing an extraordinarily high number of the students to enter the leading universities on their way to leadership positions in all sectors of Japanese society.

Another feature of the British and American secondary schools that I found so different from their counterparts in Japan was the significant number that were boarding schools, a rarity in Japan. In other words the western schools influence the student literally twenty-four hours a day and most weekends as well. Each student dormitory had an advisor, often with spouse, living in the dorm with the students. Certain traditions of the dorm were upheld under the watchful eye of the faculty advisor. Most of the Japanese students in this survey, on the other hand, return home each day or to a relative's house if home is too far for commuting to school. Weekends they're on their own.

This brings us to the most fundamental issue in education and leadership that I encountered while carrying out this comparative study in Britain, America, and Japan. The vast differences between the education of future leaders in America and Britain with that in Japan can be attributed primarily to the interpretation of leadership and the role of a leader in their respective societies. Education for leadership, therefore, necessarily follows a divergent path among them.

First of all there is an unstipulated practice among the outstanding schools of Japan not to actively promote leadership qualities among their highly select student body. Rather than appearing as a negative feature of these schools to the students and their parents, many of whom themselves have attained positions of influence, it is a virtue. In a word, the school is not expected to promote education for leadership. This approach toward leadership contrasts sharply with that followed by the outstanding schools of America and Britain. These schools make every effort to encourage leadership tendencies within the students and to instill aspirations to lead.

The contrasting approach to leadership in the Japanese schools reflects the cultural mores and traditions of Japanese society itself. To stand out among one's peers as a leader invites widespread criticism. Modesty is a trait greatly admired within the society. A successful leader in Japan is often one who exhibits a degree of reticence, especially about personal leadership capabilities. A successful leader is often the one who does not appear to be a leader but, in fact, has gained power and influence through quiet negotiations behind the scenes.

An attribute of a Japanese leader is the ability to work cooperatively within a group to promote a sentiment of unity and, of singular importance, harmony. Although the leader's influence may be the dominant factor, the supporters must not feel that their opinions were ignored in the final decision-making process. It is a subtle art of leadership in Japanese society, not dependent upon sharp intellect, clever speaking and debating skills, or wit, characteristics admired among Western leaders.

It is precisely the intangibles in developing leadership qualities among the Japanese that cannot be readily incorporated into the classrooms of the nation's leading preparatory schools. It is, as it were, subconsciously learned that most successful Japanese leaders do not stand out conspicuously. They rarely exhibit leadership traits associated with that concept as normally understood in Britain and America. For example, many of the prominent American and British leaders have come through outstanding schools that cultivated debate through which students honed their skills of discourse and persuasions. That simply is not the case in the outstanding schools of Japan.

Comparing the overt process of instilling leadership qualities in the future leaders of America and Britain in their leading secondary schools with the covert process the future leaders of Japan undergo was a fascinating adventure for me. My ultimate conclusion was rather modest. Other than the overriding motivation for university preparation to enter the best universities that all of the schools I visited harbored, there is little the future leaders of Japan share in common with the future leaders of America and Britain in the education they are receiving in the outstanding schools in their respective countries.

MEMOIR 29

THE BITTER DISPUTE
BETWEEN ICU AND THE CITY OF TOKYO

- CHAIRING THE COMMITTEE TO
PRESERVE NOGAWA KOEN -

I n early September, 1989, newspapers reported that the Tokyo City Assembly had approved a plan submitted by three heavily populated communities in the western suburbs to construct a huge incinerator in the middle of Nogawa Koen, the 150-acre city park bordering the ICU campus. The new facility, including twin 100-meter high smokestacks, was intended to replace the current incinerator located less than a half mile from the new site that had reached its capacity as the population in the area increased sharply in recent years. A major obstacle in upgrading the current site was the height of the smokestacks since the facility happened to be located in the flight path of a small nearby airport that catered to private planes. Construction was scheduled to begin within a few months.

On learning about the plan my instinctive reaction, naïve as it seems years later, was that the decision had to be reversed no matter what that entailed. From that moment I vowed that I would do everything possible as Chairman of the ICU Environment Committee to prevent the incinerator from being built in the middle of Nogawa Koen. Little could I have foreseen that a bitter confrontation with the city of Tokyo would continue for two years consuming a great deal of my time, and that it would take on an international aspect involving Hyde Park in London and Central Park in New York.

Nogawa Koen was originally part of the ICU campus that had first been used as a farm, then turned into the ICU Golf Course in 1964, which was sold to the city for a public park ten years later. The city named it Nogawa Koen after the Nogawa River that ran through the site. The transition from farm to golf course and finally to a public park is worthy of a brief historical review. It also lays the basis for ICU's unswerving opposition to the new incinerator and the campaign to preserve the natural environment of the area.

At the very beginning of the university in 1949, the founders came across the huge tract of land in the western part of Tokyo that was considered ideal for a campus site since most of it was undeveloped. Histories of ICU chart the course of action taken to obtain the estate from the Fuji Corporation which is too detailed for this memoir. The geographical formation rendered the site unique. The property was rather neatly divided through the middle marked by a long bluff. The upper half, often referred to as the upper campus, was heavily forested with the center of it cleared for the laboratory and hangers used by the Fuji company during the war to develop some of the nation's fighter airplanes. The laboratory became the ICU Honkan, the Main Building, where I taught most of my courses during my long tenure at the university.

The other half of the ICU property, the lower campus below the long bluff, had already been partially cleared for rice patties when the site was purchased. It was expanded to accommodate the cattle barn with a herd of about thirty cattle donated from America, plus pig pens and a large chicken coop, all of which became known as the ICU Farm. It was equipped with tractors and small trucks, one of which was used by the ICU Dairy to deliver milk to campus residents. Nogawa River, actually a stream in most places that overflowed its banks during the annual rainy season, wound through the lower section of the ICU property.

Since the edge of the bluff of the upper section overlooked the lower section and beyond to the glorious mountain ranges from which Mt. Fuji emerged, homes for the ICU faculty were purposely built along the bluff. It provided magnificent views not only of the lower section of the campus, that is, the farm with the picturesque Nogawa River winding through it. It also provided stunning views of Mt. Fuji to those of us who had the good fortune to live in a faculty home located on the bluff.

Because the university, with its large contingent of foreign faculty and a significant imbalance of senior scholars among the Japanese faculty, was committed to a low faculty-student ratio, the annual budget deficits were impossible to overcome during the economic depression in Japan during the 1950s. Tuition had to be kept at very low rates in order to attract students to the new, and unproven, university. Means to stabilize the university finances were constantly being explored.

By the 1960s golfing had become a craze in Japan as well as a very expensive sport catering to the increasing numbers of businessmen who could afford the fees. In order to reduce the deficits the university converted the 150-plus acre lower campus, the ICU Farm, into the ICU Golf Course in 1964 with a magnificent clubhouse and a first-rate 18-hole golf course. Uniquely, four of the holes were located at the back end of the upper campus accessible for the golfers by an electric escalator from the lower section up the bluff.

The membership was quickly filled primarily by businessmen who could afford the exorbitant fees that quickly climbed to $100 per round plus a road tax, caddy fee, etc., a considerable amount at the time. But to be able to play a round of golf on such a magnificent course that included a splendid clubhouse with its own ofuro (bath) for the golfers, a must in Japan, all within Tokyo was most attractive to the expanding golfing community. For the ICU faculty, however, the cost per round was the equivalent of $5.

Not only did we look down upon the golf course from our home on top of the bluff, one of the fairways ran directly below us only about fifty meters away with the Nogawa River located on the other side of the hole. I took up the sport and began to practice shots from our back yard after six o'clock when the course closed. Our three children then ran down the short hill to the fairway, collected the balls, and fished out the few that went into the shallow Nogawa River. In other words the ICU golf course was within a stone's throw from the faculty homes and a bit further from several dormitories.

Once a week or so at 7:15 AM I pulled my golf cart along the path from our house to the nearby 13th hole, one of the four holes located on the upper campus, located about three minutes from our house. I'd play the four holes on the upper section and the last two on the lower section, arriving at the clubhouse as the course opened at 8 o'clock to pay my $5 fee. I then completed the course by ending with a ride up the escalator to the 13th hole that led to the path back to our house. When I first invited the ICU President, Dr. Ukai, the great constitutional scholar who loved golf, to join me on my special route, he was overcome with joy since he lived three houses away on top of the bluff. It was, without doubt, a golfer's heaven for the ICU faculty.

The ICU Golf Course was also a perfect neighbor for the university. Not only was it a quiet neighbor, it also preserved a large border of the campus from development. Already virtually every site around the upper campus encompassing the university buildings had been developed for housing, resulting in a huge increase in the number of people living in the area of our open campus. In addition, the Golf Course had been designed exquisitely with trees, bushes, and flowers to fit into the gently rolling nature of the site, which was further enhanced with the long winding river around which many fairways were cited. It fit perfectly into the natural environment of the upper campus covered mostly with trees among which the university buildings had been located. From the air, the ICU campus and the ICU Golf Course presented a stark contrast between a sea of greenery and a sea of houses built closely together that surrounded the entire site. We proudly referred to it as the ICU Greenbelt determined to preserve the magnificent campus.

By 1974, after a ten-year experimental period as a golf course, the cost of operating the facility had spiraled out of control even with increases in fees, and the amusement tax on golfing had sharply increased. During the same period ICU's budget deficits increased significantly as the university found it necessary to broaden the curriculum and upgrade the facilities when it became apparent that we could attract top students in competition with the famous well-established private universities. The annual deficits reached a dangerous level threatening the existence of the institution.

To tackle the deficit problem, a Japanese businessman and an active Christian, Tabuchi Minoru, was hired as the first Vice President for Financial Affairs to come from the Japanese business world. Tabuchi san, a tiny elderly man who negotiated with the United States government over tariffs turned out to be a gentle man who earned the respect of the staff and faculty by his quiet, patient, but determined manner. He also spoke excellent English having studied at Chicago University which meant that he could fully interact with the non-Japanese faculty.

After Tabuchi san surveyed the bleak financial situation in depth, he came to the conclusion that the golf course had to be sold to generate a permanent endowment for the university. Word got out that he was secretly negotiating the sale with various potential investors at a time when the economic miracle of Japan was moving into a higher stage that sparked rapidly increasing real estate prices. The ICU golf course on 150 acres of open space within Tokyo attracted influential developers prepared to make the investment.

I was among those on the faculty who became deeply concerned that Tabuchi san would sell the golf course to the highest bidder such as the Mitsubishi Real Estate Corporation which had the financial depth to build high rise apartment complexes all over the site that bordered the ICU campus for about a half mile. As Chairman of the

ICU Environment Committee, I was particularly concerned that the concentration of tens of thousands of people packed into an area right up against our campus would have an inordinately negative influence on our quiet wooded campus. Without doubt, the fact that highrise apartments would block out the spectacular view of Mt. Fuji that all the faculty homes built along the bluff enjoyed, was certainly a factor in our opposition to selling the ICU Golf Course.

I became very active in the opposition movement. In desperation I met with the three economists on our faculty, two Japanese and one American, to discuss the proposed sale from a long-range perspective as real estate prices were rapidly rising. They extrapolated what the 150-acre tract would be worth ten years later at the rate of increase. It was a staggering figure. I then asked Tabuchi san to meet with the four of us to give the economists the opportunity to lay out their case that selling at that time would be shortsighted. In his usual manner Tabuchi quietly listened to the case. We left with some satisfaction that the critical individual in the negotiations had been exposed to compelling logic.

Several weeks later Tabuchi san's office announced that ICU had agreed to sell the ICU Golf Course in 1975 to the City of Tokyo exclusively for a public park to be named Nogawa Koen for $200,000,000. Moreover a verbal agreement had been made by city authorities that no buildings would be constructed in the park other than the golf course club house already there to become the park office.

What a shock. Tabuchi san had been able to keep the negotiations with the city unknown to us. We had assumed that he was negotiating with developers to negotiate the maximum selling price possible. To learn that he had been negotiating the sale of half of the ICU property specifically for a public park was beyond our strongest hopes. He had literally pulled off an environmental coup, which I considered the greatest contribution he made to ICU. I wrote him a letter after he retired expressing my deepest admiration of him. This was his revealing reply.

Dear Duke San:

Thank you very much for your kind letter. As you can imagine the sale of the golf course to Tokyo was not easy. When I came to ICU in 1970, the financial future of the university was desperately gloomy. I studied what can be done. After that I asked several ICU Trustees including the late Mr. Ichimada to review my plans. It took several weeks before they agreed. I met (Tokyo) Governor Minobe's assistants many times at the Press Club to discuss, without being known by others, the possibility of the sale of the golf course for one purpose; a public park. In the meantime offers from business firms, real estate people, and other developers came, often backed by pressure from politicians. Another worry was the tax on Endowment Income. Shiritsu Daigaku Renmei (Private University Association) worked with me all these years and so far we have succeeded.

With best wishes,

Minoru Tabuchi

Within a short time after the transfer of the land, the Tokyo City Bureau of Parks began the conversion of the beautiful 18-hole golf course to a magnificent public park. Many trees were planted in the open fairways. Walkways, trails, and paths were laid throughout the Park. For ICU's protection a fence was constructed for the entire length of the border between ICU and the park. In addition, a long section of the border at the bottom of the bluff was enclosed by a fence for a wetland preserve open only on certain days for the public to walk through on carefully constructed wooden walkways. The clubhouse was turned into the park office with exhibition rooms. And pavilions with benches, tables, and fireplaces were strategically placed throughout the park along with a sports area with 12 tennis courts.

Among the various facilities, one of the most impressive ones was a large area set aside for children. For access from all directions it was sited in the very middle of the park. A wide variety of climbing apparatus and adventurous sets and games for kids was set up. They were all painted in colorful hues that attracted children and their parents. It was used extensively by children from the neighborhood.

Within two years Nogawa Koen had become not only one of the finest city parks in Japan, it had reached the status of one of the great municipal parks in the world carefully maintained by the Tokyo Bureau of Parks. Located amidst a heavily populated area of the city, it attracted huge numbers of people especially on weekends and holidays. Since they were spread out over a 150-acre area, they could enjoy themselves in spite of the number.

Many ICU students, faculty and staff also enjoyed the park facilities. June and I often packed a lunch and rode our bikes down to the park for a glorious day amidst nature on the banks of the Nogawa River. We all agreed that Nogawa Koen fit perfectly into the natural environment of the ICU campus with its many acres of woods. The sale of the land to the City of Tokyo, which provided an ICU endowment of $200,000,000 that nearly tripled when the Japanese economy rapidly improved, turned out to be a very successful decision. It placed ICU with its half billion dollar endowment among the ranks of the well-endowed American private universities of a comparable size. It was attributable to Mr. Tabuchi's foresight, as well as his convictions and courage to ignore the opposition from within the faculty against selling the land. That, of course, included my well-intended but misguided actions.

When the Tokyo government unexpectedly announced in 1989, nearly fifteen years after Nogawa Park was established, that a huge incinerator with 100-meter tall chimneys would be built in the middle of it, and on the site of the children's playground no less, many people at ICU were enraged. I was among them. As Chairman of the ICU Campus Environment Committee, I met with President Watanabe shortly after the decision was made known. We agreed that ICU should take a public position opposing the city's plans and that an appeal should be presented to Tokyo Governor Suzuki as soon as possible.

He asked me to draw up a position paper for him as reference for the appeal. He also appointed a committee of five named the ICU Nogawa Koen o Mamoru Iinkai (The ICU Committee to Protect Nogawa Koen) to direct an ICU campaign against the city of Tokyo. He asked me to chair it.

This was my first close association with President Watanabe who, for a variety of reasons, turned out to be the ideal Japanese to hold the presidency as we began our dispute with the city of Tokyo. First of all he was perhaps the leading scholar in the field of public administration in Japan. In that capacity he served on several advisory boards for prefectural governments and had much experience with Tokyo city bureaucrats and politicians. Ironically, at one time he served as an advisor to the governor of Tokyo. From years of working in the field he had become intimately acquainted with the Japanese political world and the way both politicians and bureaucrats operated.

His own demeanor was another asset to our campaign. He did not reflect emotion. He remained calm no matter the situation. He also was shy so that he spoke infrequently. That was to his advantage since he was a poor public speaker, which endeared him to those Japanese reflecting a social aspect of the culture that regards humility with great respect. When compelled to give an opinion, it was short and carefully supported by the evidence that he laid out. His writings also reflected that manner.

In contrast to his public demeanor, behind the scenes President Watanabe was an active and very effective negotiator. He always had a goal for which he designed a method to accomplish it by arranging critical people to play critical roles to bring about the desired results. He was, for lack of a better expression, a master of manipulation. As such he never fit comfortably into the academic world at ICU nor was he readily accepted by some of his senior Japanese colleagues. That was due, I thought, because of his close relationship to the Japanese political and bureaucratic world and his specialization in an unknown discipline of public administration.

Watanabe san was not considered by many at ICU as deeply committed to Christianity nor the Christian commitment of ICU as they thought the president should be. He attended church rarely and even moved off campus so that his participation in campus social and religious events was sporadic at best. I don't remember ever meeting his wife who kept apart from campus activities of the Fujinkai, the Woman's Association of the ICU Church which June enjoyed so much.

When President Watanabe asked me take an active role in ICU's campaign against the city of Tokyo, it opened up a new era for me with a unique Japanese individual that I had not yet experienced. I found it fascinating to follow his tactics especially because he committed himself fully to the struggle to protect the natural environment taking the lead in the campaign. Unfortunately he was also physically frail who, unknown to most of us at the time, was entering a period of decline. His demanding role in the struggle to preserve Nogawa Koen may have aggravated his state of health leading to his early death while in the presidency.

I willingly accepted the president's assignment and promptly set out to draw up a position paper. I was immediately confronted with two serious issues. First of all, ICU had no legal basis for our opposition. The city of Tokyo owned the park. And although Mr. Tabuchi personally told me that city representatives during the negotiations had agreed that no large permanent buildings would be built in the park, it was only a verbal understanding and was not included in the contract. The Tokyo government had every legal right to build an incinerator in Nogawa Koen.

Secondly, the city's rationale for building a large modern incinerator in that area was supported by statistics that were not only indisputable but overwhelming. In the inexorable growth of Tokyo westward, the huge increase in the number of people, houses, apartment buildings, etc., in the three communities surrounding much of ICU, Koganei, Chofu, and Fuchu, was astounding. As a result the huge increase in garbage generated by the surge in population overwhelmed the then-current incinerator that was ironically located directly across the road from Nogawa Koen at the far southern edge of the park. That site, too, had originally been a part of the ICU lower campus which was sold to the city many years earlier for the incinerator. It was argued that there simply was not enough space at that site to rebuild the facility to accommodate the enormous and growing demand which required giant smokestacks forty meters higher than the old ones that would be an obstacle to planes taking off from the nearby Chofu airport.

The problem we faced was a strategic one. No matter how persuasively ICU could argue that the incinerator should not be built in the park to preserve the natural environment of the area, as agreed to by the city when it purchased the property, the statistics were far too dramatic to surmount. I realized that the city could counter with a convincing argument that there was no other open site in the area to accommodate a large incinerator other than the park, which was already owned by the city and therefore available at no cost to the taxpayer. The city of Tokyo clearly had the upper hand. The odds were overwhelmingly stacked against ICU.

I had to come up with some tactic that could stop a project that had already been approved by the city assembly and a large budget set aside for it. A chief engineer had also already been assigned to begin drawing up the plans. Obviously the park bureau had been working on the project long before the vote of the assembly was taken. Already a great deal of money had been spent so that upon approval the officials were ready to immediately begin the implementation. There was no turning back. In other words ICU had little time to try and prevent the bulldozers from tearing up the children's playground to initiate the project.

I finally concluded that the only chance we had, however slim, to influence the authorities in charge was to base our campaign against the city of Tokyo on 'shame' as our primary weapon, and to raise such a commotion in the process both within Japan and abroad that we could not be ignored. We would begin our argument on the positive by repeating the concept that Tokyo's Nogawa Koen is one of the finest metropolitan parks in the world comparable to Central Park in New York and Hyde Park in London; that it is a magnificent example of nature in the midst of a heavily populated area that the citizens of Tokyo have financed and are rightfully proud of; that those officials who planned to erect a giant incinerator in the center of the park involving hundreds of garbage trucks emitting a special odor entering the park every day should be ashamed of themselves for desecrating the environment of the great park; and, finally, that it is inconceivable that any responsible government official could have even thought of such a proposal.

We still had to devise some alternative to the project since the need for a greatly expanded facility was indisputable. It was this predicament that had me baffled. I finally came up with a position that I advocated with tongue-in-cheek. Applying modern technology, the city of Tokyo should upgrade the present incinerator to accommodate the demand. This was clearly a stretch since we had no technical knowledge whether that was possible. However it sounded positive and we included it in our campaign from the beginning. It was, not surprisingly, dismissed by city engineers as technically impossible.

I drew up a simple statement of principles for the president to use in an official appeal to the Governor of Tokyo with the following four points.

ICU offered to sell the lower campus to the city of Tokyo for a public park only, to which the governor's office agreed.

The city of Tokyo has developed the site into a national treasure as one the finest metropolitan parks in the world providing a magnificent area for the citizens of Tokyo to enjoy nature.

The plan to build a huge incinerator with 100-meter smokestacks is not only in violation of the original agreement between ICU and Tokyo, it is unthinkable to desecrate a national treasure with an incinerator.

ICU is committed to the preservation and enhancement of the great natural beauty of a green belt encompassing the ICU campus and Nogawa Koen, and is resolutely opposed to the city's plan. The university will immediately launch a national and international campaign to protect Nogawa Koen.

President Watanabe prepared a simple statement succinctly incorporating the main points into an official statement from the university designed as an appeal to then-Governor Suzuki. It had every look about it as an official document. In the opening statement he used the shame factor. He could not imagine that the city of Tokyo, without any consultation with ICU and the citizens who lived in the vicinity, approved the construction of an incinerator with 100-meter high chimneys in the middle of a beautiful natural city park. It ended with an implied threat. In order to protect the natural environment of the area, ICU would launch a campaign both within Japan and abroad through international organizations in opposition, concluding the appeal with "ima sugu hajimemasu,"(It begins immediately!)

On the 6th of October, 1989, President Watanabe and I went to the Tokyo City Hall to meet with reporters who were notified by his office of our intention to present a formal petition of opposition to the Governor's office at 11 AM. I well recall that day in part because I was taken by surprise at how shabby the city hall, located in downtown Tokyo not far from the Tokyo Station, appeared. Indicative of the economic miracle underway, not too long afterwards the old building was torn down to be replaced by a magnificent commercial center. At the same time a spectacular new City Hall was built in another area of the city, Shinjuku, with giant twin towers designed by the great Japanese architect Tange. It stands unrivaled as a marvel of design for a city hall as well as a tourist center.

With the submission of the appeal to the governor's office which was accepted politely by the Vice Governor, we launched the ICU campaign against the city of Tokyo. That very evening two of the major Japanese newspapers, the Asahi Shimbun and the Mainichi Shimbun, carried articles with large headlines that ICU had submitted a protest statement against the city's plan to build an incinerator in Nogawa Koen. The next morning another major paper, the Yomiuri Shimbun carried the identical headline as the Mainichi Shimbun did the night before. And on the same day the English language Mainichi Daily News carried the following headline: University Protesting Incinerator Plans - Tokyo Violating Land-Use Accord, ICU Claims.

With such broad publicity, the city of Tokyo turned to a committee headed by the mayors of the three cities that would use the incinerator, that is, Koganei, Chofu, and Fuchu, to defend the plan which had officially been approved by the Tokyo City Assembly. The lower campus that was turned into a golf course that became Nogawa Koen extended into both Koganei and Chofu. The upper campus, that is, the main ICU campus, is located primarily in Mitaka which had its separate incinerator at another site.

We then launched our campaign strategy. For the first time since the campus turmoil led by radical students provoked such dissension among the faculty and students a number of years previously, the struggle to preserve Nogawa Koen struck a harmonious accord among administrators, faculty, students, and staff that proved healing. It was ICU at its best. Faculty members including Saito Kazuaki and Katsumi Masayuki, along with Vice President for Finance Shibanuma joined the effort by participating in all kinds of activities. For example, Professor Hirose Masayoshi led a campaign to get as many student signatures on a protest statement as possible. He called a meeting of students to encourage widespread participation reporting that during a one-week campaign, a total of 1,379 students, faculty and staff had signed an appeal to be submitted to city officials. Students were then asked to join in a campaign to get as many local citizens to sign the appeal by knocking on doors throughout the surrounding communities, which they did with great enthusiasm.

All of this activity and the widespread publicity helped to generate a powerful movement among the local residents who had no relationship to ICU but supported our campaign. Several local organizations were spontaneously formed holding protest meetings to which we sent representatives such as Professors Hirose and Aoyagi who encouraged them to join with the ICU campaign in submitting appeals of protest to the city. As a result we formed an umbrella association incorporating many non-ICU groups into the movement.

Ironically the local community surrounding ICU and bordering Nogawa Koen on one side, Osawa, is administratively a part of Mitaka City. Mitaka administratively lies within Tokyo on the same level as nearby Fuchu, Chofu, and Koganei whose local assemblies had originally developed the incinerator plan that Tokyo's legislature had approved. The organization of citizens living in Osawa that included some ICU faculty led a movement that resulted in the Mitaka Assembly voting unanimously against the plan approved by the Fuchu, Chofu, and Koganei assemblies. It was carried in all the newspapers further buttressing our campaign.

I contacted my dear friend, Ray Downs, longtime Headmaster at the American School in Japan that bordered Nogawa Koen on the opposite side from ICU, soliciting his support in gathering signatures from as many foreigners as possible, to include students, faculty, and parents. He immediately launched a campaign that resulted in over 1,500 non-Japanese joining the campaign that stood out among the thousands of names we submitted since they were not written in Japanese script. There was widespread support among the ASIJ community because Nogawa Koen bordered the ASIJ campus on three sides. This, as anticipated, attracted much attention among the media with the non-Japanese involvement.

President Watanabe and other members of our committee appeared on TV and radio to explain ICU's position. I wrote an article incorporating all of my ideas entitled 'From a non-Japanese Perspective' which was carried in a Tokyo newspaper word for word in translation with my picture. I invited a reporter from the English newspaper, The Japan Times, to visit the site with me. A young female reporter was sent out to cover the story. I took her to the children's section of the park with its impressive and colorful equipment with many children enjoying the facilities, precisely where the incinerator was to be cited. I said simply, "Imagine a huge incinerator with 100-meter chimneys and fifty trucks full of garbage lined up on that very spot."

Within a short time we stirred up so much commotion that the city quietly postponed indefinitely the beginning of the construction work. That was a positive signal that we had at least gotten the city's attention. The delay continued on for a year. We were then encouraged when our ICU committee was invited to a meeting called by the three-mayor committee to be held at, of all places, the offices of the old incinerator building. Other local groups involved in the protest were also invited. We were all hoping for a positive announcement.

It turned out that the mayors had sent the chief engineer and his staff assigned to the project to present a detailed case why the city had to build a larger incinerator at the earliest possible moment. Although there was nothing new, the report was impressive. But the chief engineer made an amazing statement. He recognized the concern of many people over the 100-meter tall smokestacks incorporated in the plan. Consequently he planned to cover the chimneys with images of trees painted in green to fit in with the surrounding natural environment.

At that meeting which Professor Saito Kazuaki and I attended from our ICU committee, we purposely made the point that Nogawa Koen, as a metropolitan park, was at the level of Hyde Park in London and Central Park in New York in its beauty. We reported that I had personally contacted the bureau of parks in both cities during a summer trip abroad to ask them whether they had ever considered building a huge incinerator with 100-meter smokestacks in the middle of their famous parks. Their reply, as we reported, was that it was unthinkable. We emphasized the point that since Nogawa Koen was on a standard with these great western parks, it should be preserved as they are. Nevertheless we left the meeting recognizing that there was not the slightest hint of compromise. We still had a long road ahead of us. The odds remained heavily against us.

The next day the Asahi newspaper carried a report on the meeting. For the first time the issue of Nogawa Koen being favorably compared with Hyde Park in London and Central Park in New York as a shame factor had reached the Japanese press. In fact, during the previous summer we returned to America via the Trans-Siberian Railroad, the subject of another memoir, and on through Europe to London. While there I got the idea of calling the park officials responsible for Hyde Park and asked them if there was ever the suggestion of building an incinerator with huge smokestacks in the middle of the great metropolitan park. The official responded with incredulity. It was unthinkable.

We then went on to New York where I was able to talk to the official in the city's park bureau. I asked him the same question about an incinerator with huge smokestacks in Central Park, perhaps the most famous metropolitan park in America. Hi response was about the same as that in London. Upon our return to Japan in the fall I reported the results of the conversation with the two park officials to President Watanabe. He decided that we should incorporate that issue from then on in our campaign.

To make a long and bitter story shorter, ICU's confrontation with the city of Tokyo continued for over two years as the city officials remarkably kept postponing the beginning of the work. Unfortunately during the latter half of the second year, President Watanabe's health prevented him from carrying out his presidential duties. Vice President Oguchi became Acting President. Along with Vice President Shibanuma, he maintained a firm position against the city of Tokyo.

Finally, after two years, two months, and one week since ICU launched the campaign against the city with our appeal to the governor, we received a call from the city near the end of January, 1992, asking for a final meeting between the ICU committee and the Tokyo committee of three mayors to be held at the president's office. From the tone of the request we concluded that city officials had reached the end of their patience with ICU.

There was great significance in the meeting. It meant that city officials had recognized ICU as the key institution in the battle over

Nogawa Koen. Although during the two-year struggle, there were many private organizations of citizens who joined the appeal representing thousands of citizens, none of their representatives were invited by the city to what they termed 'the final meeting.' We concluded that they had decided to negotiate only with ICU.

That recognition was important to us. ICU had stood up for the great principal of protecting the environment under enormous pressure from city officials. We maintained a resolutely firm position throughout the two-year campaign. The entire ICU community had coalesced in opposition to the plan which would desecrate a great city park. The image of ICU to the general public that was widely reported in the media was a very positive one.

Prior to the final meeting with the mayors, I convened a meeting of our ICU committee to prepare for what we all felt was probably the last chance to convince the local mayors to drop the plan. I well recall my final piece of advice to my colleagues before the mayors arrived. I urged them to make it clear to the mayors that although our campaign had gone on for over two years, and we greatly appreciated the delay in the project, that the three mayors should walk out of that meeting with the feeling that, as I graphically put it, "We have just begun the campaign."

The three mayors all arrived in chauffer-driven black cars dressed in black suits for the 11 AM meeting. They entered the meeting room with their aides in a very somber attitude. Their chairman, mayor of Fuchu City, who had a gruff manner about him, opened the meeting with the statement that this was, indeed, the last meeting they would hold with us. He made it clear that they would have to move ahead promptly with the project. He called upon the chief engineer to restate their case which he did in no uncertain terms. During the two-year delay, the increase in garbage had become enormous. Future projections showed that the amount of garbage would increase many times over the current rate. He stated that there would was no possible way that the present site could be modernized to handle the future growth of garbage predicted for the area. He was convincing as usual.

Our positions were restated concluding with the fact that we were planning to increase our efforts particularly abroad through international organizations. At precisely 12 o'clock the chief mayor stood up interrupting the proceedings and declared that the meeting would have to end since he had an official commitment at one o'clock. He then made one last appeal to cooperate with them since they had no choice but to proceed with the original plan. With that, the three mayors and their entourage promptly got up, bowed stiffly toward the Acting President Oguchi, and walked out.

It all happened so quickly that we were taken by surprise. Everyone agreed that the end of our campaign had finally arrived. We were convinced that city officials had reached a limit to their patience with our opposition movement. They were fully aware, as we were, that we had no legal basis to support our case. We had based our position on the shame factor. The mayors showed no shame. We went home that day disillusioned that we had lost the long battle over the incinerator. However we took some consolation in the fact that ICU had fought a good fight and made a valiant effort to preserve Nogawa Koen.

And now the rest of the story . . .

President Watanabe died on January 30, 1992, at the age of sixty-five after a prolonged illness. Two weeks later, on February 13, a member of our committee called me in an excited mood. "We won! We won!" "We won what?" I asked in disbelief. He explained that he had just read a very brief article in the Japanese newspaper, the Asahi Shimbun, reporting that the authorities decided to withdraw their plans to move the incinerator from the old site to the proposed site in the middle of Nogawa Koen. Their position was carefully crafted obviously to save face. The boldface title of the article under the heading of the incinerator, Iten wa Toomen, Tooketsu, was vague but revealing to those of us involved in the issue. "The move (To Nogawa Koen) has temporarily been frozen." Both temporarily (Toomen) and frozen (Tooketzu) implied that the project was being delayed, not abandoned.

The details in the story were most revealing. Because of the growing opposition to the plan, it was decided to carry out a total reconstruction of the present incinerator over the next two years to accommodate the increase in garbage for the following ten years, precisely as we recommended from the beginning. At that time the city planned to reevaluate the necessity for a new incinerator with the tall chimneys. Reading between the lines, the plan to build a huge incinerator in the middle of Nogawa Koen had not been temporarily delayed or frozen. It had been essentially abandoned.

In retrospect, the meeting with the mayors two weeks earlier was their final attempt to get our cooperation by bluffing that they would no longer delay the project. Our response that we had just begun the struggle must have convinced them, as we intended, that the battle would continue and become even more aggressive. In reality we were also bluffing since we had few options not already pursued. The city of Tokyo backed down, not ICU. In effect we called their bluff. ICU had indeed won the battle to save Nogawa Koen. President Watanabe would have been pleased.

Shortly thereafter the Japan Times carried the following article.

Thanks to an aggressive citizens' protest effort organized by International Christian University, Tokyo's finest city park has been saved from senseless desecration, In mid-February, after 2 ½ years of struggle, the city backed down from erecting an incinerator with one-hundred meter high chimneys in the middle of Nogawa Park. City officials reluctantly decided to rebuild the old incinerator.

Now, looking back the chairman of the ICU committee to preserve Nogawa Park, Professor Benjamin Duke, views the original plan to move the incinerator with a wry sense of humor. One of the group's main purposes was to embarrass the Tokyo Metropolitan Government. "This is one of the finest city parks in the world," Duke pointed out. "We wanted to confront the city and say, how could you ever dream of doing this? We tried to make the protection of the park an international issue, " noted Duke. "Often gaiatsu" (external pressure), is most effective."

Finally, at the end of January, Tokyo officials met with Duke's committee. "We held our ground," said Duke, but one of the mayor's final pleas was "cooperate with us, we have no choice." "Our impression was that they were planning to barrel ahead with the plan," said Duke "They were very severe, very stern, when they turned and left."

Nearly twenty years have passed since the Japan Times article was carried. The city of Tokyo's announcement to temporarily freeze the plan to build the incinerator in the middle of Nogawa Koen for ten years masked a reality that could not be made public to save face amidst our successful attempt to shame them. During the intervening twenty years, no mention has been made of reconsidering the plan. I like to think that the Tokyo politicians and bureaucrats will never retrieve the proposal to build an incinerator in Nogawa Koen that could provoke ICU to launch a national and international campaign against it, as we did in 1989.

MEMOIR 30

CONDUCTING THE FIRST ICU STUDENT ORCHESTRA TOUR TO AMERICA

- FROM POMONA COLLEGE TO HARVARD UNIVERSITY –

The ICU student orchestra is a unique organization. Representatives elected by the members serve on committees that manage and finance its activities, which include a fall concert on campus and a spring concert at a public auditorium. Committees determine the western classical program and hire a director from among advanced graduate students enrolled in the course on orchestral directing at a school of music. They also set the fees that all members are subject to in order to cover expenses above ticket sales for the spring concert. Tickets are not required for the annual spring concert at the ICU Church.

When we first arrived at ICU in 1959 the orchestra, then under the name of the Chamber Music Society, was newly formed and struggling for its existence as the university entered its seventh year of operation. Few students participated and few people attended the yearly concert. The musical quality was very low. The director was chosen from among the students. We attended our first concert in 1960 deciding to forego the opportunity the following year.

By the 1970s the orchestra had decidedly improved. The number of students participating increased dramatically. We began to attend the concerts then offered twice each year. By that time a graduate student in orchestral directing at a conservatory was hired to handle the baton. By the 1990s we wouldn't miss a concert.

The 1990 concert performance was so impressive that I came away with a powerful motivation to have the orchestra tour American university campuses. Without thinking through the ramifications, I rashly asked the student steering committee to meet me in my office where I began the meeting with a very strong compliment on the recent concert. That set an amiable atmosphere that relaxed the students who were puzzled to be called to the office of an American faculty member unrelated to the ICU music program. I then immediately plunged into the purpose of the meeting. I told them the orchestra had attained such a high musical standard that it was time to conduct an American tour of university campuses.

The student officers were stunned. Their immediate reaction was curious in itself. They claimed that the orchestra was not good enough to perform before American university audiences. Although I had no evidence to support my response, I countered with the bold assertion that the ICU orchestra was better than 95% of all student orchestra in America not related to schools of music. They found that analysis unbelievable but fortunately did not ask for verification. I asked them to at least think it over. And then I made a commitment that I had not really thought through. If the orchestra decided to perform in America, I would take complete responsibility for conducting the tour. The students left my office far more puzzled than when they entered an hour earlier.

Two weeks later members of the steering committee asked to meet me again. By that time they had held a meeting of the full orchestra to relay my proposal. It provoked hours of discussion. After a long and sometimes heated debate, a consensus ultimately emerged. A special committee was formed to pursue the possibility of performing before American university audiences depending on the circumstances and costs. And of greatest significance, it was directed to work with me to develop an initial plan for the trip which all members of the orchestra would vote on. Fortunately the chairman of the committee was my own academic advisee, Kono Yutaka, who played trombone in the orchestra and with whom I had already developed a good relationship. The ball was now in my court.

I immediately sent out letters to the music departments of three American universities and colleges where ICU had developed especially close relations to get their reactions about a concert on their campuses in the spring of 1991. I specifically mentioned that if a tour could be arranged, I would need local assistance to arrange housing for our students with members of their student orchestras. The response from all three, that is, Pomona College and the University of California at Davis on the west coast and Harvard University on the east coast, was positive. Indeed the enthusiastic response from all three music departments stimulated me to pursue the project with determination.

Pomona College was chosen because of its status as one of the leading private liberal arts colleges in America, and because of our close relationship to Professor Curt Tong, Director of Physical Education, and former Visiting Professor at ICU. Harvard was chosen because the distinguished head of the ICU music department and close friend, Kanazawa Masakata, earned his doctorate in music from Harvard University and maintained a close relationship with the head of the music department. The University of California at Davis was contacted since ICU and UC Davis had already developed a very successful student exchange program.

I reported to the committee that these three institutions welcomed the proposal to hold a concert on their campuses and would assist with housing. The student president of the Harvard-Radcliff Orchestra even committed his members, over half of whom were Asian-Americans, to hosting the entire ICU orchestra with their students in the dorms. The committee members quickly called a meeting of the whole orchestra and voted overwhelmingly to approve the next step involving a concrete proposal with a projected budget. The die was cast. The word quickly spread on campus that the ICU Orchestra was going to America in the spring. Much to my surprise, the number of students in the all-volunteer orchestra jumped dramatically within the next several weeks from 85 to 110.

I then responded to the representatives from the music departments of the three American institutions informing them that the members of the ICU orchestra had approved of the tour and that we were now ready to work out the many details. With that a barrage of correspondence was unleashed between me and the three music departments concerning scheduling, housing, travel arrangements, and a host of peripheral issues required to take a hundred and ten students to America to perform three concerts from Pomona College in California to Harvard University in Massachusetts.

I was keen on arranging home stays for as many of the 110 student participants as possible. As Director of the American Studies Program at ICU, I felt a deep sense of responsibility to enable our students to experience life in America. With the invaluable assistance from Onishi Naoki, Assistant Director of American Studies, the plan was to house as many students with American students in the host orchestra as well as with local volunteer families who agreed to provide housing for our students.

I then approached the Southern California ICU Alumni Association, the largest and most active alumni organization in America, for assistance not only in arranging housing but for financial support. The members under their chairman, Owada Yasuyuki, currently Chairman of the Japan ICU Foundation Board of Trustees in New York, generously contributed many hours in planning arrangements for the Pomona concert as well as contributing $2,500 to help cover the expenses. His deep interest in our project grew out of his experiences as one of the first graduates of ICU in the 1950s, and as Assistant to the President of ICU in the '60s before joining the faculty of Johnston College, University of Redlands, where he became the Chancellor. The Owadas, in fact, were our neighbors on the ICU campus many years earlier.

I also took the opportunity to contact our dear friends, Jinx and Curt Tong at Pomona College, where Curt was Director of the Physical Education Department. As noted previously, Curt had been a Visiting Professor at ICU years earlier when he and wife Jinx established a close relationship with many faculty families including the Dukes. Not only did they enthusiastically welcome our visit as I anticipated, they committed themselves to help arrange the dorm and home visits. Beyond that commitment, however, Curt offered to provide buses from the Physical Education Department to transport our entire orchestra when necessary during the visit to Pomona. Curt even volunteered to drive one of the buses. I knew that I could count on the Tongs to make our visit to Pomona College a success.

It was decided early on by the students that the same program for the regularly scheduled spring concert at a public hall in Tokyo in 1991 would be performed on the tour. In other words all of the many rehearsals preparing for the annual concert in Japan would serve as preparation for the American tour. The student committee had already selected for the spring concert Wagner's Die Meistersinger von Numberg and Dvorak's 8th Symphony with its gorgeous melodies.

I was pleased with the selections for the American audiences. However I felt that there should be something 'Japanese' in the program by a Japanese university orchestra, even though it was designed strictly as a western classical organization in which the students took great pride. There was resistance to my proposal by many of the students. Nevertheless one of them came up with the suggestion to have the famous and melodic Japanese song Sakura (Cherry Blossom) arranged for a western classical orchestra by a Japanese arranger. With my most positive reaction, the students voted their approval and it was included in their budget to hire the arranger. Within a month an arrangement of Sakura for full orchestra was ready for rehearsal. It was decided that Sakura would be used as an encore.

There was one major problem. The arranger included critical sections in his piece that called for the use of traditional Japanese drums (wadaiko). When the student committee explained their predicament that the orchestra had no Japanese drums, I was stumped. However one of them had just learned that a student wadaiko club had recently been formed by several students who had taken a new course on the drums offered by the ICU physical education department. A set of Japanese drums for the course had recently been purchased by the department.

I immediately called the faculty member in physical education who was responsible for the course having agreed to advise the club, Mitsuhashi Ryoko. I explained our predicament and asked if we could borrow the drums for the spring concert in America. She replied that that would be impossible since the newly-formed club was planning to have its first training camp during the spring vacation when the concerts in America were scheduled.

I was stumped. Shortly thereafter I got an inspiration and called Mitsuhashi san again. I proposed that we take the new Waidaiko Club with us to perform in America with the orchestra. The drums could then be used for the club's performance as well as with the orchestra for the Sakura composition. Her immediate reply was that the club had just been formed and the members were definitely not ready to perform in America. Since we still had six months before the tour I urged her to reconsider the offer. I told her that the American audiences would not be aware that the club had just been formed. She was amused by my logic.

A week later, after she had notified the Wadaiko Club members of my proposal, they became so excited about going to America that they voted to accept my offer and to begin practicing immediately. Suddenly the number of students going to America jumped from 110 to 130, plus six Japanese drums added to all the instruments for 110 musicians. Because of the difficulty of transporting the bass violins, it was decided early on to rent six of them at each of the three concert sites to be paid for from the student budget.

I had one more proposal for the student committee. I had become acquainted with one of our senior students, Ueda Satoshi, who majored in humanities and who had become an accomplished pianist without attending a school of music. After hearing him practicing on one of the ICU pianos, I was so impressed that I asked him to give a concert in our home for faculty members on our new Kawai grand piano that I enjoyed playing in my spare time. We had arranged other 'Duke Home

Concerts' with student performances. Ueda's concert in our home was magnificently performed leaving an indelible image on my mind.

I proposed to the student committee that we take Ueda san to America with the orchestra and that he perform Grieg's famous piano concerto. The student committee was opposed to the idea on the grounds that Ueda was not part of the ICU Orchestra, and that to rehearse with a grand piano complicated matters in moving one in and out during rehearsals. But I remained adamant. Since the students by now had to rely completely on me to carry out the project, they agreed to give it a try by purchasing the arrangement and holding a rehearsal. After the first rehearsal with Ueda san, they voted to include him in the program. That, I assumed, completed the program for America.

Shortly thereafter the student committee surprised me with a proposal of its own. They wanted to buy an arrangement of The Stars and Stripes Forever to play as the final encore. They explained that they had four piccolo players who could handle the famous section devoted to piccolo for which the song is known. They also wanted to have all 110 members of the orchestra included in the final song of the performance. I thought that was a terrific idea. With that the orchestral program was set.

The one remaining issue concerned how to fit the Japanese Drum Club into the concert. Because of the physical problem of moving chairs as well as a grand piano on and off stage, I finally decided that the concert would begin with the drums. The concert would open with the curtain rising to a stage set with the drums in place. The student drummers appropriately dressed in costume would run out to their drums and the concert would begin for a twenty-minute wadaiko performance. The curtain would fall while the drums were removed from the stage and the chairs and stands for eighty-five musicians would be put in place for the Wagner piece. Following that, the grand piano would be wheeled in to place for the Grieg concerto. After an intermission when the piano was removed, the final part of the concert would feature the magnificent Dvorak symphony. Sakura and The Stars and Stripes completed the concert as the encore.

I needed faculty support with a contingent of 130 students. I asked the following to accompany the tour: Kanazawa Masakata, head of the ICU music department and a Harvard graduate, Mitsuhashi Ryoko, Advisor to the Wadaiko Club and a faculty member, Tim Winant, Dean of International Studies at ICU, and Onishi Naoki, faculty member in the American Studies program and ardent supporter of the proposal. They proved to be essential for a successful tour.

By the middle of February, 1991, plans for the American tour had been essentially completed. We were scheduled to leave for the United States on United Airlines on March 10 during the spring vacation at ICU. However an unexpected event of enormous consequence took place in world affairs at the beginning of 1991. In August of the previous year, Iraq under President Saddam Hussein had invaded neighboring Kuwait. In retaliation a coalition of nations led by the United States launched an aerial attack on Baghdad on January 17, 1991. On February 23 President George H. W. Bush ordered a massive military attack on Iraq dubbed Operation Desert Storm to overthrow the Hussein government. The Gulf War was underway. It was, of course, given major prominence in the Japanese media. A significant sector of the Japanese society was critical of the military invasion.

Although the Middle East was thrown into chaos, I had no concern that it could influence the American tour. I completed all the plans for the orchestra to depart for the United States two weeks after the invasion of Iraq led by American military forces. However a day after the invasion was launched I was informed by the chairman of the student committee, my advisee Kono san, that parents of two members of the orchestra in the violin section had decided not to allow them to make the trip to America. They had become concerned that planes by American airlines both to and from America and within the United States could become targets of Muslim terrorists who deeply resented the invasion of a Muslim country by a Christian country.

I was taken by complete surprise. I never thought about the possibility of a terrorist downing an American airliner as a result of the invasion of Iraq. I did not take it seriously especially since there were thirty-five violinists in the orchestra. I figured the two dropouts were expendable.

The word quickly spread among the students that two members of the orchestra had withdrawn because of parental opposition to the tour to America as a result of the Gulf War. Suddenly several more members notified the officers of the orchestra that their parents had decided not to allow them to participate in the tour. I then became concerned that this could become serious. By the time the invasion of Iraq ended with a military withdrawal after Baghdad was captured and Hussein fled, which all took place by February 28, the number of students who notified the officers of the orchestra that they would not be able to participate in the tour had reached a critical level.

Ten days before the scheduled departure, a majority of the oboe, bassoon, flute, and horn sections had withdrawn in addition to some from the other larger sections. We held many frantic meetings trying to figure out how to handle the crisis with which we were suddenly confronted. The majority of the students were willing to fly on an American flight but understood the position of those who were not, or were compelled to withdraw because of parental opposition. With the greatest reluctance we concluded that we had no recourse but to cancel the tour since the defections were increasing.

I immediately notified all those who had worked so closely with me in America that due to circumstances beyond our control, the tour would be cancelled. To my great relief, the reaction by our American colleagues was one of deep regret but of understanding. America was at war and extraordinary consequences were understandable. I concluded my notification to soften the blow that we all hoped that the tour could be scheduled for another year.

A major concern was the reaction of United Airlines since firm reservations had been made for 130 students and five faculty members. I met with the head of the Tokyo office, a Japanese, who graciously understood our situation and agreed to cancel the reservations without any penalty. That was a tremendous relief. I assured UAL that if the tour is scheduled for another year, United Airlines would again be designated as The Official Airline of the Tour. With that, the 1991 concert tour to America by the ICU orchestra came to an unexpected ending before it began.

And now the rest of the story . . .

By the beginning of the April 1991 semester at ICU, the Gulf War had been effectively ended. There had been no terrorist threat to American airliners. Sometime later a committee of students from the orchestra came to my office to ask me to consider the possibility of arranging the tour to America during the spring vacation of 1992. Under the circumstances, and based on my experience of the previous year, I once again agreed to conduct the tour. To make a long story short, all of the arrangements were made for the tour to take place in the spring of 1992 as originally planned for the spring of 1991.

The students had the following program printed in Japan for the 1992 tour.

PROGRAM

Tuesday, March 10, 8 PM   Wednesday, March 18, 8 PM
Pomona College   U.C. Davis
Sunday, March 15, 8 PM
Harvard University
Japanese Drums

Festival Songs   K. Suenaga
Umi no Taiko – Drums of the Sea   K. Suenaga

Prelude to First Act "Die meistersinger von Nurnberg   R. Wagner
Piano Concerto in A Minor, Op. 16   E. Grieg

INTERMISSION

Symphony No. 8 in G Major, Op. 88   A. Dvorak

I took the opportunity to invite Michael Armacost, U. S. Ambassador to Japan and former Visiting Professor at ICU, to write a note for the program, which he kindly did. Since he lived two houses down from our house on campus during his year on the faculty, I knew Michael well enough to ask him for the favor. I also contacted the new Japanese Ambassador to the United States, Kuriyama Takakazu, whose wife was an ICU graduate, for a statement for the program. He promptly submitted one.

Finally I invited United States Senator John Rockefeller IV to write a note for the program. A former student at ICU, he readily complied with the following statement along with a picture. It should be noted that his comments included a most revealing assessment of the influence that his experience at ICU had on his personal development.

I welcome the ICU symphony orchestra on its America tour. My years at ICU were probably the three most important of my life in terms of my own development. ICU opened my eyes to Japan and to the world beyond my own experience. ICU gave me the chance to understand Japan, its language and its people at a time (1957-1960) when very few American citizens were making that effort. For many reasons ICU is a fundamental part of my life. This tour will be an exciting event for the orchestra members and all of us in the United States connected to ICU.

I wrote the following statement as Director of the tour that summed up my commitment to the orchestra.

As director of American Studies at ICU, and the initiator of this first concert tour to the United States by our student orchestra, I am delighted that it has reached a formal stage of performance. Several years ago I became convinced that this volunteer association of like-minded students who loved classical music so deeply had a musical level worthy of a concert tour to the United States. As one who has enjoyed the ICU orchestra concerts for so many years, it is my deep pleasure and great satisfaction to have worked with the students in carrying out this tour. I feel that I have, in a small way, repaid them for the enjoyment that I have received from them through my own love of classical music that we mutually appreciate.

Finally the president of the orchestra, Shimakawa Takeshi, a senior at the time, wrote the following statement for the program.

On behalf of all the members of this orchestra, I would like to thank you all for coming to our concert this evening. We originally planned to make our first concert tour to the United States in March 1991. However it was regrettably cancelled at the last moment as a result of the Gulf War. We all feel very fortunate that we finally are able to carry out this ambitious project. It is our wish that this performance will serve as a bridge of understanding between your country and ours. We hope that through this music we will be able to communicate the joy we experience in playing the great classics. It is our desire to convey to you how much this music stirs our hearts, as we hope it does yours. We hope that you will remember this concert, as we will, as a period of mutual enjoyment.

The tour to America was a great success. Upon returning to Japan I wrote an article for the Japan Times carried in the April 26, 1992 edition under the title of American Colleges Welcome ICU Student Orchestra. The final part summarized our experience.

Looking back on our three concerts in the States, there is only one way to describe the reaction by the American audiences to the ICU orchestra. Perhaps the Japanese expression, daiseiko, a great success, fits most appropriately. At each of the 3 universities, the audiences responded with long standing ovations. The reaction to the opening

Japanese drum team was overwhelming. And the pianist Ueda san played brilliantly receiving a standing ovation at all three concerts. But with the final encore, when 110 members launched into the old sentimental favorite, the Stars and Stripes Forever, the audiences could not contain themselves.

All in all, the response of the American university audiences to our music went far beyond our hopes and expectations. Our students were simply overwhelmed by the reaction they received on American campuses. But the home stays and dorm stays were equally rewarding both to the guests and the hosts as well. For example the French horn player of the San Francisco orchestra specifically asked for a horn player from our orchestra as his house guest. They had much to talk about. This aspect of the program also far exceeded our expectations. As our student chairman repeated again and again, "I can't believe our hosts would do so much for us." Before the decision to carry out this tour, we were all aware of what some consider a temporary period of strained relations between Japan and the United States. Reports of American workers hammering Japanese cars, and even physical threats to Japanese Americans, could not be dismissed. However, our Japanese students handled themselves both on and off the stage with great composure as well as eager friendliness. And our American hosts responded to them with unrestricted hospitality.

If ever there was an opportunity to enhance mutual relations between the United States and Japan, the 1992 ICU orchestra tour to America proved to be an outstanding example.

MEMOIR 31

NIGHTMARE ON MT. OYAMA

- JUNE'S PIGGYBACK DESCENT WITH TWO BROKEN LIMBS -

I n late October, l995, we decided to hike up Mt. Oyama in Kanagawa Prefecture, well over two hours from ICU by train and bus in those days. A member of my weekly seminar at Keidanran, Mr. Yamamoto Yasashi, Vice President of Kiren Beer, had gone halfway up Mt. Oyama by cable car a week earlier and highly recommended the trip to us because of the great views of the Kanto Plain. We appreciated the recommendation since over the years at ICU we had become ardent mountain hikers in a land where hiking is one of the great pastimes of the people, and understandably so. Geographies of the country invariably characterize Japan as a mountainous country. And indeed it is with only 14% of the land level enough for people to live on. That explains in part the necessity for the Japanese to live in close proximity to each other, and why real estate prices are unbelievably high.

The magnificent Japanese mountains are readily accessible to everyone. For example, the appropriately named Japanese Northern and Southern Alps that traverse the main island of Honshu are within an hour's train ride from the Kanto Plain, home to millions of Japanese living in the Tokyo-Yokohama megatropolis. In the midst of that great span of mountains, Mt. Fuji rises majestically and most visibly from our living room window just 60 miles away in Tokyo.

As a result of the accessibility of mountains to all Japanese no matter where they live, and the citing of thousand of temples and shrines on mountain peaks attracting worshippers, millions of Japanese have become mountain hikers. Accordingly they have laid out thousands of hiking trails that cover the country from north to south and east to west. In particular, as can be imagined, the glorious mountain ranges near Tokyo are blanketed with hiking trails that are not only well marked but widely publicized with detailed maps available. As a result Tokyoites have an amazing choice of hiking trails within an hour or so from home, many of which include spectacular views of Mt. Fuji. Among them, Takao San (Mt. Takao) has been climbed by virtually every Japanese child brought up in Tokyo on one day field trips conducted by their elementary schools, which included our three children several times during their Osawadai school days. All six paths up Takao San are full of excited, and very noisy, kids nearly every spring day.

We were first introduced to hiking in Japan after arriving in the country when my graduate students invited us to join them for a farewell party for a colleague on top of Mount Fuji in the summer of 1960, described in an earlier memoir. From then on we began a regular routine of hiking on the many trails accessible by train from ICU. Among them was our plan in October, 1995, to hike up 6,000 ft. Mount Oyama.

The path we chose was estimated to take between three to four hours to reach the top from the bus stop. The first two hours were uneventful although several sections of the path were steep and slippery from recent rains. But we had no particular concern about the conditions. There were, however, many rocks and boulders that you had to walk over or climb around. Climbing conditions got worse as we continued upwards. Nevertheless we were determined to get to the top for lunch and hopefully take an easier path down.

We finally reached the top of Mt. Oyama at 12:30. The views in all directions were tremendous. We ate our lunch and concluded that the ordeal getting there was worth it. Surprisingly there were only a few people at the top on a weekday afternoon.

Since we had to get off the mountain before dusk, which set in around 5 o'clock at that time of the year, we started down a different path at 2 o'clock. Others told us that this path was easier than the direct route straight up that we had taken. But even the longer path turned out to be quite steep in places with narrow sections strewn by roots sticking out of the ground. We walked for an hour without meeting anyone.

While carefully maneuvering through a particularly steep section that had become slippery from earlier rains, I heard a scream from June who was following me down. I instantly turned to find her slumped on the ground where she had fallen after losing her step on a steep slippery curve. She was holding her left arm up in pain. I immediately realized that we had a serious problem since her hand was bent out of place. I suspected that she had broken her arm or wrist since her hand was pointing in a slightly different direction from the arm. Although deeply concerned, I didn't mention it in order not to frighten her further since she was obviously in severe pain. I tried to console her.

After about ten minutes, and realizing that the sky was getting a bit darker with an increasing cloud cover, I told June that we must get started again or we'll get caught on the mountainside after dark. I figured we had at least two more hours to reach the bottom. I also realized that no other climber had come up or down our path for the last half hour or so. We were alone about half way down the 6,000-foot mountain.

June's response brought me to a gripping sense of reality. She said she couldn't walk due to the intense pain in her right leg. "We have to move." "I can't move." I knew that we were in very serious trouble. I couldn't possibly carry her down that steep path and I couldn't leave her to try and get help because she was getting dizzy with pain. I hadn't a clue what to do. It was a nightmare.

Just about that time I heard voices coming from the path above us. At last someone was coming down behind us. It turned out to be a Japanese couple in their early twenties who were taken by surprise by what they had come across. When I explained the situation, and they could see that June's hand was out of place, the young fellow said we should lift her up and try helping her down the mountain. He got under one arm and I the other and we gingerly brought her to her feet. She began to hop on her one good leg and we started down. But it was so slow and painful that this Japanese hiker, who weighed about 130 pounds, instructed me to put June on his back. He'll carry her down the mountain piggyback-style. I couldn't believe that he was serious.

We had no choice. His female companion and I lifted June up on the back of this courageous Japanese. It was an unforgettable sight with an American woman, her left hand bent in the wrong direction, hanging tightly on to the back of a small Japanese man halfway down the side of Mt. Oyama on a Friday afternoon in the fall of 1995. Off he went slowly and carefully down the slippery path. As I looked at his small legs I envisioned him slipping with the two of them sprawling on the ground. But he seemed confident and I was grateful and relieved that we were at last moving down the mountain as the clouds began rolling in.

About every forty yards or so our new Japanese friend stopped to catch his breath when we lifted June off his back for a short break. After several stops his clothes were dripping with sweat. On one break he mentioned that he had a car at the bottom of the mountain and would take us to the nearest hospital in Atsugi, indicating that he would get us down for sure. It was reassuring.

Just then we met a middle-aged hiker dressed in mountain-climbing attire coming up the mountain. He saw our predicament and told us he had medicine, to put June down, and to take off her shoe and sock of the injured leg. He opened up his backpack and there was a full assortment of medicinal supplies. I asked him if he was a doctor. He explained that he wasn't. However on one of his many hikes he fell and injured his head. He decided never again to go hiking without a full medicine pack. What luck to meet such a seasoned climber on a lonely trail with a seriously injured person.

He reached in his backpack and pulled out a plastic box full of medicinal supplies fortunately including ace bandages. He applied ointment on the swollen leg. He then mixed some pain-killing medicine with water for June to drink. The Japanese woman suddenly came up with the idea of using chopsticks, which she carried for their lunch, to apply on June's wrist as a splint. An ace bandage was wrapped around the wrist which held the chopsticks firmly in place so that the hand was now at least stabilized. I thanked the second hiker profusely and off we went again with June hanging tightly on to the back of her Japanese carrier with her good right arm.

After what seemed like a never-ending nightmare, and with June in constant pain the whole time, we finally arrived at the parking lot at the bottom of the mountain. Our Japanese savior was by then soaked from head to foot and totally exhausted from the ordeal, but in high spirits over his remarkable accomplishment. We were able to get June into the back seat of his car where she sat quietly in a daze. It was now around 5:30, darkness was setting in, and we got caught up in rather heavy traffic as we neared the city of Atsugi, well known for the large American airbase located nearby.

By that time we had decided not to go to a local hospital since we didn't have our national medical card required for treatment with us. It would be quite a hassle without it. Rather, we decided to try to get to the Red Cross Hospital located close to ICU where we often go for medical treatment. Our Japanese friend agreed to drop us off at the Atsugi train station.

Since we were caught in the evening traffic moving along slowly, I finally had an opportunity to ask our new friends who they were and why he was so confident that he could carry June down the mountain on his back. His story revealed it all. He and his girl friend had graduated from the Yokohama National University the previous year in physical education. He was in his first year of teaching. During the four years at the university he played on the varsity soccer team that carried on a tradition of high performance. The practice sessions were particularly grueling in which every player had to carry a teammate on his back the length of the field several times alternately, not only to strengthen the leg muscles but to build up endurance capability. He knew that he could carry June, who weighed less than his average teammate, particularly going downhill. As a physical education teacher, he kept in good shape with a regimen of daily exercises.

I was overwhelmed by the story. I wondered what the odds were that in the dangerous situation we were in halfway down Mt. Oyama, we would not only meet a Japanese who carried a full medical pack but another Japanese who had been trained to carry a human being on his back. I couldn't help but think that of all the Japanese in the land, we would encounter one with an unusual physical capability and endurance which was exactly what we needed. I shutter to think what we would have done if that particular Japanese had not come along the mountain path at that exact moment.

But the nightmare was not yet over. It took an hour to get to the train station where the couple left us for the long drive home to Yokohama. From then on June and I were alone. June hopped on one leg with my assistance to the train, a local to Tachikawa station on the main Chuo line to Tokyo. It was a single-track line so we had to stop for several minutes at each station until the train coming the other way arrived. June was in a daze in part from the ordeal and perhaps also as a result of her pain-killing medicine. At the huge Tachikawa train station I called daughter Kim, who was staying with us while teaching that year at the American School in Japan, to get to the Red Cross Hospital with our medical card and wait with a wheel chair at the taxi stop to take June to the emergency center.

We finally arrived at the hospital at nine o'clock. At last we could breathe a sigh of relief. It had taken over six hours to get from the site of the accident to the hospital. Kim was there and wheeled June, now completely numb from it all, into the emergency center. X-rays were taken but the orthopedic doctor was in surgery. Another hour delay. Finally the doctor read the x-rays to discover that both the left wrist and the right ankle were broken. He then put a cast on each. We got to our home at ICU at midnight. The nightmare on Mt. Oyama was finally over.

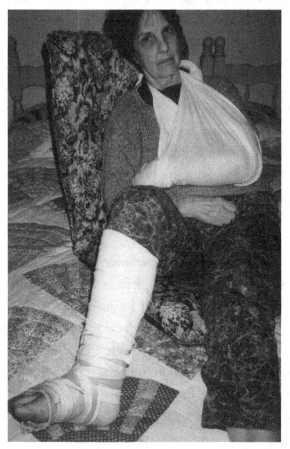

June with two broken limbs

MEMOIR 32

THE YOUNG MOMIJI (MAPLE) TREES ON THE ICU CAMPUS

- A SECRET REVEALED -
(ICU Gazette, December 14, 1995)

We have just experienced another glorious momiji foliage season at ICU. Many people from off campus came to enjoy the gorgeous reds and yellows of the maple trees located throughout the campus. But few people either from ICU or otherwise are aware of the origin of the hundreds of younger momiji trees. That has been an unintentional secret known by only a few during the past decade. It's time to reveal the secret of the young momiji on the campus.

It actually began in 1966 when our family moved from the old East Grove Apartment House to the campus home number 346. That house was originally the home of Dr. and Mrs. Maurice Troyer. Dr. Troyer was the first Vice President for Academic Affairs who retired from ICU in l966. He moved back to America and we moved into that splendid house, our first experience in a private residence on campus.

One of the features of the early campus houses was an open fireplace. We were determined to use the fireplace in our new home not only to provide extra heat and reduce the enormous costs of heating the spacious house with extremely expensive kerosene. We also wanted to enjoy the cozy atmosphere of a live fire burning in our living room during the winter months. I began building a fire in the fireplace every morning as soon as we got up. We kept it burning most of the day until we went to bed at night. We thoroughly enjoyed our fireplace. And so did the many students who came to our home for 'open house.' They loved the atmosphere of a fire burning in the living room.

Anyone who has ever used a fireplace is well aware of the problem of keeping a constant supply of firewood. Since we used the fireplace from morning till night throughout the winter, we needed an enormous supply of firewood each week. Luckily there was dead wood all around us on the ICU campus covered by trees that made perfect firewood.

The problem was how to collect the dead wood on campus and bring it to the house. That was done with the help of our young children, Noriko Susan, Kimiko Anne and Christopher Kenji. We searched all over the campus for dead trees lying on the ground, cut them up into smaller pieces, piled them on the wheelbarrow, and brought them back to the house to be stacked around the back of the house.

There was also a supply of dead trees still standing. When we ran out of wood on the ground we cut down the dead trees. That gave us a good supply of firewood throughout the winter months while keeping the woods clear of dead trees. Each winter we used about twenty or more dead trees for firewood from throughout the campus. Working with our children to bring in the firewood was also great fun.

About ten years ago when I got the idea of starting the ICU Campus Environment Committee, I realized that although we were using about twenty dead trees each year for firewood , we were not replacing them. I then decided that for every dead tree we cut up for firewood, we should replace each of them with a live tree. But the problem was what kind of tree and where would we get them.

One day while walking through the campus woods behind the home where Dr. and Mrs. Kidder lived, I noticed many small momiji saplings growing tightly together in one area. That gave me the solution to replacing the dead trees. We'll use the small momiji samplings growing right here on campus. In other words we could simply transplant them from one area of the campus to another, and at no cost. So the first year we did just that. Whenever we found a dead tree for firewood, we dug up a momiji sapling behind the Kidder house and planted it in the same place where we found the dead tree.

The first year we transplanted a total of 25 momiji saplings. The following year another 25 were transplanted from behind the Kidder's house to different parts of the campus, replacing the dead trees we cut down or those blown down by the annual typhoons. Then we began planting them along the walkways in front of the dormitories as well as along some of the roads in appropriate places. I felt we were improving the campus environment and began to take pride in the work every springtime increasing the number of sapling transplants each year.

The saplings were easy to dig out of the ground and easy to transport in the basket on the back of my bicycle. We did the work during late Sunday afternoons when few people were walking on campus. Once the former Manager of the Buildings and Grounds, Mr. Takahashi, came riding by on his bike. As one can imagine, he was surprised to see me digging in the ground in back of Maple Grove and asked me what I was doing. So I explained. Although looking a bit perplexed, all he said was "Soo desu ka," and rode on. I interpreted his response as an approval from the official in charge of the campus grounds so I continued replacing the dead trees with live samplings over the years.

Last year during the momiji season I realized that my maple saplings were no longer saplings. In fact the earliest transplants were by now three or even four meters tall. And their color was becoming quite noticeable. Out of curiosity I decided to count them. Much to my amazement, the number came to over 400.

Within ten years into the 21st Century, the ICU campus may become as famous for its momiji trees, and the splendid colors of the late autumn season, as the magnificent cherry blossoms along the main entrance in the spring. Many who will enjoy those gorgeous fall scenes on the ICU campus in the 21st Century, when all of the momiji trees finally reach their full size, will not know the origin of the 400 samplings that were transplanted from one part of the campus to another in the latter half of the 20th Century. Those of you who read this will.

MEMOIR 33

CHAIRING THE ICU FACULTY MEETING
FOR EIGHT YEARS

- ROBERT'S RULES VS CONSENSUS -

T he ICU faculty is a unique combination of Japanese and non-Japanese scholars from many countries. Japanese make up from 70 to 80 percent depending upon the period. Among the non-Japanese faculty members, about half come from America. The remainder originate from, among others, Armenia, Australia, Britain, Canada, Germany, France, Korea, and the Philippines.

The Japanese are usually long-term faculty members with tenure from the beginning of their contract. The non-Japanese vary from long-term such as myself who spend their academic career at ICU, and short-term faculty who range from one year or less as Visiting Professor or Guest Professor, to three years as the initial period required for tenure.

ICU prides itself as an international university not only in the composition of faculty and students, but also in the language of the classroom. The institution is bilingual. Japanese faculty teach in Japanese. Non-Japanese, regardless of nation of origin, teach in English. This policy places great emphasis on preparing Japanese students to take some of their courses in English, and non-Japanese students, other than junior-year abroad students, to take a fair amount of their courses in

Japanese in order to graduate. It does not require non-Japanese faculty to speak Japanese or Japanese faculty to speak English, although the vast majority of the Japanese do so at an impressive level.

One of the problems of this arrangement from the beginning of ICU was the working language of the faculty meeting. When I first joined the faculty in 1959, there were about fifteen non-Japanese and thirty Japanese on the faculty. Few of the non-Japanese were sufficiently capable in Japanese to conduct business of the faculty meeting in Japanese.

A workable solution emerged with all non-Japanese regardless of their nationality, and those Japanese faculty capable in English, and most were, using English at the meeting. Some Japanese spoke first in English and then repeated their thought in Japanese. Several were so adept that they incorporated their ideas into a combination of Japanese and English in the same sentence so that the listener could understand the content whether Japanese or non-Japanese. I was not affected by that problem. As the youngest member of the faculty dominated by senior scholars, I did not say a word at the meeting for the first several years, never imaging that someday I would serve as chairman.

Faculty Meeting when I joined it (far left rear)

The chairman of the faculty meeting when I arrived was the Vice President for Academic Affairs. However, in the reaction to the crisis of the student uprisings in the 1960s, when the faculty meeting could not function properly as divisions among us developed over how to react to the periodic occupations of academic buildings by students, a committee was appointed by the president to reform the faculty meeting itself. Among the members appointed to the committee were my close divisional colleague, Nakano Terumi, and myself.

Nakano san and I presented a reform proposal on the management of the faculty meeting to adopt Robert's Rules of Order as the method for conducting the meeting. Until that time there was no official procedure governing the decision-making process of the faculty. In a non-controversial setting, the method at arriving at a decision was not tested. Controversy threw the meeting into uncharted territory that proved unworkable in times of crises.

Our second proposal concerned the process of selecting the chairman of the faculty meeting. At that time the Vice President for Academic Affairs automatically served as chairman. Under our proposal, the faculty elected the presiding officer by a simple majority. In addition, since the faculty chairman came under heavy pressure during the student crises, our proposal introduced a system of co-chairmen to include a Japanese and a non-Japanese presiding alternately over the bimonthly meetings conducted in Japanese or English. The co-chairman not presiding served as the parliamentarian in determining the proper application of Robert's Rules of Order.

At that time, however, a translation system was installed in the faculty meeting room. From then on both Japanese and English could be used with a simultaneous translator providing the alternate language to those who needed it through an earphone. That action greatly speeded up the meeting.

Our proposal was approved by the faculty meeting and implemented from 1972. With non-Japanese numbering around twenty by then, those with most seniority were inevitably drawn into the nominating process for the non-Japanese co-chairmanship. The first one voted to the position was my good friend and senior colleague, Ted Kidder. However for some reason he had to be absent during one semester of his term. As an associate professor with twelve years on the faculty, I was elected to serve as the non-Japanese co-chairman during his absence.

In 1974 I was elected as co-chairman when Ted became a member of the administration. From then on until retirement, I served as co-chairman for a total of eight years, far longer than any other faculty member, Japanese or non-Japanese. That record has stood the test of time.

When my first adventure at chairing the ICU faculty meeting was about to begin, I borrowed a copy of Robert's Rules of Order from the library to make certain that I understood the provisions. Since I was instrumental in proposing that Robert's Rules govern the conduct of the faculty meeting, I now had the responsibility to make sure they were applied properly as the presiding officer. By the time I called the ICU faculty meeting to order for the first time, I was prepared to conduct the meeting according to commonly accepted procedures outlined by Robert's Rules. I soon learned that some of my Japanese colleagues were not.

My basic understanding of Robert's Rules of Order was that every faculty member should have the opportunity to present motions before the meeting for a faculty vote, and that every member who wishes to do so should have the right to give an opinion on the merits of any motion that has been seconded. I particularly wanted to have both sides to motions that involved controversial elements make their positions, and the ramifications thereof, clear before calling for the vote. I encouraged as many faculty members as possible to participate in the deliberations.

Monthly faculty meetings normally ran two to three hours long beginning late afternoon following the day's classes. When a motion reached the floor involving a controversial issue, not infrequently related to a personnel matter, I was usually aware of the possibility that it would require more time than usual. In other words I was mindful of the issue and the timing that would be required to arrive at a decision. The challenge for me as chairman was to make sure that all sides of the issue were made clear in a reasonable amount of time before calling for the vote. It did not always transpire that way.

The problem arose during meetings that involved a controversial issue when I, as chairman, felt that all sides of the motion had been presented and that time was being wasted with the same views being repeated. Although the faculty may have been divided, the time to vote had arrived. At that moment, according to Robert's Rules, I called for the vote. "Are you ready to vote on this motion?" Not infrequently the response was a chorus of 'No!" I then reluctantly continued with further discussion of the motion.

The first time I was confronted with the problem of bringing the faculty to a vote on a controversial issue according to Robert's Rules, I realized the reason for the reluctance of many members to vote. The Japanese faculty, reflecting a cultural trait that places emphasis on arriving at a consensus before decisions are made preserving a sense of harmony, balked at making a decision when a consensus was clearly not yet achieved. In that case the sense of the meeting was to continue the deliberations or postpone the vote. The latter provided an opportunity for those sponsoring the motion and those opposing it to arrive at a consensus behind the scene, nemawashi-style, by either revising the motion or applying enough pressure on a sufficient number of faculty to assure that the motion would comfortably pass a vote at the next meeting.

As I recall the details nearly twenty-five years later, one of the most divisive motions that I encountered as chairman of the faculty meeting took place in 1987. It remains vividly in my memory as an example of how Robert's Rules conflicted with the desire for consensus among the Japanese faculty members. It concerned the motion presented by the head of the International Division, who happened to also be my Japanese co-chairman of the faculty meeting that academic year, to approve a candidate to fill the vacant post in diplomatic history.

The candidate was an American with considerable experience as an academic recommended by his professor, a leading authority on Japan then heading the Japanese Department at a premier American university. The credentials were very impressive including a doctoral thesis on the Japanese Self Defense Forces. It appeared as a routine motion when first placed before the meeting with a rather thick packet of supporting materials.

As faculty chairman I was prepared to move expeditiously on the motion when a Japanese faculty member in an unrelated division posed a question about a statement in the candidate's employment record. He noted that the candidate had worked for several years with the American CIA, the Counter Intelligence Agency. He then asked this question. "Was the candidate a spy for the American government? If so, would it be appropriate to have him on the ICU faculty?"

That response set off a buzz throughout the faculty. The sponsor of the motion, who had not anticipated such a sensitive question, could not answer yes or no without asking the candidate's professor the awkward question whether his student was a former spy. Others began to question the candidate's appropriateness for the position. Some wanted to know more about the candidate's relationship with the Japanese military. I could see that the meeting was getting out of hand. There was no possibility that I could then call for a vote according to Robert's Rules. The deliberations continued for nearly two hours when the sponsor of the motion, sensing a consensus developing against it, withdrew the motion. The meeting was adjourned without any action.

The following faculty meeting was convened by the Japanese co-chairman. However, when the time came to take up personnel matters, the chairman announced that he was presenting a motion and would turn the meeting over to me to handle the deliberations. As the original sponsor of the motion to fill the diplomatic history post, he presented the same candidate for faculty approval. He therefore could not chair the deliberations on his own motion.

In his presentation, he explained that the CIA is responsible for the spying activities of the American government. However, it was pointed out, the CIA employs many recognized scholars as analysts. Since it was felt that to question the integrity of one of the most distinguished American scholars on Japanese studies whether his student was a spy would bring embarrassment to the university, it should be assumed that his candidate was an analyst. Otherwise, it was reasoned, the American professor who had close ties to ICU would not have recommended his student for the post. The motion to approve the candidate was again placed before the faculty meeting as the most qualified applicant for the opening.

As before, the comment about the possible spy connection set off a barrage of questioning that continued late into the night. Finally amidst a heated debate, one of the senior Japanese faculty members sitting in the front row quietly nudged his chair to the chairman's table and asked in a whisper, "Ben. This could go on forever. How can we end the meeting?" I quickly looked over my chart of motions under Robert's Rules of Order and spotted the provision on "motion to adjourn the meeting with no debate or amendment." I replied in a whisper that he could say, when recognized by me, that, "I move to adjourn the meeting. A vote would be taken immediately without debate." His response: "Really?"

He returned to his place and waited for a speaker to end his comments. He immediately raised his hand. I called upon him over others with raised hands since he had not spoken on the motion as yet. He made a motion to adjourn the meeting. I announced that a vote would be taken immediately on the motion without debate or amendment. That caused an uproar since few members knew the intricacies of Robert's Rules. I reminded the meeting that Robert's Rules had been approved by the faculty meeting and then read the exact clause in the regulations governing the motion to adjourn the meeting without debate or amendment. The vote was taken amidst some confusion. A large majority approved, partly to close the long meeting nearing midnight, as well as to return home for a very late dinner.

During the following week the sponsor of the proposal, my fellow co-chairman, decided that a consensus in favor of his candidate to teach diplomatic history could not be achieved in the faculty meeting. He reluctantly notified the candidate and his professor of the decision. The matter had been resolved without a vote. Robert's Rules of Orders in the western-style had been carefully followed. In the process, however, a consensus in the Japanese-style prevailed. It exemplified the process of decision-making at ICU.

MEMOIR 34

A PASSION FOR KABUKI

- TERAKOYA AND THE ULTIMATE ACT OF LOYALTY -

During our many years at ICU we gradually developed a deep and abiding passion for the Kabuki theater. It did not come easily. Performances that last four hours, often with interminable conversations, require endurance beyond imagination. Dialogue between two male actors in female roles sitting on a tatami floor that not uncommonly continues for twenty minutes or more in falsetto voices taxes one's patience to the fullest. And during dance routines when the performer suddenly stops and stares off in space at a precise moment in the routine, provoking applause and outbursts of vocal appreciation among the audience, strains one's sense of credulity to the maximum.

And yet we grew to greatly appreciate not only the magnificent costumes, the elaborate scenery, and the clever stage maneuvers, but also the themes that ran throughout virtually every play written and originally performed during the samurai era of Japan from the early 1600s to the late 1800s. Among them was the enduring act of loyalty through sacrifice that resonates throughout Japanese society to this very day. The play which poignantly portrays the act of loyalty to one's lord or master is entitled simply Terakoya, the cherished temple school for the common folk of the samurai era, often dubbed the village school.

Before reviewing the Terakoya and its underlying theme of loyalty and sacrifice, the routine we experienced in attending the Kabuki plays and dances in the old venerable Kabukiza Theater just off the Ginza in downtown Tokyo was an adventure in itself. Before arriving at the entrance, we bought an obento for lunch for the 11:30 AM to 3:30 PM performance, or for the evening performance from 4:30 to 8:30. In a truly incredible act of timing and staging, the two daily performances unrelated to each other that run for nearly an entire month typically include two dances and a lengthy play each, such as the Terakoya in the morning and the well known Forty-Seven Ronin in the afternoon. The two plays require a complete change of scenery and cast within the one hour interlude from 3:30 to 4:30.

Depending on the play, one chooses either the morning or afternoon performance. Both performances require an obento, a small wooden box of cold rice, cold vegetables, and cold pieces of chicken and/or fish. There are many obento shops near the Kabukiza that cater to the Kabuki enthusiasts that fill the theater for nearly every performance throughout each month.

Thirty minutes before show time with obento in hand, one lines up at the entrance to the magnificent Kabukiza Theater decorated with chochin, colorful lanterns strung along the upper level of the theater. Few other scenes in the glittering metropolis of modern Tokyo remind the contemporary Japanese of the old Japan as does the Kabukiza Theater in the evening when the chochin are lit up. Another world comes alive both on the outside and the inside of the Kabukiza.

Upon entering the theater, the first place most non-Japanese head for is the desk where earphones are available for rent ($6) to hear excellent English translation of the plays. Curiously, nearly all the translators have British accents. One trend that we witnessed over the years is the increasing numbers of Japanese who rent earphones to listen to a version of the plays in modern Japanese since much of the dialogue originates from an earlier period using stylized accents and diction. The earphones are color-coded to identify the language. The English translations are so complete that a full understanding of the plays is available at a reasonable price.

Kabukiza is a large theater with three floors that survived the devastating air raids of World war 11 that destroyed much of Tokyo. It has an old classical look about it as it should. The stage is huge extending about twenty-five meters wide, fifteen high, and fifteen deep. It's marked by a large round section of the stage which rotates to change scenery when one scene rolls around to the rear exposing the next scene within ten or fifteen seconds. The stage is also marked with several escape hatches when the floor opens and a performer disappears, or rises from below the stage to enter the scene, always amidst great applause since virtually everyone knows the routine.

For dances accompanied by the shamisen, the Chinese flute, and the small Japanese drums that are struck with the hand, there may be five or up to twenty or more musicians lined up across the full stage in the rear sitting on a low platform. The background is often painted with cherry trees frequently with blossoms falling softly on the stage for the entire routine. It's usually a breathtaking panorama when the huge curtain opens.

For certain plays, however, the curtain may open to a simple room of a peasant house. With that background one can expect long and tedious dialogues between two or more peasants commiserating over their lowly status in life. Or it may be two or more samurai bearing swords hatching some plot amidst the ever-shifting alliances among warlords.

Around 12:30 of the morning performance and 5:30 of the afternoon performance, usually after the first dance, as the splendid curtain with the famous Kabuki colors of rust, gold, and green close, a light flashes at the side of the stage. The figure 25 denotes a 25-minute break to eat. The sign sets off a frenzy of movement especially in the balcony seats where we always sit. The lower floors are far too expensive especially when you go as often as we did.

Outside each of the three floors there are western-style sofas lined up along the outside wall. The rush is on to grab a seat to eat one's obento, with ohashi (chop sticks), of course. June became particularly adept at skillfully maneuvering herself to a sofa reserving space for two where we quietly ate our obento. This was followed by a bathroom break since we had two and a half hours more of the performance. The procedure must be completed within 25 minutes when the buzzer sounds and everyone rushes back to their seats for the next dance or play.

When the curtain opens for the cherished play Terakoya, the scene is of a bare classroom with ten students seated on the floor around a table. They're all dressed in simple peasant-style clothing practicing their kanji (calligraphy). The teacher is identified as a struggling lower level samurai who runs the terakoya school in his home to make a living, not uncommon during the feudal era. We learn that he was a warrior from a clan whose lord was on the losing side of the ever shifting entangling alliances that marked the Tokugawa period.

Loyalty by the samurai teacher to his defeated lord is demonstrated daily by harboring his beloved master's son in his terakoya classroom, dressed in peasant clothing so that the new lord of the clan cannot find him. If the boy, considered a threat to the new ruler of the clan, is discovered, he will be killed. What makes the story truly dramatic is that the teacher's son is also in the class dressed in the same style.

When the new lord of the clan dispatches a mission to search for the former lord's son, they receive a tip that this particular teacher, known as a follower of the defeated lord, is secretly hiding the missing son at his home. The inspection party arrives at the school ceremoniously inspecting each child in the class in an attempt to identify the proper lad for execution. Since all of the students are dressed in peasant clothing, and the inspectors do not know what the missing child looks like, they are unable to identify him.

Fearing to return without completing the mission, the leader upon departure orders the teacher to demonstrate his loyalty to the new lord of the clan. He must present the head of the boy they're looking for in a box to the leader upon his return the following day. And that sets the stage for the ultimate act of loyalty to one's lord that virtually all Kabuki plays entail, and which the contemporary Kabuki fans greatly appreciate.

The final scene opens to the bare terakoya classroom with a simple black box in the middle of the room, presumably containing the head of the former lord's son. The teacher is sitting next to it grief-stricken, pleading that he be forgiven by his own son. Through that plea the teacher reveals that the head in the box is not that of his former master's son that he was harboring from the authorities. It was, in fact, the head of his own son.

When the mission returns to pick up the box, the teacher regains his composure and ceremoniously turns the box over to his enemies having sacrificed the life of his own son to protect the life of his true master's son. It was the ultimate act of loyalty of a samurai. There's hardly a dry eye among the audience that fills the theater for Terakoya, a favorite Kabuki play of the Duke's.

THE FINAL MEMOIR 35

THE HISTORY OF MODERN JAPANESE EDUCATION

- CONSTRUCTING THE NATIONAL SCHOOL SYSTEM 1872-1890 -

I n January 2009, Rutgers University Press published my 18-chapter manuscript on The History of Modern Japanese Education. It represented the first book in English to analyze how the public school system was organized within a two-decade period between 1872 with the Gakusei, literally the educational system, to the Imperial Rescript on Education in 1890. It was a remarkable historical episode when the Meiji Government, four years after the overthrow of the feudalistic Tokugawa regime in 1868, launched the nation's modern public school system.

With no public school buildings, no textbooks, no curriculum, and no trained teachers, a newly-designated Ministry of Education was responsible for organizing a public school system with one elementary school serving every child per six hundred residents. No country east or west set such a goal for a national system of education by decree under such circumstances. By 1890, when the Imperial Rescript on Education was adopted, the country had achieved a mass standard of literacy commensurate with the most advanced nations in the world.

In 1990, as I entered the fourth and last decade at ICU, I decided to write a book on the history of modern Japanese education between 1872 and 1890 to mark my final publishing contribution to the field of education. At the time I was serving as Chairman of the Graduate School Division of Education. I was also chairing the ICU committee involved in the bitter campaign against the City of Tokyo over building an incinerator in the adjacent Nogawa Park, the topic of an earlier memoir. Under the circumstances it was a rash decision to undertake such an enormous research project with so little time to devote to it. It was destined to become a twenty-year adventure, my last one at ICU that began in Japan and ended in America.

I designed a plan to carry out the project in two phases. In the first phase I set out to collect as many materials on the subject as possible while still on the faculty of ICU with excellent library resources at my disposal. The writing would take place during phase two after retirement in America. As time permitted I began the project by rereading sections of history books on Japanese education since the Meiji Era from 1868 that I had used as reference material for my courses on education over the years. I also referred to my notes on the two courses on the history of Japanese education that I took at Columbia University thirty years earlier under Dr. Herbert Passin, author of the classic Society and Education in Japan.

After an initial survey I set up a routine to gather pertinent materials for phase one. I hired my graduate student, Arai Hajime, as my research assistant. Arai san, a serious scholarly student, had served as an assistant in the Education Division for several years. He was also employed part-time at the ICU library during his undergraduate days. By 1990 he was in his late twenties working on his doctorate thesis at a leisurely pace. Helping to care for his ailing father at home, he supplemented his ICU income with part time lecturing at a local nursing school. Academically inclined and well versed in Japanese education, he welcomed the assistantship. It proved to be the wisest move I could have made.

During my last decade at ICU when I was fully occupied with teaching duties, launching the ICU International Forest, fighting the

City of Tokyo over the incinerator, etc., I worked closely with my assistant to search for relevant materials in Japanese on Meiji education. I engaged him in translating key documents that we analyzed together during our thrice-weekly working sessions. I gradually became more skilled at determining key factors in modern Japanese history books on the Meiji era, of which the ICU Library had a major collection. The more we worked together the more I was able to use Japanese sources with dictionary in hand. At the same time I hired other graduate students to copy thousands of pages of Japanese materials to take with me to America for phase two, writing the manuscript.

While in America during summer vacations in the 1990s, I traveled from our mountain retreat in Pennsylvania to Rutgers University where one of the major resources on Meiji Japan, the William Griffis collection, is located. While duplicating many documents I learned from the librarian that a Japanese scholar, Yoshiie Sadao who taught Japanese educational history at Keio University, had recently visited the library searching for similar material from the Griffis collection as I was. He was completing the Ph.D. program at an American university on the life of Dr. David Murray, Superintendent of Education in Japan during the Meiji Period who was originally on the Rutgers College faculty in the 1860s.

Upon my return to Japan I contacted Dr. Yoshiie at Keio University to introduce myself and explain my research studies for a book on Meiji education. We agreed to meet at the National Diet Library in Tokyo to discuss our mutual interests. Dr. Yoshiie turned out to be not only an invaluable source of information and analyses; he very kindly agreed to serve as an advisor on my project. Unexpectedly I had found a Japanese authority on the subject of my book who was most willing to assist me in gathering reference materials. Moreover he agreed to read every chapter of my manuscript to react to my ideas, conclusions, etc. I couldn't have found a more knowledgeable individual to act in that capacity. From that first meeting at the National Diet Library, we began to periodically meet during the 1990s at the Diet Library, at Keio University, and during the final years at his home an hour south of Tokyo.

When we shipped our furnishings from ICU to our new home in retirement near Harrisburg, Pennsylvania in 1999, five large crates of materials on Meiji education were among 212 boxes of Japanese antiques including twelve chest-of-drawers (tansu), and a Kawai grand piano. As the 21st Century began I was ready and eager to begin the writing of my final book on Japanese education concerning the origin of the public school system during the Meiji era. For the next eight years I returned to Japan each spring with chapters in hand to review them with Dr. Yoshiie, and to gather needed documents to have the manuscript ready for publication before the end of the first decade of the 21st Century.

In The History of Modern Japanese Education: Constructing the National School System 1872-1890, I divided the period into the 1870s and the 1880s. The 1870 period was the most interesting to me for several reasons. First of all I characterized it as the 'American era' since the Meiji government, after 300 years of enforced isolation from the outside imposed by the Tokugawa feudal regime, turned to America as the primary model for developing a modern school system. Although other western countries contributed to the process, the influence from America overshadowed that from the rest.

The two most intriguing figures who played the leading roles in the early modernization period were Tanaka Fujimaro and David Murray. Tanaka led the Ministry of Education from 1873 to 1879 when the first public school system was organized, and hence can be characterized as the 'father of modern Japanese education.' Dr. David Murray served in the Ministry of Education as Superintendent of Education and senior advisor to Tanaka during that period. I became fascinated with this unlikely couple, one a former local samurai of little consequence during the Tokugawa era, and the other a professor of mathematics and astronomy from an American college, who formed a close professional relationship in Tokyo that overcame cultural differences.

Their wives were as different as were their husbands. Mrs. Tanaka, a renown beauty, had no schooling other than that for the life of a geisha, which she was when she met her future husband at a teahouse where she performed. Mrs. Murray came from a socialite family in the New York-New Jersey area and was living the life of the wife of a distinguished professor when she traveled to Japan with her husband. The Tanakas and Murrays formed a close personal bond enjoying many social events and taking sightseeing trips together. Mrs. Tanaka actually moved in with the Murrays during weekdays for several months to learn western customs and the English language while teaching Mrs. Murray Japanese customs and manners. I found their relationship to be a touching story of intercultural relationships that transpired in Japan a hundred fifty years ago. I dealt with it at some length in the book.

One of the most interesting discoveries of the period that was not included in any Japanese history books on education concerned Tanaka's first trip to America. He was dispatched with the Iwakura Embassy, a mission of fifty ranking government officials sent to the west in late 1871 for a two year research study of modern institutions. Tanaka's assignment was to study education by visiting schools and interviewing teachers and administrators in America and Europe. He was to return to Japan to assume responsibility for launching the first public school system in the nation's history as head of the new Ministry of Education with Murray as his senior advisor.

During a week or so in Washington, Tanaka, as a member of the Iwakura Embassy, met their host, President Ulysses Grant, former commanding general of the Union forces during the Civil War. He toured local schools guided by Superintendent of Education George Eaton, also a Union general during the Civil War. As a former samurai brought up in the tradition of a Japanese warrior, Tanaka was in good company.

Tanaka then set out from Washington on a tour of American schools in the east. It so happens that his translator, a young samurai named Niijima Joo, was studying in America at the time. Years later he founded the great Christian University, Doshisha, where Dr. Yuasa served as president before becoming the first president of ICU prior to my arrival. In my research I came upon a letter sent home from Philadelphia by Niijima never encountered in Japanese history books. It noted that he and Tanaka, on their way from Washington to Philadelphia, had stopped for three days in Harrisburg in April, 1872, to meet the Pennsylvania State Superintendent of Education, James Wickersham, whose office was located in the state capital of Pennsylvania. I immediately drove over to the Pennsylvania Department of Education library ten minutes from our home and discovered the notes of the three-day meeting. The discovery intrigued me when I realized that Tanaka Fujimaro and Niijima Joo had been to Harrisburg in the 19th Century, long before I arrived after retirement in the 21st Century.

Wickersham took an immediate interest in Tanaka who was deeply impressed by the Pennsylvania system of educational administration. It was his first opportunity to hear about the locally elected school board system as a fundamental instrument of American democracy. He learned that school board members must reflect the will of the community in developing educational policy. Otherwise they face the prospect of being voted out of office at the next election. Tanaka spent a year and a half observing schools in the eastern United States, England and Europe looking for the best system as a model for Japan. He chose America.

During the extended trip to the west, the Iwakura Mission leaders hired David Murray as Tanaka's senior advisor in organizing and administering the first public school system in Japan. Murray was surely an unusual choice for the assignment since he was educated in private schools, including one of the most elite institutions in America at the time, Union College. Moreover, he taught only in private schools beginning with the position of Headmaster of Albany College in New York before his appointment as professor at Rutgers College in New Jersey, the forerunner of Rutgers University.

I trace the story of how Tanaka and Murray, as the two senior officers of the Ministry of Education, launched the first public school system in 1873 when Tanaka returned to Japan from his sojourn through Europe and the Murrays arrived from America. The main stipulation of the new law required each community of six hundred residents to establish a public elementary school to serve every child from six to ten years old. I detail how the Ministry hired an elementary teacher from San Francisco, Marion Scott, to teach English in Japan in 1861-2 but who was unexpectedly transferred to the new national teacher training college. He taught the first class of trainees how to teach exactly as he taught his elementary students in San Francisco. It became the standard teaching methodology in the new schools. In addition, he introduced the curriculum he used in California that became the standard curriculum in the new public schools of Japan from 1873.

The second section of my book takes place from 1880 to 1890. I document the dramatic 'reverse course' that was initiated against the rapid modernization of Japanese education with a western curriculum, translated western textbooks mostly from America, and teaching methodology adopted from California. Both Tanaka and Murray had left the Ministry of Education by then. Tanaka was ignominiously replaced as head of the Ministry of Education at the beginning of 1880 held responsible for the trends underway by then considered by powerful forces as inappropriate for Japan. Dr. and Mrs. Murray returned to America in 1879 after completing two contracts as Superintendent of Education in the Ministry and senior advisor to Tanaka.

I then turn my attention in the book to the causes for the sharp criticism of modern Japanese education that was originally implemented by Tanaka and Murray on the American model in the 1870s. According to my analysis of the reverse course, the leader of the opposition was no less than an elderly former samurai, Motoda Nagazane, Confucian tutor to the young Emperor Meiji. Motoda claimed that during the late 1870s Emperor Meiji became increasingly concerned by the emphasis on western technology at the expense of Japanese customs in the new public schools under the Ministry of Education led by Tanaka and Murray. In particular, the disregard for cherished Confucian principles contained in traditional morals teachings became the center of the controversy over modernizing Japanese education on the American model. Motoda argued that morals (shushin) should be the number one course all children must take in the new schools. Under the western curriculum promoted by Tanaka and Murray, morals was relegated to the bottom of the curriculum.

During the 1880s, Motoda, from his position within the Imperial Household and in Emperor Meiji's name, was able to bring about a major revision of the curriculum through like-minded officials appointed to the Ministry of Education to replace Tanaka. The critical revision elevated morals education from the bottom of the curriculum to the top. Motoda then wrote a book on Confucian morality employing ancient stories from China to illustrate revered concepts such as loyalty and filial piety. It was intended as a reference textbook in the new morals course now dominating the curriculum in all schools. Nevertheless the courses in western science and mathematics from the Tanaka-Murray era retained a significant position in the curriculum.

Through Motoda's profound influence, the most famous document in prewar Japanese education, the Imperial Rescript on Education of 1890, was incorporated into the school as the foundation of all teachings. It was a brief statement of Confucian teachings of loyalty and filial piety embedded in imperial ideology that Motoda championed for the modern school system. With the approval of the Imperial Household itself in 1890, it brought to a close the first period of modern Japanese education and set the course of modern Japan that continued until World War II.

The major conclusion of my book was that the most influential figure in modern Japanese education was not Tanaka Fujimaro, progressive head of the Ministry of Education with David Murray from America as his trusted advisor. Although he was responsible for launching the first public school system in Japan after a lengthy first-hand study of western schools, Tanaka's remarkable accomplishments of the 1870s were overshadowed by a most unlikely figure. It was Motoda Nagazane, elderly Confucian scholar, who engineered a reverse course in educational modernization in the 1880s. He effectively implanted Japanese customs and traditions as the foundation of the new public school system from 1890, while recognizing the essential role of western science and technology in preserving the nation's independence as western countries carved up Asia into colonial empires. It was the unique combination of eastern morality and western science that formed the foundation for Japan's success in the modern era.

Motoda Nagazane

My interpretation about the critical role of Motoda Nagazane in modern Japanese education is not without controversy. It has not been interpreted by Japanese historians as conclusively as I did. One of the reasons may be related to the traditional understanding of Emperor Meiji's role in Japan's modernization after the overthrow of the feudal Tokugawa government in 1868. The youthful Emperor is commonly portrayed as an enlightened monarch leading his people from centuries of isolation into the modern world by catching up to the west industrially and militarily. By arguing that Motoda led a movement from the Imperial Household to reinterpret modernism, that is, from the western perspective to modernism with the preeminence of science to the eastern perspective with the preeminence of Confucian principles, my book is in one sense an indirect criticism of Emperor Meiji's enlightened rule.

My last adventure at ICU that began in 1990 with the research on the modernization of Japanese education finally came to a conclusion in 2008. In August, Chapter 18 was completed during our annual summer retreat to the Endless Mountains of Pennsylvania. It was entitled The Imperial Rescript on Education: Western Science and Eastern morality for the Twentieth Century. Who would have imagined when the first adventure at ICU took place with our unexpected arrival on campus in December, 1959, that the last adventure would end sixty years later at Lake Mokoma in August, 2008, ready for publication in January, 2009?

ICU campus upon our retirement